# What's a Dog For?

### The Surprising History, Science, Philosophy, and Politics of Man's Best Friend

~

## JOHN HOMANS

PENGUIN BOOKS

Published by the Penguin Group
Penguin Group (USA) LLC
375 Hudson Street
New York, New York 10014

USA | Canada | UK | Ireland | Australia | New Zealand | India | South Africa | China
penguin.com
A Penguin Random House Company

First published in the United States of America by The Penguin Press,
a member of Penguin Group (USA) Inc., 2012
Published in Penguin Books 2013

A portion of this book appeared as "The Land of the Labradors" in *Condé Nast Traveler*.
Grateful acknowledgment is made for permission to reprint excerpts from the following
copyrighted works:
"The Early Purges" from *Poems 1965–1975* by Seamus Heaney. Copyright © 1980 by Seamus Heaney.
Reprinted by permission of Farrar, Straus and Giroux, Inc. and Faber and Faber Ltd.
"Another Dog's Death" from *Collected Poems 1953–1993* by John Updike. Copyright © 1993 by John
Updike. Used by permission of Alfred A. Knopf, a division of Random House, Inc.

*Photograph by Randy Harris*

THE LIBRARY OF CONGRESS HAS CATALOGED THE HARDCOVER EDITION AS FOLLOWS:
Homans, John.
What's a dog for? : the surprising history, science, philosophy, and politics of man's best friend /
John Homans.
p. cm.
Includes bibliographical references and index.
ISBN 978-1-59420-515-6 (hc.)
ISBN 978-0-14-312412-2 (pbk.)
1. Dogs—Social aspects.   2. Dogs—Psychology.   3. Human-animal relationships.   I. Title.
SF426.H63 2012
636.7—dc23   2012009278

Printed in the United States of America
1   3   5   7   9   10   8   6   4   2

DESIGNED BY AMANDA DEWEY

PENGUIN BOOKS

WHAT'S A DOG FOR?

John Homans has been the executive editor of *New York* magazine since 1994, and previously worked at *Esquire, Details, Harpers,* and the *New York Observer.* He lives with his wife, son, and dog, Stella, in Manhattan. This is his first book.

PENGUIN BOOKS

# Praise for *What's a Dog For?*

"A remarkable chronicle of the domestic dog's journey across thousands of years and straight into our hearts, written with equal parts tenderness and scientific rigor. . . . Beautifully written and absolutely engrossing, *What's a Dog For?* goes on to examine such fascinating fringes of canine culture as how dogs served as Darwin's muse, why they were instrumental in the birth of empathy, and what they might reveal about the future of evolution."　　　　　　　　　　　　　　　　　　　*—The Atlantic*

"Through careful observation and analysis, *New York* executive editor Homans opens the door into the world of dogs, from the scientific to the humorous . . . illuminating nuggets of information on the ever-changing and complex world of people and their pets."　　　*—Kirkus Reviews*

"Writing in an engaging, straightforward manner, Homans combines great personal charm with an intense interest in his subject matter."
　　　　　　　　　　　　　　　　　　　　　　　*—Publishers Weekly*

"A fascinating tour through ever-changing perceptions of dogs as pets."
　　　　　　　　　　　　　　　　　　　　　　　　*—New York Post*

"Retraces [the] journey from Darwin's study of canine emotions to puppy mills to a canine-science conclave in Vienna . . . covers doggie consciousness and evolution . . . Homans hits his stride on topics like the red-state (pro)/blue state (con) divide over euthanasia and the aristocratic origins of canine pedigree. Sprinkled throughout are charming anecdotes that will delight dog lovers and even likely appeal to die-hard cat people."　　　　　　　　　　　　　　　　　　　*—Mother Jones*

"John Homans has written an intensely readable, thoughtful look at man's best friend and its place in our world. Factually fascinating and emotionally satisfying, *What's a Dog For?* is a great gift for dog lovers and those who wonder what they're about."
　　　　　　　　　—Julie Klam, *New York Times* bestselling author of
　　　　　　　　　　　　　　　*You Had Me at Woof* and *Friendkeeping*

"John Homans's *What's a Dog For?* is a romp across time and space and evolution that ends right up right in our own living rooms—a book as winning and companionable as the canines snoozing on our sofas. It's a fresh and amicable look at dog science, history, and training, both an indispensable guide for dog lovers and a terrific read for anyone looking for an enlightening glance at the world we live in."

—Melissa Fay Greene, award-winning author of *Praying for Sheetrock* and *No Biking in the House Without a Helmet*

"A few years ago, John Homans and his family walked into a Long Island animal shelter petless and emerged, fortunately for readers, with a lovable, slightly skittish mongrel named Stella. Her almost instant transformation from stranger to a family member with 'honorary human' status inspired Homans to plumb the mysterious, age-old bond between humans and canines—a quest that takes him from Darwin to Updike and from New York City dog runs to a Vienna conference on 'canine science.' The result is a beautifully written natural history of the complex and evolving relationship between dogs and their owners and a sort of thinking man's *Marley & Me*. It will enlighten pet owners not just about their beloved animals but also themselves."

—Warren St. John, author of *Outcasts United: An American Town, a Refugee Team, and One Woman's Quest to Make a Difference*

*For my parents*

# Contents

# What's a Dog For?

## *One*

# Entering the World of Dog

Stella's world is in turmoil—not that you'd know it by looking at her. She's on her spot on the rug, looking at me, waiting for the next thing, as usual. A couple of milk bones that I gave her earlier are arrayed in front of her. She took them somewhat reluctantly, knowing I had steak in the refrigerator—sometimes she refuses such offerings altogether, turning her head away in what I imagine is disdain.

All seems placid, a dog on a rug, but beneath this tranquil scene, large forces are at work, and Stella, I've been learning, is at the center of them. The very definition of who she is, what goes on in her head, how she should be treated, and what rights she might deserve have all been shifting rapidly. Today the dog world is in the throes of political and ideological convulsions of a kind not seen since Victorian times, when the dog as we know it was invented. Put simply, the dog is now in the process of being reimagined.

I wasn't aware of any of this when she arrived in our home. Stella was, to begin with, just a dog—although in many quarters these days, "just a dog" are fighting words. She came into my life for the usual reasons. My wife, Angela, and I had an acute sense of time passing. Our son, Charlie, was about to turn ten, hurtling toward teenage-hood and then God knew where. We'd had a dog when he was born, a West Highland terrier named Scout, a proud, ridiculous creature who'd tried not to let on just how upset he was when this squalling interloper and rival for our affections arrived. But Scout was old—thirteen at that point—and was dead before Charlie's first birthday. If Charlie was ever to have a childhood dog, it was now or never.

The dog we planned to get was, like most things we wanted for him, as much for us. We wanted another family member, someone to fill out the cast, a supporting actress. And while our son would one day inevitably spin out of our little nucleus, we could count on the dog to stay. After dropping Charlie off at college, our dog would, in all likeli-hood, come back in the station wagon with us—a reassuring thought. It was all pretty simple.

A purebred dog was never really part of our concept—it seemed an anachronism, a bit stuffy. There were plenty of dogs that needed homes, and we'd osmotically learned that pet store animals might be products of puppy mills—not institutions that we wanted to support. And so on an unseasonably hot Friday afternoon in September, the week of Charlie's tenth birthday, Angela and Charlie and I drove out to the North Shore Animal League in Port Washington. We'd heard that North Shore, unlike some of the other shelters in the area, always had adoptable puppies. We'd seen their trucks in Union Square, me-nageries of dog whimsy with pits and basset crosses and all manner of mongrels, waiting for somebody to change their lives.

There's a cheerful seriousness in a place like North Shore, a whiff of destiny: lives are being determined. Adopting a pet is a big step, a family ritual, an obligation entered into joyfully but not lightly. As we pulled into the parking lot, we saw a boy of about seven crying as his mother tried to explain why the family wouldn't be getting a dog that day—there was just too much going on in their lives, and they weren't ready for the added responsibility. But we were ready. Or at least, there didn't seem to be any prospect of our getting more ready. Now was the time.

North Shore is a fantastic place to get a dog. This is by design. At a great shelter, the adopters' emotions are carefully managed. You feel the dog's need for companionship, without that feeling ever spilling over into guilt if you go home empty-handed. The trick is to make you want to save these dogs without it seeming like a burden.

To get to the inner sanctum where the puppies are kept, you have to pass by the pens of the older dogs, a cheerful cell block arranged around an interior courtyard where prospective adopters can take an animal they want to get to know better. The concrete floors are warmed in front, so the dogs will nap where the people can see them, not cower in a back corner. But most don't nap. They beseech you, pressing their noses through the chain links, trying to make a connection or barking exuberantly. You know you could change one of these dogs' lives, take it away from its caged existence—but which one of the pits and Lab mixes and shepherds, each fixing you with eyes that seem designed to connect with you, to force you to fall in love, will you choose? It's a big decision, because by making it, you're leaving the rest of them to their lives in this place, loud and crowded but a bit lonely, waiting to be selected.

We'd thought for a while about getting an adult dog, imagining the satisfaction of doing a noble thing, the gratitude we'd reap. But a puppy—what a joy! As a friend said, getting an adult dog would be like sex without the orgasm. A puppy would be ours, loving us above others, imprinted with our ways. I steeled myself, swallowing the guilt, and kept moving. Back in the inner sanctum, volunteers bustled about in blue scrubs as a few families evaluated their options amid a cacophony of puppyish barks. There was a wall of puppy condos, cages stacked three high, floored with newspaper. The dominant smell was cleaning products, with farmyard undertones, not at all unpleasant, though you got the sense that maintaining the place was a big job. Some of the cages' occupants napped, especially the younger ones, but more of them were fully engaged, pressing against the bars, looking for contact, yipping eagerly.

And there she was, big-pawed and a little slow moving compared with some of the other dogs, peering out at us from her cage, her head slowly bobbing and craning like a little black brontosaurus. She had a glossy, jet-black coat and big, brown, expressive eyes. A beautiful dog. Hard to resist, even if she seemed a bit under the weather. The paper on her cage said Lab mix, twelve weeks old. She was at that point just a number: puppy T68782, from Tennessee, a fact that I wondered about for a minute—how had she wound up here?

There was a male puppy in the cage next to her—a winning, shaggy black and white animal that I thought might have had some border collie in his ancestry—loudly and energetically seeking our attention. He'd be a handful—in a good way, I thought. Stella's charms were subtler. She seemed self-possessed, happy for attention but not demanding it. I imagined, with no evidence whatsoever, that she would be sensible—the Labrador as a kind of nanny, a helpmate for the adults, the dog of my childhood.

We milled around, poking our fingers into other cages, trying to imagine a bond, making ourselves fall in love, the common activity in the puppy rooms at North Shore. We're not exactly believers in love at first sight, though retroactively it's a story one might like to tell. I'd grown up with a Lab, but truthfully, I hadn't thought we'd end up with one this time. Then another couple came in and eyed her, then began whispering in the corner. They might have been talking about the weather, and not the new apple of our eye, but we couldn't take a chance. The loud little border collie would have to keep waiting— Stella would be ours. We filled out the paperwork and waited as the volunteers called our references. They take these checks seriously; they want to make it seem as much as possible like an adoption, not a purchase—a life you're taking responsibility for.

Back at a house we were renting on the North Fork of Long Island, we set her loose on the lawn. She took a few wobbly steps and then lay down, a position she spent quite a bit of time in over the next month. She had a bad case of kennel cough; any shelter or kennel, even the cleanest and best run, is not the healthiest environment for a dog. But after a while she was on the full puppy program, for good and ill—chasing butterflies, snatching gloves from passersby, and chewing up shoes and furniture, which was annoying, but it was what we'd signed up for. In the first weeks, that was about as far as my dog horizons extended—but they quickly expanded.

Stella was going to be a New York City dog, and in this she would be joining a large and growing population. Our downtown street is a nonstop dog parade, part of the urban scenery, along with New York University students and hipsters and the men at the garage on the corner and the guy in the grungy gray coat and taped-up sneakers who shouts "Zirzu!" at the traffic passing on Bowery with an emphatic, not-unhappy certainty.

In the dog parade were dogs from all walks of life: a pair of glossy brown-and-gray Great Danes as big as ponies; a gorgeous orange chow, as cheerful a dog as you could find despite the fact that she had three legs, always accompanied by a little Maltese wingman; and a thirteen-year-old shepherd mix who made her circuit with an impossibly dignified slowness, still sniffing at all her favorite spots. On the next street over, in front of the most glamorous building in the neighborhood, we sometimes ran into a pair of yellow Labs that spent weekends at their owners' spread in Montana, then returned to the city for their workweek—a dog's life. Some dogs were walked with orange smocks that read "Adopt Me." There were plenty of pits, some from a little dog-rescue place on Fourth Street, others from Alphabet City to the east, where the pit could serve as the neighborhood emblem, much as the bulldog does for England. And there were a good number of dogs that looked a lot like Stella, Lab mixes, many a little whippier than Labs, with white blazes on their chests and white toes.

It was not my imagination that the parade was getting ever more crowded. Something has been happening with dogs in the last couple of decades. New York, along with just about every other city in the Western world, is overrun with them. There were some 77 million dogs in the United States in 2010, compared with about 53 million in 1996. Pet food and products were a $38 billion industry in 2010. At the Greenmarket one afternoon, I bought some lamb chops from a woman who told me wonderful stories about the intelligence of her border collies, their foresight and uncanny responsiveness. These were qualities I wanted to believe my own dog possessed, if only I'd take the time to develop them—but I couldn't see how Stella would use such qualities in her mostly urban world, even if she had them, which I sometimes questioned.

But the numbers tell only part of the evolving story. Dogs have been moving into households in ever more intimate arrangements. Close to a hundred percent of dog owners talk to their dogs (and the few who say they don't must be lying). Eighty-one percent view their dogs as family members, according to one study. And many of these family members, I began to notice, were sleeping right in the bed, a privilege Stella didn't get and, at any rate, didn't seem to want—she prefers a floor-based lifestyle. But she gets plenty of human privileges, starting with her diet, which features leftovers—sometimes, I'm sorry to say, straight from the table. A shockingly high number of people say that in certain life-threatening situations they would save their pet before they would save a fellow human. I hope I know what I'd do if facing that choice, but I'm glad I'm not likely to be put to the test.

Because, immediately, Stella *was* a family member. We couldn't deny it. All of us spent a lot of time walking her, talking to her, analyzing and reanalyzing her quirks, her combustible mix of fear and excitement in the dog run, her dislike of the car, her abject terror of thunder, her varied and exuberant vocabulary. We worried about how she would spend the weekend if we weren't with her. We imagined what her concerns might be and tried to accommodate them.

Stella is an elegant creature, with a high-gloss black coat and the runway model's trick of looking simultaneously gorgeous and ridiculous. She's mostly a Labrador retriever—certainly in her goofball ways—but her splotchy purple tongue, curling scimitar tail, and brownish undercoat suggest chow blood, and sometimes I think there's a hint of pit bull in her muscular, slightly bulging cheeks. She's a Lab, definitely, but she's also a mutt, although that word, with its whiff of contempt for the mixing of breeds, is used much less than it once was.

I don't think of Stella as a person in any conscious way. Yet I treat her as if she were a very unusual toddler. I endeavor to fill in the cartoon thought bubble over her head as well as I can. Sometimes the message is fairly clear: *Want chicken!* If she wants a run, she stands in front of me, ears slightly cocked, and fixes me with a hard stare, not angry but very definite. If the delay is too long—sometimes an hour, sometimes five minutes—she unfurls an ululating whine, all o's and u's, the meaning of which is unmistakable: *Why won't you take me?* That's one of her communicative vocalizations: she also has a splendid baritone bark, used in spirited play; a yip of fear; a low, long growl that she sometimes employs while begging; and another sort of ululation, a delightful half bark, half growl of several syllables that she usually uses to signal her presence to certain neighborhood friends—the firemen next door, or the guy at the dry cleaner who always has a biscuit.

Stella seems to get most of her big ideas across (although who knows what's really going on in there), but the closed captioning doesn't really work very well. Is she depressed? Angry at us for taking her back from the country? Jealous that our cats get to climb on the furniture? She stares at me, waiting for me to figure it out. Making sense of it all is my job. The relationship inevitably involves imagination.

There is plenty of found comedy in the cognitive dissonance of treating Stella as if she were a human; it's a sitcom we're constantly in the process of rewriting. But the laughter is of the slightly uncomfortable variety, because underneath, we mean it—we treat her as a person, as part of our human group in some ways and as a dog in others.

But the boundaries of these categories are unclear and constantly shifting. Over time I came to think that what once seemed a mistake— *Your dog is not a human being!*—was actually a mystery, giving rise to a series of cascading questions that were never far from my thoughts: *Who, or what, is she? What goes on in her head? And what's going on in my head that I can't help but treat her as something she clearly isn't?*

As I began to investigate these questions, I learned that a dog's honorary personhood was a kind of battleground, and not just in my head. The fact that the dog is a dog and not a person but is treated like a person is a recipe for misunderstanding, miscommunication, and interspecies neurotic interchange. With Stella's arrival, I started to pay attention to the vast people-are-from-Mars, dogs-are-from-Venus industry, trainers and books and TV shows devoted to addressing this issue, all with different prescriptions but trying to bridge the same gap. The dominant mode of dog literature these days is not about dog training, necessarily, but about how to better understand your dog.

An even bigger industry is trying to confuse the issue, because what's partly considered a person gets a better—and more expensive—brand of dog food than one that isn't. Beneful, that doggie junk food, even has an ad directed specifically at dogs, using insidious dog-whistle-type sounds to attract your dog's attention. In New York, there are dog bakeries, haberdashers, and luxury kennels, everything that the marketing mind can dream up—a vast and ever-growing junkyard full of kitsch, with names (Paw-tisserie, etc.) that are more annoying than the products themselves, if that's even possible. I don't think there's anything wrong with buying your dog all this stuff—it's nothing direr than a game of dress-up—but it's probably prudent to ask who you're buying it for. Your dog doesn't care if it's wearing a funny hat or traveling in a sequined dog purse—no one loses anything but their dignity. Treating your dog as a person can be a kind of aesthetic error, albeit one that's becoming ever more common.

My first impulse was to ignore the kitsch, push all of this away. I thought of the dog's ubiquity in our culture, and its partial personhood, as another minor sadness of the modern world, something to avoid if we could and to accept if we couldn't. With Stella, there would be no bed sleeping, and no climbing on the furniture. She would get no birthday cakes. And though it pained me to think it, there would be no five-thousand-dollar medical treatments, no doggie hip replacements or chemo or long hospital stays. Stella was a delight—but humans were humans and dogs were dogs. A line had to be drawn.

But as our life with Stella went on, I began to understand that this large and growing flood of kitsch contained, or concealed, interesting changes in the dog world—it was all part of the same current. I could see the comedy in our unlikely human-animal partnership, but I also began to take her seriously. In this respect, I found I had illustrious company. Charles Darwin was obsessed with dogs, not only for their amazing variety of form, which suggested some mechanism of change—dog breeding was a basic model for his theory of evolution—but also as companions, as family members, with emotions and affiliations and cognitive abilities, however limited—as creatures that were somehow like us. They were at the core of his science, as subject and metaphor and philosopher's stone. Darwin was, not incidentally, an unabashed dog sentimentalist who thoroughly anthropomorphized his animals—that sentiment too was a large part of his scientific inspiration.

But not long after Darwin, science rejected the premise that the dog was in any way humanlike. In an effort to cleanse science of the corrupting influences of sentimentality and anthropomorphism, the dog's role was drastically limited too; the household and the laboratory became two completely different spheres, ones that seldom touched.

The fact that the dog is a product of human culture, linked to us in ways that are impossible to tease out, made it even more of a scientific pariah. The dominant way of thinking post-Darwin was that the dog, like the chicken or the cow, had been subject to so much human

imaginative intervention that it couldn't tell us anything about the natural world. Why study something that humans had cobbled together?
The sample was compromised, hopelessly polluted by human interference. Trying to separate out what had been engineered from what had
evolved was pointless. The wolf, serious and dangerous, howling at the
moon, is profound; Stella, begging for treats at the dinner table, is ridiculous, if sweet. What could she tell us? But that attitude, I learned,
has been changing very quickly.

Just in terms of sheer numbers, it had to be observed that the dog
had completely outcompeted the wolf, its ancestor. A thousand years
ago, and for fifty millennia before that, the wolf was the king predator
in most of its range, and its range was most of the world. Now wolves
number as few as one hundred thousand, in a range that continues to
shrink. The last wolf in the British Isles was killed in Ireland in the
eighteenth century. The king predators there are now foxes and bad-
gers, creatures that know more or less how to keep out of our way. In
the United States, the last truly native wolf populations in the lower
forty-eight are in northern Minnesota and Michigan. But there are,
worldwide, some 300 million dogs (as compared to 7 billion people,
1.3 billion cows, and 1.3 billion sheep). Evolutionarily speaking, that's
success.

And the amazing thing about this success is that dogs—sorry,
Stella—aren't good for much of anything that can be readily measured,
in terms of their economic contribution. A very small percentage of
them do useful work, and an even smaller percentage currently serve
as food, an intermittent fact of canine existence ever since they first
entered the human story. But mostly what they do is hang around,
whether they are invited into our homes (as is increasingly the case) or
lurking around outside, looking for a handout.

Ordinary folks may praise the intelligence of their dogs to the
skies, but scientists long tended to view this attitude as a sentimental
superstition, or an illusion that would disappear in the clear light of
the laboratory. Edward Thorndike, the turn-of-the-century British psy-

chologist on whose insights behaviorism was founded, set the tone. "The question is not how smart animals are," he wrote in characteristic killjoy style, "but how dim."

Though her intelligence is not the primary reason I love Stella, statements like Thorndike's sting. I like to joke about my dog's IQ as much as the next person—she doesn't take it personally. But believing your dog is an imbecile does tend to spoil the party a little bit. What would it mean to take as a premise in my ordinary activities the notion that my dog is much dimmer than I think she is? Some scientists still say that animal consciousness is little more than a fantasy, that what's going on in their brains is mostly a matter of rote programming, and that all our everyday anthropomorphisms—*Stella is sad, Stella is mad at the cats, Stella wants to go out*—are fancy human notions about a much simpler reality. In this view the dog's honorary personhood is an illusion.

But there are other ways of thinking about animals. Ever since Jane Goodall, whose love for her dog Rusty largely inspired her to pursue her scientific interests, the pendulum has been swinging back, gradually at first, but lately very quickly. Scientists in the last couple of decades have revisited Darwin's interest in the dog, armed with a new set of tools. The dog has escaped from the veterinary schools, where it was locked up for decades, and has become a subject of serious investigation at some of the country's most prestigious universities, such as Duke, Harvard, and Columbia. These studies are conducted not only to figure out why Fido is so mopey or keeps biting the mailman but also to tease out the differences and similarities between dogs' cognitive and emotional equipment and our own.

As never before, the fact that the dog's history over the millennia has been shaped by its relationship with humans is precisely what makes it interesting to scientists—in part because its social nature can mirror our own predilections. Intense debate rages over whether dogs have a primitive moral sense—a sense of fairness, or humanlike feelings like envy. Some scientists are fascinated by dogs' ability to cooperate with us: to watch our gestures and act accordingly. Learning what makes dogs so comfortable in our households may also tell us something about ourselves. But just as some people think giving a dog a birthday cake is a bit *de trop*, many scientists still believe that even asking how a dog might be like a human being involves anthropomorphism—the cardinal sin in animal studies for most of the past century.

Stella pushed open the door to these worlds, and the farther in I went, the more the questions raised there seemed worthy of real consideration. Indeed, the dog has been central to human imaginings for aeons. Fourteen thousand years ago, and possibly much earlier, people were fascinated by dogs. For prehistoric humans, as for Darwin, as for Jane Goodall, and as for a new generation of scientists, dogs are a kind of mirror species. The dog's honorary personhood may seem ridiculous, a William Wegman romp. But underneath is something fundamental about both dogs and people. It was Stella who began to show me what this mystery is.

Stella took me down other paths too, ones that intertwined in complex ways. Several of them have led into the past. As for many a dog owner, for me Stella lives partly in a haze of nostalgia, reminding me of dogs I've previously had. Here too it's obvious that dogs—along with the rest of us—have been undergoing rapid change.

My first childhood dog was also a Lab, a purebred named, unaccountably, Putzi. She died when I was twelve, and I cried for a day, for her but probably more for myself: the event seemed somehow to demarcate my childhood from my adolescence, evidence that the world wasn't always going to stay the same. And of course Stella may someday serve a similar, life-marking purpose for Charlie. Dogs measure human eras, stages of our lives.

The nostalgic feelings that Stella awakened in me were partly of the things-were-better-in-the-old-days kind, a longing for the green fields of my childhood—which actually were pretty green, and for dogs too. Putzi lived in a leashless, fenceless, laissez-faire dog paradise.

Never spayed, she had multiple litters of puppies over the course of her life, some of which we marketed with a sign—FREE PUPPIES!—in our front yard. A Norman Rockwell scene, definitely, although Rockwell never painted the whole truth. In those days, dogs chased down cars as if they were so many moose or musk oxen and often died in the attempt. And in 1970, the year Putzi died, some 70 million dogs were euthanized in American shelters—but no one paid too much attention to statistics like these. All this death was simply seen as the cost of their freedom in suburban America. And sick dogs most often simply died on the rug—old Putzi lingered for a couple of days, barely able to move, before she passed. She was old—it was her time. High-tech medicine was reserved for humans.

That world, for good and ill, hardly exists anymore. In the town where I grew up, dogs almost never run loose on the street. They bark at passersby from behind invisible fences or are power-walked on leashes. I haven't seen a dog chase a car for decades.

I had mixed feelings about this change. Sometimes I thought that the dog, in becoming more of a person, had become less of a dog, its freedom much diminished. An urban dog, or a dog always confined by fences and leashes, doesn't need all its sublime, finely tuned faculties, the speed and agility, the joy of pursuit. These, I imagined, would atrophy. Of course, my notion of the canine past was partly fantasy. And in certain ways, life for dogs now is quite a bit better. The worst part of the good old days was that taking a puppy to the local shelter often amounted to carrying out a death sentence. Now, at least on the East and West coasts, there's a shortage of adoptable puppies. The number of dogs euthanized in America in 2010 was about one-eighth of what it was in 1970.

In concert with these changes, the big institutions that have dominated the dog world since the late nineteenth century have also evolved quickly. For the better part of the last century, the prime directive of the ASPCA and its sister organizations was to give unwanted dogs a humane death—and as the statistics attest, they did it very well. But the changing status of the dog, its new honorary personhood, has made this enterprise seem hollow and compromised. In the new world, every dog, even the ugliest, even the meanest, deserves a chance at life. And being humane can't mean killing.

This new ideology was everywhere I looked, once I started looking. If you wanted to save the world, the dog was a place to start. Animal rights have a beachhead in the universities but a much bigger presence on the street, where one can, surprisingly frequently, encounter freelance moral philosophers who shape their worldviews around their dogs. One day, outside an East Village used-bike store, a cheerful white-haired woman in a blue windbreaker, seeming to belong behind the wheel of a vintage Volvo, came up to me with a couple of golden retrievers and a fistful of vegan brochures—and delivered a rap about the connections between dogs, pigs, feminism, industrial agriculture, and world peace. Forty thousand people die of starvation every year, she said, yet we're feeding cows to turn them into McDonald's hamburgers that make people sick. I could agree with her that this system didn't make a great deal of sense. Her dogs were vegans, she announced, subsisting on a diet based on rice and lentils with plenty of flaxseed oil. And they're doing quite well, she told me: she'd just buried a dog who'd lived twenty years, an assertion I wanted to fact check. The woman's friendly manner allowed me to feel not too much shame when I told her that Stella was a carnivore. If you wanted to preach to the converted, a used-bike store on Third Street between First and Avenue A was a good place to find them.

For others, saving dogs was an end in itself. The dog-rescue world is full of volunteers and heroes, people who lose sleep and travel huge distances, infiltrating kill shelters to extricate at-risk animals, then finding homes for them or even caring for them themselves. It's a gargantuan underground railroad. For these activists, dogs are their thing, and they're doing their part. Helping dogs that have not found their own family is a calling, a contribution to the good of the world.

But conflict lay just below these heartwarming sentiments. Some people thought that dogs monopolize concerns and money that belong more justly to humans. I occasionally thought that if all the energy dogs monopolized were devoted to, say, teaching math to underprivileged kids, we'd be a nation of engineers in a decade. Some of the most vivid images in the aftermath of Hurricane Katrina were of dogs—on roofs, in the water—awaiting rescue or struggling to survive. After the catastrophe, Barack Obama spoke of an "empathy deficit," but there was no deficit when it came to the animals. An army of animal rescuers descended on the city, going house to house looking for abandoned pets, marking the houses as they searched them in exactly the same way the national guard did when searching for people. The work of these rescuers is legend in the animal-rescue community. But among some locals, their intervention was further proof, if more was needed, that not enough value was placed on the lives and concerns of the area's human inhabitants. One could be a dog lover and still see that these people had a point.

As the animal-rescue movement grew it seemed to take the oxygen from the old dog world order. The American Kennel Club (AKC) was founded in 1884, modeled after the British organization the Kennel Club, which had been founded a decade earlier. Its well-worn stories of breed origin seem increasingly quaint and distant from the concerns of modern dog owners. AKC dogs themselves could be problematic—some of them, a long way from their imagined country past, had been refined to the point of freakishness. Critics tried for decades to get the organization to pay attention to the problems of inbreeding. Now, finally, people were paying attention. As more and more dog breeds were found to have heritable diseases, inbreeding had became a humane issue, and the number of people registering their dogs with the AKC, or with the Kennel Club in Britain, had begun to drop.

Stella had a paw in each of these worlds. As a Labrador, with its nautical associations, she embodied fantasy ancestors leaping from fishing boats to fetch buoys—not that Stella was useful, but she might be if I gave her the opportunity. But the more I learned about dogs, the more I wondered about their origin stories. Who was Stella, really? What was it, exactly, that had been transported from the past?

Her Lab heritage was only half her identity—one that, at any rate, the AKC wouldn't certify. Because really, she was a mutt. And, not incidentally, a "rescue dog," as the modern vernacular has it—a dog that had been rescued from abuse or neglect and also from euthanasia. And she was a Tennessee dog, a refugee from a red state. The world of my yard sign reading FREE PUPPIES! seemed a long way away. Stella's arrival in our home initially seemed so uncomplicated—but as I explored, I found that her origins and identity weren't simple at all.

My questions about Stella's origins weren't just personal ones. The dog's place in the world, and its personhood, or lack thereof, were something to fight about. People got angry about dogs. Most vividly, they were angry at the American Kennel Club. And a lot of people were angry at the dog shelter regime. The language could be extreme, peppered with words like *holocaust* and *eugenics,* as if all the horrors of the twentieth century had somehow converged in the canine world.

The problems of one dog don't amount to a hill of beans in this crazy world, but the existence of 70 million dogs inevitably means: politics. The politics were vicarious—it was people who are arguing about dogs and making decisions and judgments about them—but that rendered them, if anything, even more intense. Stella's arrival on my rug was the arrival of great forces of history.

The dog world is aflame with conflict. Breeders battle humane organizations. Pit bulls, the most common dogs in urban animal shelters and also in dog maul statistics, are the subject of a long-running debate and legal struggle as to whether nature or nurture produced their problems. Some people use their dogs to help hunt and kill animals. Others, who keep their dogs vegan, find this the rankest hypocrisy— how can you love one animal and kill another? And no one knows just how dogs will be produced in the future, what the rules will be, and who should be in charge.

The fierceness and impacted rage in some of these disputes suggested to me they were about something else, and they are: the politics of dogs are a reflection, distilled and distorted, of the politics of people. They're surrogates for our own conflicts, being fought by conservatives and radicals of many stripes, all trying desperately to put their own ideological stamp on the future of dog.

*Two*

# The Family Dog

The public world of dogs, with its noisy, swirling politics, was not the core of my experience with Stella. She was, to start with, a family member, Angela's and my child and Charlie's sibling, though of a different species. Her personhood, and its consequences, began in our home—and it turned out that the dog's place in the family—down to the basic chemistry of bonding, friendship, and family emotion—was as intellectually contested as are kill shelters and animal rights.

The basic ritual by which our family's relationship with Stella is built and reinforced occurs every time one of us walks through the door. The whole greeting thing is really the best reason to get a dog, as most dog owners know. It's not that the other members of my household don't make an effort—Angela's greeting is most often cheery, while Charlie has a stylized grunt of hello, an elaboration on my own monosyllabism. But for Stella, the opening of the front door is, unfailingly, the occasion for an elaborate family festival. There's no how-was-your-day competition, no feeling that one's unburdening is making the other feel burdened. She trots down swiftly from wherever she happened to be resting, head slightly bowed in supplication. If you turn away, she'll paw the backs of your legs. Sometimes she backs away, as if the charged field of our bond were too intense, but eventually she'll come over and sit in front of me and put her paw on my arm as I scratch her chest. That lasts for thirty seconds minimum—afterward, she'll go and greet everyone else, as if they had just come through the door too. Sometimes treats follow, which doesn't mean she does it for food. The greeting is probably our purest, clearest communication. It's who she is, and who we are. It's what makes her family.

It's never been a secret that a dog is a nice thing to come home to. What is a bit more surprising, given the paved and fenced and isolated nature of our urban and suburban environments, is the increasing number of dogs we seem to be welcoming into our homes. The dog as family member has become the norm, to a degree that it wasn't even in the age of Lassie. Stella is part of an enormous canine migration. "We've seen a linear explosion in pet populations in Western countries over the past forty years," James Serpell, a British professor at the University of Pennsylvania, told me. Serpell, who's the leading scholar of the dog-human relationship, noted a correlation with the depressing statistics in Robert Putnam's *Bowling Alone*. "People are living more isolated lives, are having fewer children, their marriages aren't lasting. All these things sort of break down a social network and happen to exactly coincide with the growth in pet populations. What's happening is simply that we're allowing animals to fill the gap in our lives."

In New York, where people can postpone life choices like getting married indefinitely or ignore them altogether, one can observe these effects on a granular level. And indeed, dogs do fill gaps, help build communities. On the street, Stella multiplies my acquaintanceships— though the names I learn are more often those of the dogs than the owners. Dog owners are a community of the like-minded, the dogs a ready-made reason to stop and talk about something besides the weather. Non-dog-owners find it bizarre, this incessant dog-themed yammering and frequent attempts to include the dog in the conversation. *Oh, Stelly, who's your friend!?* Yes, quite dopey, but comfortable too, part of the fabric of the neighborhood.

Dogs fill other gaps as well. A century and a half ago cities were filled with animals, being driven to market, pulling wagons. Stables—now mostly relegated in Manhattan to the far West Forties, among garages and car washes—were once upon a time on every other street. E. O. Wilson, in his 1984 book *Biophilia,* argued that people have an inborn need for and fascination with the natural world, a vestige of our need to understand the ancestral environment. We're riveted by animals; we can't look away. New York is home to plenty of rats and pigeons and seagulls too, living on our filth. And quite a number of hawks live here, some of which, in their natural grandeur, have become urban celebrities. But mostly we have dogs. From their beginnings, dogs have been a kind of emissary, ambassadors between nature and human culture. Certainly this is true of my New York experience with Stella—as a wolf, she is connected to a world I don't live in as much as I'd like to.

That a wolf has arrived on my rug, and now rolls over for a belly scratch, is a frequent subject of wonder. But Stella's an unusual sort of friend in other ways. For one thing, as Cole Porter would put it, she's easy to love—much easier than my other friends and family members, wonderful people though they are. My relationship with Stella is simple. Even when I'm disappointed in her, with her occasional inanities, it doesn't greatly disturb our bond. She doesn't take much offense if I step on her paw—she's unflappable. None other than Sigmund Freud pointed out this excellence with his usual boldness, damn the evidence. "Dogs love their friends and bite their enemies," he wrote, "quite unlike people, who are incapable of pure love and have to mix love and hate." In a letter to his friend Marie Bonaparte, he elaborated on these emotions: "Affection without any ambivalence, the simplicity of life free from the conflicts of civilization that are so hard to endure, the beauty of existence complete in itself."

Well, yes, Doctor. I'm not at all sure that what Stella feels for me qualifies as pure love—plenty else is involved, like her occasional playful anger at the leash, the emblem of my control. Besides which, let's not forget all the treats. But after all that, I know she loves me, above and beyond.

There are amazing anecdotes of dogs' attachment to humans—dogs that go to train stations, or lurk at graveyards long after their masters are deceased. More recently, a video of a dog staying by its wounded comrade in the aftermath of the tsunami went viral. Stella is not going to be one of these hyperloyal dogs, I can safely predict. But what is true is that human relationships with dogs are uncomplicated—there's less understanding, maybe, but less misunderstanding too, which leads to the purity Freud was pointing to. Because the bandwidth is limited, it's possible to communicate only the important things.

Freud, so often chilly about people, could get a little goopy about dogs. He came to his love for them late, when Hitler was consolidating his power in Germany and Freud's own misanthropy was burgeoning. By that point, he had mouth cancer (besides dogs, his other great love was cigars), and as he retreated inside himself—dealing with the pain of multiple surgeries on his jaw—his dogs became his most trusted companions and even colleagues. He believed in and relied on their insights about people, and they became participants in his practice.

His later analyses were often attended by one of his handsome, leonine chows, particularly Yofi, a gift from his daughter Anna, who he came to care for so much that Anna thought the dog had replaced her in his affections. Yofi "has a very psychoanalytic mind," he asserted, telling one patient that when she detected resistance, she would leave the room, and that when it was time for the session to end, she would yawn. And after reprimanding Yofi for licking her genitals, he told another patient it was hard to get her to stop, a difficult problem. "It's just like analysis," he said.

Yofi played perhaps her most famous role in the analysis of the

American poet Hilda Doolittle, serving, according to her, as a kind of mediator of the transference and countertransference, an emotional go-between, as well as an inexhaustible subject of analytic grist. Doolittle also wondered whether "the Professor was more interested in Yofi than my story."

As usual, Freud was on to something. Yofi's role as Doolittle described it in that therapeutic setting is one that dogs play in many a family. In our household, Stella is a central figure. She's a totem of family love and a mediator, allowing feelings to be expressed that might otherwise be kept under wraps. She draws them out and helps them flower. She's also a safety valve in arguments—it's hard to maintain a state of white-hot rage at your partner when the dog comes and puts her head on your knee, eager for her evening walk.

The triangle is an important concept in family systems. Developed by a psychologist named Murray Bowen in the 1950s, the theory of triangles holds that when two people are in conflict, they inevitably involve a third to displace some of the tension. When our son arrived in our lives, he was the third point in the triangle—which is a lot of pressure to put on a child. Whatever issues we were embroiled with inevitably affected him too.

For us, Stella complicated this web in mostly happy ways, making our relations more fluid and less brittle (in my highly unempirical view). We didn't have to worry about scarring Stella for life if we fight, the way we did with our son, and her comic presence kept things light. Just by being on hand, she can change the subject. We didn't develop a dynamic of you-love-the-dog-more-than-me, or too much conflict over who walks her. And Stella now treats Charlie as her master, as just another adult, which I like to think is good life practice for him.

Things don't always work out so well. Some dogs end up as scapegoats, convenient receptacles for an adult's rage, their behavioral inadequacies reflecting a human's own shortcomings. And watching this occur is almost as ugly as seeing that dynamic between a parent and a child. When Stella was young, I sometimes wondered what it was about me and my family that made her misbehave. I envisioned a life of leash wars and low-level conflict and shouts of STELLA!!!—*A Streetcar Named Desire* in constant rerun. I didn't want to resent my dog. For her part, Angela often felt that Stella was a bit remote emotionally, focused on her own pursuits and insufficiently attentive. At times she didn't seem to care whether she was with us or not. You could go through life disappointed in your dog, and for a time I worried about these behaviors and wondered what the consequences might be. But luckily, they turned out to be passing teenage phases. I'm still miserable and blame myself when she gets overexcited in the dog run and speeds around growling like a mad dog—what's a parent to do? But mostly, with some training and the wisdom of her current four years, she became a really great dog: "a good girl," as Angela likes to say.

I certainly treat Stella like a child, but she's clearly different in significant ways. Her current family position, if not all her physical gifts, is liable to continue, whereas a child grows up and necessarily grows away. There are fewer human satisfactions, but there's also less risk, and fewer opportunities for conflict. She's easy to love, indeed. And that quality makes a dog very useful in New York City.

One wet early winter morning, I went to see Barbra Zuck Locker, a New York psychotherapist who's been thinking about dogs and people for the better part of three decades. Her office is in the Beresford on West Eighty-first Street, the biggest of Emery Roth's Central Park West dream castles, with three towers to the San Remo's two. It's one of those city places that's gorgeous in all weather. Mist hung low in the trees, some of which still held a few sprays of orange leaves. At that hour, the dogs of the Upper West Side were returning from their morning walks, streaming out of the park's Eighty-first Street entrance. It was quite a show. This is one of the dressier parts of the city, and about half the dogs were wearing rain slickers, their bright colors contrasting with the dark livery of the doormen they often stopped to greet.

The Beresford and its neighbors are the stagey backdrop for many a New Yorker's personal fairy tale. Some of them come true—Jerry Seinfeld lives upstairs, as do a quorum of other New York glitterati. But when dreams don't turn out quite as imagined, the dreamers end up in ground-floor therapists' offices like Locker's, with its discreet entrance just west of the main awning where, behind almost-closed venetian blinds, personal dramas can be rewritten, and dreams and reality can be brought into better balance.

It's long been Barbra Locker's contention that dogs can play many roles in this process. Locker, petite and auburn-haired, dressed in flats and New York black, has been amazed to watch the world come around to her point of view. In the early 1980s she wrote her Ph.D. dissertation on the possible health benefits of dogs, part of the first wave of such studies. At the time she and her grad student husband were caring for a sick cocker spaniel, "ferrying back and forth to the Animal Medical Center, spending money we didn't have. You couldn't even talk about it," she said. "People would think you were nuts." One acquaintance from Texas, she told me, suggested a cheaper solution: "A bullet only costs a dime."

Locker had made us some tea. Her right hand played absentmindedly with the fur on the head of her lamblike little Havanese. Gussie is a rescue dog, treated terribly by her former owner, but she's now calm and self-possessed, showing no obvious signs of her troubled past. Gussie has become ubiquitous in Locker's practice—"my copilot," she calls her. One thing the dog can bring into a therapeutic situation is comedy. "Oh, he doesn't want those wet paws on him," Locker said in a singsong, very unshrinklike voice when Gussie greeted me at the door. "Not with those wet paws!"

But often with dogs, whimsy can be a gateway to the deepest of secrets. Locker told me of a client, a daughter of an august family from an eastern metropolis, who was very walled off and hard to reach. During one of their sessions, the woman spent the entire time on the floor of the office, petting Gussie. After that, said Locker, "she told me a story that she'd never told me before. At seven or eight, she'd had a puppy. Her mother was very, very proper. And the puppy made messes, as puppies do, and no one ever trained it. And she came home one day and the puppy was gone—it had been given away, or so the mother said. Her mother told her that the dog was too messy, too dirty. She never had a chance to say good-bye. It was character forming for her. She worried that if she did something wrong, she too might be given away, with no warning."

Children, Locker said, learn about their parents from how they treat other children—a category into which dogs can fall too. In New York dogs often can keep couples together just as children do, making a family out of two people. Locker told me a story about a couple she'd once counseled who'd bonded over a cocker spaniel and then married. It wasn't a happy marriage, "but the dog was a bridge between them," Locker said. When the spaniel died, the marriage did too.

Gussie had moved to the other side of the office and was happily chewing a bone almost as long as she was. It got me thinking about dogs in my own relationship. Our first dog, Scout, a cheerfully cantankerous Westie, played the role of our first child while we dreamed our Beresford dreams and did whatever else we were doing until we finally got around to producing Charlie. It's a pretty standard New York City pattern, and it was ours—and I was happy about it.

"It's the old saw," said Locker. "If you can't take care of a plant, you can't take care of a dog. And if you can't take care of a dog, you can't take care of a child." Possibly this was true in our case, although a squalling little bundle of love definitely has a way of concentrating the mind. Sometimes, Locker says, the ease and lack of judgment involved in loving a dog is so satisfying that nothing more is needed. Locker doesn't judge these people—contentment is contentment, whether it's produced by a dog or by a wife or by a child. But all of us know people for whom a beloved pet is an excuse to retreat from the human world, the frustrations of dealing with friends and partners who talk back.

While a therapist's job may be to gently deflate a patient's more outlandish dreams (the high-floor Classic 8 in the Beresford, looking down on the tiny figures and their dogs on the walkways of Central Park), it's not always to deliver the whole, unvarnished truth. "Some people," she told me with her gravest look, "are very, very boring." This must be the secret pain of the psychotherapist. And for such people too, a prescription can be: *Get a dog*. Instantly, their conversations and their lives (and the therapist's too) improve.

In families and in therapists' offices, a dog can be a surrogate, a stand-in, an old memory, a conduit, a symbol. But it's also true that the dog's flesh and blood realness brings a kind of animal solidity to our abstracted lives. In the world of e-mail and texting and videoconferencing, a relationship with a dog is unmediated by technology (except maybe an invisible fence or one of those appalling radio collars). Unlike with people, with a dog you have to have a physical, personal, one-to-one interaction—even the cats can sort of play with the iPad.

Locker believes that this intimacy is the key to dogs' appeal in a city like New York. They take us back to simpler modes of interaction—and meanwhile we want to dress them in coats and keep them in apartments for hours on end, bringing them into our unanchored modern lives. One reason Stella goes crazy in the dog run is that, no matter how hard I try, I can't give her as much exercise on a leash as she needs. Yet many dogs don't have it as good as she does. Dogs are built for life with people, but they're also built for outdoor life, pursuing their own ends, not sleeping on the rug while we're at work. It's a basic conflict in the canine-human relationship. No wonder so many New York dogs need psychopharmacology.

Stella's unusual place in my household, with her preposterous humanlike status, reminds me of Woody Allen's joke about relationships at the end of *Annie Hall*. A man goes to a psychiatrist, complaining that his brother thinks he's a chicken, and when the psychiatrist suggests getting the brother some help, the man replies: "I would, but I need the eggs." An outsider looking at the place of dogs in our culture might think we were all suffering from some kind of mass delusion—but we definitely need the eggs.

At a chemical level, it may not matter that the dog is not a person. An increasing amount of evidence points to oxytocin, the all-purpose bonding hormone, as the crucial mediator in these effects—exactly the same mediator that underlies many significant human contacts, including the bond between mother and child. A 2009 study by Miho Nagasawa of Azabu University (near Tokyo) found that people's urinary oxytocin spiked after interactions with their dogs. Interestingly, the length of the gaze was significant—those who looked longer into the eyes of their dogs got a bigger dose. The gaze is fundamental to the interaction between mother and infant—it's the basic communicative building block. A dog's willingness to gaze at a human is also one of the basic differences between dogs and wolves. Nagasawa and his colleagues suggest that dogs and humans may have "a common style of attachment," which would be a key to understanding this unusual relationship.

The role of oxytocin in dog-human bonding has interesting corollaries. While the hormone increases trust and attachment, it apparently doesn't make people love everybody. In fact, it tends to reinforce the cohesion of our social groups, partly at the expense of outsiders. A Dutch study even found that the hormone can play a role in ethnocentrism. Oxytocin, the authors wrote, enhances not only in-group favoritism "but to a lesser extent, out-group derogation." The love for one's friends and family is accompanied by an increased dislike for those who are not in the group. This alarming yin-and-yang makes a lot of sense. I often wonder if I would save Stella before I'd save a stranger. I'd like to think not, and I hope never to have to choose—but it would certainly be something I'd struggle with.

Dogs actually do pretty well at providing our needed eggs—better than people in some respects. A long and fascinating thread of research, after three decades, has demonstrated that dogs produce measurable positive health effects on people. Though many aspects to this research are still disputed, the stress-reducing power of dogs is increasingly acknowledged.

In a 1980 study of ninety-two patients who'd suffered either heart attacks or angina, Brooklyn College researcher Erika Friedmann, now at the University of Maryland, found that the patients with pets (any pet—even a snake) had measurably higher survival rates than those without. (As it happens, Barbra Zuck Locker collaborated with her on one of these studies.) Friedmann coauthored a larger study in 1995 that came to a similar conclusion, except she found that dogs offered better results than other pets, possibly because they have to be walked. Their results have winked in and out in subsequent studies, but the consensus is growing that dogs, while not quite a wonder drug, have measurably beneficial effects on human health. This influence is related to the growing realization that loneliness is a health problem— again, the *Bowling Alone* phenomenon. Social connections buffer stress—without social contact, our chemistry can go haywire.

Beginning in the 1990s, Karen Allen, a psychology professor at the University of Buffalo, performed a series of studies that further refine the picture of the dog's health benefits. In an ingenious early experiment designed to find out whether dogs have an effect on everyday stress, she wired volunteers with electrodes and blood-pressure monitors and had them count rapidly backward by threes from a four-digit number, a task that seems simple enough but is actually fairly challenging after a few repetitions. People's stress response when frantically counting backward was significantly reduced if a dog was on hand—even simply wandering the room—than if not.

In a refinement of this test, Allen compared the calming effects of dogs with those of spouses and found that dogs were significantly better at reducing certain measures of stress. In one experiment, she measured the blood-pressure spikes of people, all of whom had hypertension, who had to take care of brain-damaged spouses, a highly stressful activity. She found that the blood-pressure spikes of people with dogs were only a fifth as high as those without. And more recently a Japanese study found that walking or otherwise interacting with a dog (not necessarily the owner's dog) enhances heart rate variability, which is associated with stress reduction. The dog walkers experience a "parasympathetic surge"—essentially, engaging the nervous system's brake, allowing the person to relax.

James Serpell has suggested that this oxytocin effect may broker the various health effects of dogs. Oxytocin is the body's stress reducer, calming people down and lowering their anxiety. Because our stress responses, so useful in dealing with conflict, are highly unhealthy over the long term, the oxytocin produced by petting our dogs may also help us live longer.

Some scientists dispute these results, of course. But most of what I read tended to confirm my happy preconceptions about my relationship with Stella, and those between people and their dogs more generally. This research is real science, but it can feel like cheerleading, especially when amplified in the media, which loves nothing more than a heartwarming dog story. Sentimentality can't help but creep into the results, as one optimistic hypothesis after another is proved, a kind of scientific preaching to the converted. But other scientists think the research is tainted by the yearning to uncover a purpose for these animals that people have taken into their homes. "Don't do this if you don't have tenure," Karen Allen said at a UCLA symposium on pets and people. "Don't even try it."

Yet the science marched on. One study found that children who are raised with a pet are more empathetic than those who aren't. The dog—no secret here—is also an excellent wingman. A 2008 study found that a man with a dog has a much better chance of getting a woman's phone number than one without. Dogs can even tell you whether you're a good person: people who strongly dislike dogs score significantly higher on the measure of anal character and lower on the empathy scale of the California Psychological Inventory, indicating "that people who liked dogs have less difficulty relating to people." Numerous studies have found that for autistic or emotionally damaged people, dogs can serve as a kind of gateway back into the social world.

Dogs have also long been associated with human damage, with people who are lonely or have trust issues, with misanthropes (Hitler was a dog lover), and with people with lots of money who think—perhaps accurately—that that's the only reason anyone could love them. Leona Helmsley's little dog Trouble, the richest dog in the world until his death in 2011, is the obvious example. The only charitable cause specifically mentioned in Helmsley's will—her fortune was estimated at $5 billion at the low end—was to "provide for the care of dogs." The document is testament to a moral impoverishment of mythic dimensions—the last bird the queen flipped at the little people. She outsourced the work of distributing the money to her trustees, who have so far not seen fit to bestow very much of it on canine causes.

As in Helmsley's case, a dog can be a last refuge for lost people. Everyone knows people for whom a dog is a chosen escape. A kind of therapeutic solipsism is at work in this type of relationship, needs met and unmet. The dog fits perfectly into this sort of calculus because its needs are so simple—and of course, your dog doesn't know you're a narcissist. Loving a dog can be like looking into a mirror that strips away your bad qualities, your human spikes, reflecting only the pure, caring person you believe yourself to be. Relatedly, Nicholas Epley, Adam Waytz, and John T. Cacioppo, psychologists at the University of Chicago, have confirmed what is obvious to anyone observing the dog's place in the modern world: that loneliness amplifies our propensity for anthropomorphism. In the absence of people to interact with, we transmogrify our dogs into people.

It's easy to think, looking at canines like Helmsley's Trouble, that dogs are a species of emotional con men, wheedling their way into the hearts of weak people and extracting their bounty, whether it be a huge fortune or an extra piece of steak and a place in the bed. People get something out of these relationships, it's true. But dogs look as if they are getting more. John Archer, an evolutionary psychologist at the University of Central Lancashire, has gone so far as to suggest that dogs are social parasites. "Pets," he wrote in a 1997 paper, with the hint of a killjoy's glee, "can be considered to manipulate the human species. They are similar in this regard to social parasites such as the cuckoo. . . . The affection, food, and time and energy devoted to a pet is not repaid in terms of related offspring and it could have been more profitably spent caring for human offspring and relatives." Archer judged our relationships with our pets as "maladaptive behavior," and though his argument is about evolution rather than about the day-to-day life with animals, it tended to reinforce the notion that there was something amiss with these increasingly intimate relationships. Stella, he seemed to suggest, was duping me, selling me a bill of goods with those big brown eyes, getting something for nothing.

Drawing on ideas developed in the 1940s by Konrad Lorenz, Archer suggests that the "infant schema" of a dog's face—essentially, the high forehead, big eyes, short snout, and floppy ears—might have evolved to take advantage of humans' innate responses. These features, known as "social releasers," elicit a human caregiver's response—and some studies have maintained that women are slightly more susceptible to them than are men. It's a compelling theory, if a bit unsettling: *Did he just call my dog a parasite?* And there are an abundance of dispositive arguments one might make against Archer. For one thing, the spreadsheet over the centuries also contains many reasons humans choose to have dogs—for hunting, herding, and guarding. But the simplest reason might be *because we want to.* Dogs are a part of human culture in a way that is not reducible to simple calculations of cost and benefit—somehow they're involved, like art or religion, in our higher functions. Stella is, for me, more than the sum of her cost in dog food.

Sometimes I thought people like Archer wanted to wish away the presence of dogs in our homes: all an illusion, nothing to see here.

But the contrary evidence was right there, on the rug. Stella was more than a trickster—she was a friend, less communicative than those in my human circle, but this gave her her own distinctive excellences. Whatever Archer's intentions, I could concede that he was right that somehow, by design or by evolutionary accident, dogs have become sublimely suited for life with us. They've been part of our ecosystem for millennia—and we are the central feature in theirs.

*Three*

# The Search for Stella's Brain

I was convinced by much of the science I'd been reading: Stella was my friend, somehow imprinted in my chemistry as well as my conscious sentiments. But what exactly was this creature that I was now having a relationship with? Friendship involves commonalities, and I wasn't at all certain what these were. With people, language provides a window into another mind, cobbled together and limited and illusory though the view may be. But with Stella, all I had were her brown eyes and elaborate vocalizations—richly expressive but still limited—and her various expressions, including the dreaded Mad Face, head slightly lowered and turned away, held absolutely still, which means: *It's really time to take me out.*

To find out what was going on in Stella's brain, one week in late July I went off to attend the second Canine Science Forum, held at the University of Vienna, whose Clever Dog Lab is one of the field's central institutions. The Great Hall of the University of Vienna is a preposterous venue for a conference on canine science—no dogs are allowed. Really, it's a preposterous venue for any purpose, mixing as it does the comic and the august. Looming, cheerful marbles of Duke Rudolf IV, who founded the university in 1365, and Empress Maria Theresa, the eighteenth-century lady bountiful, such as she was, of this Joseph Cornell–box city, beckon from either side of the dais, where the lecturers speak from under a dark wood gazebo the size of a small summer cottage.

When I told people I would be attending the Canine Science Forum, they laughed. It's a cross that this young field has to bear. Dogs have certainly long been considered worthy of study—think of Pavlov, and all the many vivisectors for whom the dog was the easiest avenue toward anatomical knowledge. But mostly the study of dogs has been a means to other ends. The suggestion that dog science is a field of study, with its own conventions, to be done largely for its own sake, continues to surprise people.

The researchers regard the dog's presence in our cultural lives as a fact worthy of study and pursue it wherever it may lead. This means they poke their noses into provinces where science has seldom gone— the living room, the street corner, the dog run. The research produces plenty of comedy (as always with dogs), as the language of science and its complexities cloak the most ordinary of activities. It's hard to keep a straight face when you're looking at a dog trying to get a treat, no matter how that particular dynamic is described. In the past, science has tried to untangle what was human from what was natural—but investigating the dog means investigating the tangle.

I can't say that, on some level, when I went to the conference, I wasn't looking for some eureka moment, some leap forward that would clarify in scientific language this whole question of Stella's humanlike social talents and the strangeness of having this predator in my home, lying on her back, waiting to get her stomach scratched. But science doesn't work that way. More often it's a trudge through the fog.

The big established labs, the Clever Dog Lab in Vienna and the Family Dog Project at Eötvös Loránd University in Budapest, were the dominant groups in attendance. The Brits were blustery and confident, possibly as a result of getting to operate in their native language. A group or two from most of the European countries were present, and also a group from Japan, which has a thriving dog research community. But even in the Great Hall, with several hundred Ph.D.'s listening raptly, ordinary human perceptions and sheer ordinariness often threatened to overrun the science. The scientific reality of our relationship with the dog is hidden in plain sight, which means looking at things that seem obvious, measuring the most evident qualities of our connection.

A group from the University of Pisa had investigated whether owners or nonowners were better at understanding canine interactions like play-bows and mounting—they found that, yes, owners do have a knowledge advantage when it comes to their animals. So far, so good. Another team of Italian researchers showed a series of videos of dog-on-dog aggression in a dog park. In one of them, a little Jack Russell-ish dog sets upon a big, friendly black and white shepherd that wanders in too close. "That dog is crazy," said someone in the audience, to laughter throughout the hall. Female dogs, they found, are significantly more likely to engage in defensive aggression, a fact I could have told them from my experiences with Stella, the queen of such behavior, whose normally cheerful mien changes to the snarling and lunging and squealing of a hound of Hades if a dog seems to approach her with the wrong intent. And God help the dog that tries to mount her.

A group from New Zealand who had tested whether dogs understand human expressions of emotion—whether they distinguish between happy and angry voices—found that dogs will be slower to take a treat if it is offered with an angry voice. They also seem attuned to human sadness, though what sort of mechanism might be at work is another question. A team from the French National Veterinary School that investigated how dogs react to various human facial expressions found that dogs, like children, also have to learn to interpret them; adult dogs are better at determining human anger than are puppies.

A long series of experiments was presented, often accompanied by dark Kafkaesque videos, about how dogs behave when confronted with strange people or threats of other kinds. In one of them, a man sits in a chair in the back of a high-walled, dark little enclosure. One by one dogs are sent in to confront this ambiguous and spooky new presence. A German shepherd with a shyness problem stalks back and forth nervously along the back wall, keeping his distance. Some of the other dogs have more direct methods of confronting their social anxiety. An Irish wolfhound, which must have weighed a hundred pounds, jumps right into the lap of the experimenter.

After the videos, a glamorous, long-haired Swiss man spoke excitedly about reintroducing livestock-guarding dogs to the Alps—a program necessitated by the intensive husbanding of the wolf population, which puts the local sheep in harm's way. The wolves steer clear of wandering tourists—but the livestock-guarding dogs, raised to be wary of intruders, sometimes don't, and attack. It was definitely a postmodern problem, the kind of situation that reminds us of how deeply we are involved in managing nature, even in the wildest of places.

For the first day or so, the conference in Vienna was a party at which the guest of honor was absent. But on the second night a special dispensation was made, and the no-dogs-allowed policy was temporarily rescinded. It was an antic scene, the dais turned into a kind of altar of dog love, a reminder of why people study dogs in the first place.

Just below the dais where Freud and Schrödinger and all the others long ago delivered lectures, a low, long-haired brown dog played a canine version of a video game. Pictures of dogs and landscapes flashed randomly on a screen. When the dog pressed her nose onto a picture of a dog, a treat would pop out of a chute at the bottom. When she pressed some other picture, the screen went orange and the game stopped for a while. The apparatus was developed by Friederike Range, the head of the university's dog lab, who was cochairing the conference, and her colleagues, and it can be used for a large array of learning and perceptual experiments. It's a big advance because the handler can't see the screen, avoiding the Clever Hans Effect, where the experimenter gives the animal hidden cues, thereby skewing the results. The procedure recapitulates experiments done on pigeons in the 1960s that opened a window onto how animals organize their visual worlds—how they process raw data into patterns and images. Whether the dogs are actually seeing what's depicted on the screen or merely reacting to different patterns is still an open question. Some researchers have found the rudiments of symbolic intelligence in certain brilliant dogs—they can take a smaller toy as a kind of representation of a larger one, one thing standing for another.

A crowd gathered, and Range and her colleague Zsófia Virányi, who was cohosting the conference, stood by proudly as their charges showed their stuff. A border collie stepped up, as focused and intense as a teenager with an Xbox, and pressed her nose to the screen, then bounced down to collect her reward. *Oops, that one's wrong.* Realizing her mistake, she moved her nose across to press the correct one, but it was too late. She stared at the screen unhappily, waiting for her next chance.

Range, blond and high-cheekboned, is one of the field's young turks—though everyone in it is pretty young. The Germanic definiteness of her presentation makes her a vivid emcee for the conference. Range and Virányi found, in a series of groundbreaking studies (published in 2007), that dogs have the ability to selectively imitate, in much the way a human infant can. Babies, even without the full human richness of adult perceptions of others' motives—our theory of mind and everything that goes in it—can intuit very early on that people's actions are directed at goals. By fourteen months or so, they do not simply perform monkey-see, monkey-do—they can tell whether the person they are watching is performing the action in the service of the goal, and they will choose to imitate it only if it is.

University of Washington psychologist Andrew Meltzoff, in an exploration of imitation, tested whether babies would learn to lean forward and touch a light box with their foreheads, thereby turning on the light, by watching an experimenter do it. Most of the babies did as the experimenter showed, bowing down to the light box. In the animal world, learning an unusual behavior of this kind just by watching is unusual—in a way, imitation is the basic glue of human culture. A chimp can learn to turn on the light, but it does it with its hands, not its forehead.

A group of Hungarian scientists complicated the picture by draping the experimenter in a blanket in some of the tests, as if she were cold. Without the blanket, the experimenter could easily have turned on the light with her hand. But with the blanket, using her head made more sense, because her hands were covered. The babies seemed able to make this distinction. Most of those who watched the experimenter touch the light box with her head when her hands were covered went ahead and turned on the light with their hands, understanding that the head-touch was not essential to achieving the goal.

Range and Virányi designed an experiment along these lines, training dogs to push a lever to obtain food—a dog would ordinarily use its mouth for such a task—then having other dogs watch them to see if they'd learn. In some of the tests, they'd give the experimenter dogs a tennis ball, so they couldn't use their mouth and had to use a paw. In one of dog science's most remarkable findings, Range and Virányi demonstrated that the dogs had mostly performed much like the infants, imitating the unusual action to get their reward, but only when necessary.

This result, still controversial, certainly doesn't imply that the dog is in some way smarter than the chimp. The opposite is closer to the truth—the chimp, more confident in its perceptions of cause and effect, easily discounts the odd behavior of the head-pressing hairless ape, doing it the easy way. Rather, the result suggests that infants and dogs are more gullible, albeit in a way that may be highly useful. It's a *social* talent. They think—or intuit, or feel, or whatever term omits anthropomorphism—that the experimenter knows something useful; they're ready to be helped.

Meltzoff has hypothesized that imitation is a step, the first glimmer, on the journey to a full-blown theory of mind. It'll take the babies they tested another year or so to get there. But exactly how far dogs are capable of going is still under discussion. In Budapest, researcher Josef Topal tested a four-year-old Belgian Tervuren named Philip—trained as an assistance dog for the disabled—to see if it could imitate a series of human actions. Philip turned out to be a prodigy. After he observed a handler performing an action—say, fetching a bottle or stick and moving it to another part of the room—the dog repeated it. To the researchers, the fact that the dog, not having hands, could translate the action to his mouth suggested a glimmer of understanding of the underlying semantics of the action—*Get stick*—rather than merely a rote response. Primates and dolphins, of course, are much better at this than dogs. But imitation of any kind is a fairly high-level skill, and a decade ago no scientist would have believed that dogs had anything like this capability.

Alexandra Horowitz, the Barnard researcher and author of the best seller *Inside of a Dog,* came up to ask Range about some experiments she'd been working on, investigating whether dogs have a sense of jealousy. Jealousy is one of the secondary or self-conscious emotions—along with pride, envy, guilt, and shame—that are said, along with our wizardlike cognition, to distinguish us from other animals. It's long been folk knowledge that dogs possess a few of these emotions, at least in rudimentary form—and the search for them is one of the defining questions of the field. In a 2008 paper, Range and her colleagues established that dogs are responsive to whether a handler has acted fairly: if a dog sees that another dog is getting a treat for giving its paw, while it is getting nothing, it will hesitate to give its paw or not give it at all. The effect is ambiguous and a bit hard to detect, but Range's team was satisfied enough, as any dog owner will attest that fairness is an element of a dog's moral equipment. At that point, however, Horowitz's results were still inconclusive.

In 2009 Horowitz published a now-well-known paper showing that the dog's famous guilty look is, to some degree, an anthropomorphic myth. Canine guilt is one of the oldest questions in the dog science world. Darwin believed that dogs display shame, guilt's close relative, and Konrad Lorenz wrote about guilt in 1954. Various scientists have explored the question in the intervening decades. In Horowitz's study, she had owners order their dogs not to eat a treat, then leave the room. But she tricked some of the owners: she told them their dog had eaten the treat even if it hadn't. The owners scolded the dogs, who behaved in ways identified with guilt—head downcast, avoiding eye contact, ears drooping, slinking away. Horowitz concluded that these behaviors were a response to the owners' scolding words, and not expressions of guilt because they knew they had misbehaved by eating the treat. What looked like guilt had to do with foreknowledge of impending punishment, not necessarily a sense of having done something wrong. In fact, the dogs that looked guiltiest were the ones that were being punished in error. It was, in effect—and this is of course another anthropomorphism—a false confession.

On one level, Horowitz's conclusion may look like evidence for the simplicity of dogs—as well as the very imperfect interspecial mind-reading skills of humans. But even if Stella is not going to approach Raskolnikov in her inner moral turmoil (in fact, she appears to be farther away from this condition than most dogs I know), many questions about the nature of guilt remain unanswered. I think of it in human terms. Our sense of right and wrong is constructed partly on our internalized fear of consequences—of punishment, either now or in the hereafter. Even if we feel guilty, we may be pretty confused about what we should feel guilty about. And being falsely accused produces turmoil too. So maybe that supposedly guilty look is a kind of proto-guilt, a foundation for the richer human experience.

When a dog has actually committed a crime (to tell a thoroughly anthropomorphic and unscientific story), it may be pretending it has not, while nursing a secret fear that it will be found out. Every dog owner has, at one time or another, received an especially cheerful and winning greeting at the door, only to then discover a chaotic scene in the kitchen, with the trash knocked over and remains of the roast chicken carcass in all manner of unfortunate hiding places. And then the guilty look appears. The mechanism may be just a jerk of the knee, an anticipation of punishment. But there are times when the dog *is* guilty and knows it. My admittedly anecdotal experience gives ample evidence that a dog's brain has the capability to process the fact that strewing the floor with trash may cause problems afterward, and to imagine perhaps that some slavish, submissive gestures may help make things right with the angry party. Whether inner turmoil is involved, and what kind of inner turmoil it might be, is a question science may never answer—but that some may be involved seems at least a hypothesis worth exploring. If dogs wrestle internally, they wrestle with what *we* think is right. It's also significant that the behavior—that familiar gaze avoidance and sniveling supplication—*appears to us* to mean feelings of guilt. It may be simply a matter of cause and effect. But it also may be a legacy from the wolf's social past, a way for a weaker animal to get by when a more powerful animal decrees that it's done wrong. (Even in our world, the ways of the lawgiver are not always rational.)

Whether dogs possess a humanlike sense of fairness is an even more contentious issue. A growing body of evidence indicates that humans experience unfairness on a biological level—that inequity aversion is programmed, one of the basic building blocks of our social order. Humans will punish those who perpetrate inequity, even at cost to themselves. But whether other animals share this trait has been the subject of a prolonged debate over the last decade. A famous study found that capuchin monkeys possess this faculty, but other studies maintain that the capuchins' behavior had more to do with trying to get the best possible rewards for themselves than with any kind of comparative equality: what looked complex was actually quite simple.

Twenty years ago few scientists would have believed that a dog has a sense of fairness—unlike dog owners, who have always believed that a dog that sees treats being distributed unequally will mope.

In my dealings with Stella, I certainly behave as if she has a sense of fairness—it would be unthinkable to give another dog a treat in her sight without giving her one at least as big—if not twice as big (in keeping with what I imagine to be her sense of fairness: two for me, one for you). It's possible that my behavior is as much about my own sense of fairness—and my wish to take care of my family member—as it is about anything she might feel. It's part of the anthropomorphic legend I've inevitably built around her. But there's *something* there. But the mechanisms at work are more complicated than simple hunger. If one of the cats is getting a good stomach scratch, Stella will watch closely, seemingly awaiting her turn: *I want what she's getting.* It's simple—but maybe such a feeling is one of the building blocks of the more complex emotion jealousy. At any rate, it's easy to interpret it that way—Stella is an open book, even if, as seems likely, I'm making up large parts of that book's contents.

Everyone agrees that dogs and wolves, as social animals, have various mechanisms for defusing conflict and even for distributing resources among the group. In some situations, wolves and dogs clearly adjust their behavior to the abilities and needs of their conspecifics and will enforce social norms. Dogs in play will calibrate their aggressiveness to equalize the game, and they'll avoid playing with a dog that won't toe the line. "There's no play for poor rule followers," Horowitz said in her talk at the conference. It's not quite morality—more a series of ritualized cues that keep aggression in check.

Horowitz studied at the University of California at San Diego, collaborating early on with Marc Bekoff of the University of Colorado, a legendary animal cognition researcher who'd done pioneering work on the rituals of dog play. "I didn't go to grad school to study dogs," Horowitz told me. "Initially, I was interested in the dog as a creature that would allow us to make inferences about minds. I wanted to try to determine if we see things the same way as nonhuman animals."

As she moved deeper, she had to overcome a basic skepticism about the work itself. "I wasn't convinced I should study dogs. I thought it was a nonserious subject. I've thought of different reasons why this should be. One is because it's a domesticated animal. Scientists are supposed to be interested in animals that are uninfluenced by humans, in the raw state. And humans adulterated the process—which is true, of course."

As her career progressed, she came to think of her dog studies less as a means of understanding our minds than as an end in itself. The focus of her work now, she says, is "What is it like to be a dog?" It's a controversial approach—philosophers have been fighting about whether the objective-subjective barrier could be breached in this way ever since Thomas Nagel's 1974 paper, "What Is It Like to Be a Bat?" But for Horowitz, this difficulty presents an opportunity. "It's not obvious how to answer these questions scientifically," she says. "It allows me to pursue a lot of different approaches."

Taking into account dogs' subjective experience (which is also a tenet of autistic animal savant Temple Grandin), she believes, could lead to a small revolution in how we treat them. "It could really change how we own dogs, because if you're really attentive to a dog's experience, it's hard to do things like leave the dog at home for long stretches, the kinds of things we did as kids."

Trying to peer inside their minds, detecting internal processes based on external signs, is maddeningly difficult work, often interpretive, and partly an art—which, in the realm of science, can be a big problem. When scientists are reading mental states from lingering glances, it's easy to be wrong.

When I thought of Stella's experience, I pictured something like a movie with no words, in Sensurround—and smellaround, of course—careening and intense and vivid, no ideas but in things, something Pauline Kael would have loved. But of course it's a fantasy. Some scientists at Berkeley once monitored the brain waves of people looking at pictures, then managed to crudely reconstruct the pictures from the brain waves: mind reading! Sometime in the future, will scientists find a way to map the fantastic electric pulsing and hormonal secretions going on in a dog's brain, so we can watch the movie? Another fantasy. This is a bridge I don't expect to be crossing anytime soon.

So mostly we're left with judging internal states by external behavior. People disagree all the time about what they've witnessed and what it means. Even if we're getting the results we want, a whole host of factors can trip us up. The most famous of these is the aforementioned Clever Hans Effect. Hans was a famous turn-of-the-century horse who appeared to be a genius at counting—until it was discovered that he was receiving secret cues from his owner, though the owner didn't know he was supplying them. I wondered too whether a kind of yearning for an animal connection, for bridging the gap between us and our relatives, might also be the root of newer errors. If you are in this line of work, how could you not hope that your charges would turn out to be little geniuses? Not human, exactly, but something more than bundles of instinct. In Vienna, this powerful undercurrent was a definite danger: it could tug at the science, pulling it toward a kind of cheerful fantasy of man-dog harmony.

As the Canine Science Forum went on, the veil of science seemed to slip. Many of the participants echoed my perception that change is coming to the dog world. Sometimes a great struggle seemed to be under way, in which sides should be chosen. The few dog trainers in the group, hugely outnumbered by the scientists, seemed especially susceptible to these feelings. One afternoon a lumbering white-haired Swedish woman—a legendary dog trainer and canine empath named Turid Rugaas—took the stage. Mystics have always had a place in the dog world, communicators with the hidden worlds of nature. Knowledge of animals can be like a second sight. I thought of Rugaas in those terms. An expert in dog language, and in the many forms of canine-human misunderstanding, she spoke emotionally about putting in place a new code of ethics for dog training, to minimize the stressors that cause dogs so much needless hardship, and to bring the practice into the twenty-first century. Her point was that, for all our familiarity with our pets, we treat them without adequate consideration, making gestures that they inevitably misinterpret. "Never. Hug. The. Dog," she said emphatically. "Teach your children to never hug the dog."

Stella didn't seem to get the memo about that—she seems to like being hugged, or at least suppresses her rage so it's not visible to me. But no doubt much about her, and how she should be treated, remains hidden. A central objective of the conference, and of much thinking in the dog world nowadays, is to address communication problems between dogs and people—the kind of neurotic interchange that arises from radically different frames of reference. Children are especially susceptible to miscommunicating. A study at the University of Lincoln in Britain found that 62 percent of the four-year-olds tested interpreted a dog's bared teeth as a smile. (Adults have made this mistake too, of course. In a photograph, a Russian chimp coming back from its space voyage was grimacing—widely interpreted as an expression of joy, but actually the face of a chimp in abject terror.) The point, as in many of the conference talks, was that dogs and humans have much to learn about each other.

My favorite character at the conference was Alexei Vereshchagin, a young Russian ethologist, long-haired and bearded, a glamorous figure in a crazy-quilt jacket who studies wild dogs in Moscow. I talked to Vereshchagin one afternoon during a break. He believes the wild dogs live in big packs, with clear hierarchies and richly cooperative behaviors—his photographs show them looting dumpsters, one dog passing its haul down to its waiting accomplices. It's a fantastic Dickensian vision, outlaw fraternities making a living however they can—the Dog Gangs of Moscow. Some specialize in begging, says Vereshchagin, some in scavenging; some latch on to a particular place or a particular group of people; some even ride the subway. I could see that he gets a charge out of the work and identifies with his subjects. His confident descriptions of their cooperative behavior raised the eyebrows of some of the scientists in Vienna, but he comes from a different dog culture, one that answers the question of canine intelligence in its own way.

One night a well-known British veterinarian named John Bradshaw gave a lecture called "Conceptualizing the Domestic Dog: Should We Start Again?" It was a kind of overture to the New Age of Dog. The dog today is not bound by what it once was, said Bradshaw, by the old stereotypes. Freed from these shackles, the dog can enter civilization in a more enlightened way: anything seems possible. Such happy talk finally drove the Russian a little crazy—it seemed to him like a fantasy. During the question-and-answer session after Bradshaw's lecture, Vereshchagin burst up from his seat in the center of the hall. In his research, he said, he'd seen dominance, and he'd seen pack behavior. Dominance is the way of the world, and it doesn't do any good to deny it. It's operating even here, he pointed out. "You're up there"—Vereshchagin shrugged his shoulders dramatically—"and we're down here. You've proved you have some dominance."

Later that night I happened to be seated next to him and a few other conference dissidents at a café near the university. "They're testing the dogs in such visual ways," said one of his companions.

"And they're testing things that are obvious to you the first time you see them," Vereshchagin said, his voice booming through the quiet Vienna street.

Then he took out his laptop and began showing pictures of his dogs—love for which, no doubt, he and Bradshaw could agree on.

Bradshaw's talk was, partly, an attack on Cesar Millan's be-the-pack-leader mode of dog training, with its emphasis on teaching the dog to know its place and the bad consequences that will occur if the dog doesn't learn that lesson early and often. Training is one of the main focuses of dog politics, and Millan's ideas, partly because of his enormous celebrity, are the main flashpoint: nothing except euthanasia inspires such heated arguments in the dog world, and even more in Bradshaw's native England than in the United States.

Bradshaw's lecture seemed to promise a better, simpler, happier world—one of treats and actions and responses. In the New World of Dog, the dog will feel no pain. But what *will* the dog feel? It will possibly be a happier creature, but also a simpler one, not the Manichean-souled animal of Millan's imaginings, the one who needs your help to get a hold of his demons. And not the one who lives by his wits, scavenging with his fellows on the streets of Moscow. But part of what makes dogs interesting to people, however questionable, evaporates in a conception like Bradshaw's. To some, he seems to be dumbing dogs down, reducing them to the lowest common denominator, as if the dog-human relationship were entirely based on treats.

The Old World of Dog could be harsh, but it may have taken the animals' minds more seriously. It's an odd paradox. In the old days, dogs could be moral actors, good or bad or mischievous or dull—the whole anthropomorphic kit. This wasn't a problem because science wasn't a major factor then—it was up to the trainer to manage these qualities. In the 1960s and earlier, the dominant method of training was, essentially, "Do this, or else." William Koehler, the preeminent dog trainer in the middle of the last century—he'd been a military dog handler and afterward the head trainer for Walt Disney Studios—defined this method as giving the dog "the right to the consequences of his actions." Koehler was patently a dog lover, and his epigram reflects a deep respect for the animal. His ideal was an off-leash animal, one that could work independently while still paying attention to its owner and that knew enough not to get itself into trouble. But Koehler's methods of bringing his dogs to this level of maturity—choke collars and violent jerks on the leash—certainly could cause pain. Later trainers who preferred gentler methods called it "yank and crank" and painted Koehler as kind of a monster. And it's true that his book contains some strong stuff. In counseling owners on how to deal with a dog that rebels by trying to bite, Koehler recommended that before the dog's teeth meet their target, it should be jerked to the ground. "TO LET THE BITING DOG RECOVER HIS FOOTING WHILE HE STILL HAD STRENGTH TO RENEW THE ATTACK WOULD BE ALL CRUELTY," he insisted, in all caps. "The sight of a dog lying thick-tongued on his side is not pleasant, but do not let it alarm you."

Even in those more innocent and hard-hearted times, it's diffi-cult to imagine that many dog owners followed Koehler all the way with this technique. But there was method to his madness. He had the now-old-fashioned idea that suffering might have an important place in the good life—even for a dog. And pain, or the threat of it, is an important part of wolf culture, where growls and nips and various dominance displays are used to enforce civilized behavior.

Millan is in the Koehler tradition in terms of some of his tough-minded training methods—but he's added a half-scientific, half-mystical idea about wolf-pack behavior and dominance: *Show the dog, not who's boss, but who's the pack leader.* In his worldview, dogs aren't peo-ple, so people have to act like dominant dogs, rolling the animals over on the back, learning the subtle signals that govern canine society, going native with their dogs. I saw Millan one day at a North Shore Animal League function—and he's blessed with a powerful physical charisma, with an array of crisp gestures that seem to communicate more than his words do. Anyone, man or dog, would follow him. But whether this is evidence for the accuracy of his theories is another question.

Currently arrayed against Millan are the clicker trainers, descen-dants of B. F. Skinner, who believe that positive reinforcement is the best—and most humane—way to instill obedience; and scientists like Bradshaw, who think that Millan's ideas about wolf packs are inappli-cable to the relation between dogs and owners (and possibly not even to wolf packs).

Skinner's ideas—the dream of a universal system of behavior, the infamous Skinner box—may seem to belong in the musty attic of sci-ence. But in one place Skinner's ideas are even more forceful today than they were in the 1950s, and that is in the world of animal training. During World War II, two of Skinner's graduate students at the University of Minnesota, Marian Bailey and Keller Breland, moved his operant conditioning technique out of the laboratory and put it to work. They started a business, Animal Behavior Enterprises, intending to bring civilization to the nation's dogs. But no one in the dog world listened to their newfangled ideas. They trained animals for TV, coin-operated arcades, and, most famously, the dolphins at Marineland of Florida, which was the first dolphin show. No one who has watched professionally trained animals would deny that operant conditioning is a remarkable system for channeling animal minds.

But in the dog world, it took a few more decades for Skinner's training methods to triumph over Koehler's harsher, tough-love techniques. In 1985 Karen Pryor, a former dolphin trainer, published *Don't Shoot the Dog!*, which translated Skinner's methodology lucidly for the canine training world and introduced the now-ubiquitous clicker to a wide audience. Her method, most notably, didn't rely on punishment— a huge selling point in a country that had begun to regard its dogs as family members. The clicker concept—marking a desired behavior by making a sound, then rewarding with a treat—took a lot of the drama out of dog training, the agonistic struggles favored by Cesar Millan and his disciples. With the clicker and a full bag of Bacon Bits, a trainer could manipulate a dog rather than physically grapple with it. For high-level obedience competition, some trainers believe that clicker training alone is less effective than methods that supplement the persuasive power of treats with occasional physical correction. But the clicker removes negative emotions from a trainer's relations with her dogs, and more and more trainers have adopted it.

The effectiveness of operant conditioning did not necessarily constitute a cognitive argument, but the technique showed the power of associative learning. And if associative learning was that powerful, was any other kind really necessary? It definitely simplified things—*Do x, and y will happen*. Operant conditioning provided a language that we could speak and the dog could understand. Its rise to popularity also happened to coincide with changes in our own child-rearing practices, which regarded punishments like spanking as producing fear, neurosis, and damage. The same could be true for dogs.

While its removal of punishment was a definite virtue, this training model also had conceptual problems. For one thing, all animals ended up in the same bucket regarding their learning capabilities, with no essential differences between them. The Brelands broke with Skinner in 1961 over a paper they wrote called "The Misbehavior of Organisms," a provocative play on the title of Skinner's 1938 book *The Behavior of Organisms*. Some of the animals that the Brelands were training for various performances weren't responding to behavior training: a chicken would scratch and peck rather than stand calmly; a raccoon wouldn't put down some coins it had been given to get a treat. These kinds of problems persisted over their whole Noah's ark: hamsters "stopped working in a glass case after four or five reinforcements," while porpoises and whales "swallow their manipulanda (balls and inner tubes)," cats "will not leave the area of the feeder," and rabbits "will not go to the feeder." The Brelands observed "great difficulty in many species of conditioning vocalization with food reinforcement, problems in conditioning a kick in a cow, the failure to get appreciably increased effort out of the ungulates with increased drive, and so on."

For the Brelands, these results constituted a failure of behaviorism, which had been their creed. The universal machine for mental processing wasn't quite universal after all. One must understand an animal's instincts to train it properly, and some animals are harder to train than others. This seems obvious—think of herding cats—but to Skinner, it was the rankest heresy.

Behaviorism was a powerful way of understanding the world, but it succeeded partly by ignoring things that others considered obvious, or claiming that they were illusions. It was a simple system—and simplicity is prized in science—but if you used it exclusively, you overlooked differences: rats and pigeons and dogs and even people end up as the same creatures wearing different outfits. And notwithstanding its effectiveness as a training method, it's less useful as a way of talking about animals—it seems to omit parts of the world. Even behaviorists couldn't help but talk about their dogs as if they were people: *He wants to do this, but you can't let him.* Whether one can truly, in everyday life, think of a dog as purely a creature of operant conditioning, of inputs and outputs, rather than of wants and desires, of tactics and stratagems and communicative intentions, however simple-minded, is a real question. The debate isn't only, or even primarily, about science. As with many issues in the dog world, it is actually as much about morality, about good dogs and bad dogs, dogs with free will, dogs with minds of their own, dogs that have been brainwashed with treats—and about what the dog world might look like without these kinds of concepts, so easy to use whether or not they make scientific sense.

I've certainly employed operant conditioning effectively in my own efforts with Stella. The dancing chickens and seals balancing balls and dolphins bursting from the water to jump through hoops provide too much evidence to ignore. At nine months, I made a crude attempt to train Stella, armed with a couple bags of chicken strips. It took me about a week to teach her to come, sit, stay, speak, and present her paw—the pulling and pushing and coaxing soon gave way to something that looked like obedience, at least when the chicken strips were around. Given the unruly creature she was and to some degree still is, not to mention my shortcomings as a trainer, that was magic. Sometimes, when a biscuit is in the offing, she'll do all these things in quick succession, pawing the air, then flopping down, a parody of slavish obedience. I sometimes wish I hadn't taught her to bark on command, because often she'll try it even when she hasn't been asked.

But I didn't necessarily believe I was reaching her whole brain—or rather, the parts that bonded us. She had other structures there too, ways of processing her world and reacting accordingly that click-treat didn't address. Her elaborate greeting, for instance, is a means not of asking for treats but of bonding with me. And of course, I didn't want to believe that our interaction was entirely transactional—a culture of bribery. I thought of this sort of training more as a kind of Esperanto or pidgin language, good at communicating certain kinds of things but silent on others, working on all sorts of animals—rats, pigeons, dolphins, chickens. But on the question of what makes dogs specifically so suitable for life with people, the behaviorist model is largely silent—but that also means that a new generation of scientists, like the ones I met in Vienna, can step in to fill the gaps.

## Four

# How the Match Was Made

The question of why dogs and people seem so perfectly fitted, and how this relationship may have evolved, is at the core of the new canine science. Its researchers aim to apply findings from the disciplines of ethology (the study of animal behavior) and psychology to the relationship between dogs and people, to measure precisely what had once seemed like the most ordinary of interactions. The central idea, and the most controversial, is called convergence: that adaptation to life with people made dogs become more like people, developing rudimentary forms of our social wizardry. Canine science is intended to shed light not only on what makes dogs dogs but also on what makes people people.

In the second half of the twentieth century, a smattering of scientists have been purely interested in the dogs, most famously John Paul Scott and John L. Fuller (whose 1965 book, *Genetics and the Social Behavior of the Dog*, is still a bible of canine science), but in the last fifteen years the study of dogs has exploded, especially using the ethological approach. The notion of dog ethology may seem oxymoronic to a scientist, because ethology implies the study of an animal in its natural environment—and the dog's environment seemed, until recently, anything but natural. And the new field required a much more extensive knowledge of the wolf's behavioral characteristics in order to ascertain what precisely changed in the wolf to create the dog—which may be the biggest challenge that canine science faces.

One afternoon, a cool, windy summer day, the sun winking in and out through scudding clouds, I had lunch with Ádám Miklósi, the central theorist, cheerleader, and impresario of the new field, who organized the first Canine Science Forum, in Budapest in 2008. A professor at Eötvös Loránd University and head of the Family Dog Project, Miklósi is a bright-eyed, fast-talking, Charlie Chaplin–ish character with a goatee and jeans and a many-pocketed vest. We sat at a table in the courtyard of the university's main building and talked about the early days of his young field as I tried to keep the papers in front of me from blowing away. "We had no idea what we were really doing," he told me. "Now it seems to be so simple. But it was not that simple. We started doing experiments one after the other and writing down basic statements. So this whole idea about convergence, taking seriously the idea that dogs genetically adapted to the human environment, this came together quite slowly."

In Budapest in the 1990s, Miklósi was a young researcher studying under the tutelage of ethologist Vilmos Csányi. For the better part of a decade, they did research on aggression and predator avoidance in paradise fish. But in 1994 Csányi announced that the lab would henceforth be studying dogs. Miklósi, an ambitious young scientist, was skeptical. "'My god, are you crazy?' That's what I thought, although I didn't say it," he told a reporter. "None of us were happy about it."

Csányi was an eminent evolutionary researcher but also something of a renegade. He seemed to enjoy poking at the nostrums of scientists, seeing if he could get a rise. And he had always been interested in dogs. In the late 1970s, the age of Washoe the chimpanzee, when researchers were interested in animal language learning, he tried to replicate some of those experiments with dogs but found the work too difficult. Dogs found their way once again into his science through the back door—the one that his family dogs used. At work, he would observe his paradise fish. And at home, he would chronicle the behavior of his dogs, Flip and Jerry, keeping voluminous diaries, a collection of sparkling anecdotes, and, not incidentally, painting a pretty rich picture of Csányi's home life. To a certain kind of dog person, *If Dogs Could Talk* is a heartwarming work, surrendering at many points to anthropomorphizing, and confirming in scientific language many preconceptions about the brilliant little creatures that share our lives. It's as sentimental as any Victorian tract, but it's informed by a deep knowledge of evolutionary theory. As it had for Victorians like Darwin and his disciples, science for Csányi began at home.

Flip, a stray that Csányi discovered when he was hiking in the mountains, was one of those remarkable dogs that owners love to brag about—he had an uncanny understanding of his master's ways and, according to Csányi, a full complement of intellectual and emotional gifts as well as a prodigious vocabulary. Flip found ways of wordlessly conveying what he desired. When he wanted a towel for drying after a walk in the rain, he would rub his head on the rug, then look intently at his master. He learned by imitation, understood the family's rituals, and took his appropriate place in them. Csányi phrased many of his conclusions in the language of extrascientific certainty: "Who could doubt that the dog knew," or "I think it is certain that he somehow understood this." His innovation was to prosecute these home-and-hearth observations with the tools and methods of his laboratory. "He was always coming in with some brilliant thing that Flip had done," Miklósi told a reporter, "and saying 'How could we prove this?'" Csányi put few limits on dogs' cognitive possibilities. He finally went so far as to say that it might be possible to breed a talking dog. He conveyed an air of playfulness about it all, but underneath he seemed to be serious.

Csanyi's speculations were a complicated birth for the field, containing as they do a number of scientific original sins. But Miklósi is unapologetic. "His attitude was always provocative," he told me, "and taught us to be provocative in our hypotheses. Then you can back it up or refute it by doing experiments."

The scientists took as their surprisingly radical premise the notion that the natural environment of the dog is human society. "This is what we try to investigate," Miklósi told me. "We want to find out how dogs understand their environment, in which people are central players." They made a point of working with ordinary dogs in the most ordinary of environments. They pointedly named their center the Family Dog Project. Rather than try to separate out what was innate in dogs from what they had learned in their interactions with humans, the researchers tested dogs that had grown up with people. A key advantage was that, obviously, these animals were plentiful.

This radical idea doesn't sound radical at all—the dog's natural environment is with humans. But at first the scientists had to struggle to figure out what was interesting or worth investigating, what could be measured. They had no papers to react to and few experimental protocols to follow. The kinds of animals that had traditionally been the subjects of cognitive research were rats and pigeons, on the one hand, and primates on the other.

"It took us four years to have a good idea," he told me. Their first successful study involved attachment, the most elemental building material of any social species. Freud had written about attachment, but it was the English psychologist John Bowlby who turned it into a scientific idea, in the 1950s tide of theorizing that came to be known as the cognitive revolution. Bowlby first articulated his theory in a 1958 paper called "The Nature of a Child's Tie to Its Mother." He drew on his experiences as a child psychologist working with World War II orphans, but also on his own childhood, and the upper-class child-rearing method of benign neglect and boarding school that he believed had scarred him. He had trained as a psychoanalyst but became frustrated by the field's lack of empirical rigor and looked for a method to apply to the dawning science of animal behavior.

Throughout the 1950s, Bowlby was in close contact with Niko Tinbergen and Konrad Lorenz, the Nobel Prize–winning founders of the field of ethology. Ethology essentially proclaims that a child's attachment to its mother is a kind of instinct and is a crucial factor in its development; its absence could have damaging consequences. Somewhere between dependence and affiliation, attachment is one of the vital glues that holds human groups together. Bowlby emphasized the essential animality of this basic human impulse—the same attachment behavior, and reactions of fear and anxiety upon separation, could be seen in human infants and rhesus monkeys alike.

The most influential of the tests that flowed from Bowlby's theory was the Strange Situation Test, developed in the 1970s by Mary Ainsworth, a psychologist and colleague of Bowlby's at the Tavistock Clinic in London. In the test, a child (Ainsworth tested children younger than eighteen months) is in a room with its mother or a caregiver and some toys. The mother or caregiver leaves, and a stranger comes in. During the child's various separations and reunions with the mother and the stranger, the researchers measure "secure attachment." Ainsworth found that the child will play and explore more in the presence of a "secure base"—the caregiver—than when alone or in the presence of the stranger. By now Ainsworth's detailed protocol has been tested on a vast range of infants across many cultures; her findings have been organized into several distinct personality types, and it has become a fundamental diagnostic procedure in child psychology.

In 1996 Miklósi, along with his colleague Josef Topal and others, adapted the Strange Situation Test to describe the human-dog relationship—they used "an ethological method used for evaluation of mother-child attachment," as they wrote in their study. It turned out that the Strange Situation Test worked perfectly on dogs. The dogs treated their owners like their mothers: they showed less anxiety when they were present than when they were absent, and they greeted their owners enthusiastically when they returned. The result wasn't exactly a surprise to dog owners, but now here it was, in scientific patois, the most basic of the canine virtues—the fidelity that the pre-Victorians who first lionized the dog so prized.

Some of the behavior that I see as obedience in Stella is probably better described as the result of attachment. As I get up to leave the dog run, she snaps to it—though sometimes she tries to prevent me from going. And if she's being pursued, whether by, as she sometimes seems to imagine, a ravenous pack of bloodthirsty curs, or by, as is usually the case, a couple of sweet, rambunctious animals much like herself, she seeks refuge under my legs—she's half-person, half-chicken.

Whereas the Victorians characterized a dog's fidelity as an affiliation more or less freely given, these scientists saw it as dependence. Other studies at Miklósi's Family Dog Project measured the effect of a caregiver's presence on a dog's problem-solving efforts. Miklósi found that a dog's first response to a problem is often to look at its owner, which can seem a little dim—but usually (as in the case of Stella and the refrigerator containing leftover chicken) it's a pretty good solution. It's a form, however crude, of cooperation, a useful and somewhat advanced skill.

The Strange Situation Test and other attachment experiments established a baseline for the behavior of the dog in its natural (or unnatural) environment, the human family. But they also provided more evidence—as if more were needed—of dogs' essentially childlike nature. The dog, famously, is a case of arrested development. Dogs look like children and act like children, horsing around till a ripe old age, and they are treated like children—which actually seems to amplify their childlike behavior. Miklósi and his colleagues found that dogs' dependence correlates to the degree to which its owners anthropomorphize it.

Some dogs' more extreme infantile features—the pug's flattened face and bulging eyes, the Pomeranian's miniaturized love-bomb form—exist due to semiconscious design, the result of 150 years or so of careful breeding. Cuteness can be a powerful evolutionary weapon if one wants to succeed with a species as committed to child-rearing as humans are. Konrad Lorenz invented the study of cuteness in the 1940s, compiling a list of features, including a large, round head and big eyes low on the face—the *Kindchenschema*—that trigger "innate releasing mechanisms" to caregivers. The cute response is programmed in: Stella hypnotizes me with her big brown eyes, making me forget her gleaming, wolfish teeth and the notion that, as I've been told, she's a parasite. She plays me like a violin. It's irresistible—she's really a marvel of design.

But cuteness isn't everything. No doubt neoteny, the retention of childlike characteristics in adult animals, has played a role in the dog's relations with humans. The notion that dogs' childlike appearance and behaviors are the result of human choice over millennia of breeding is less widely accepted now. No doubt lapdogs, with their wide, round faces and exaggerated eyes, have been created in a doll's image. But in the dog's descent from the wolf, cuteness may have been a by-product that then accelerated the relationship. It's a chicken-and-egg question, in which both chicken and egg played important roles.

For Ádám Miklósi and his colleagues (as for Cesar Millan), understanding dogs means understanding wolves. By studying the differences between them, they can see what makes dogs distinctively dogs. On one level the differences are self-evident. Wolves, with their long noses and impressive teeth, are not, by definition, neotenized. They can seem awfully cute in nature shows—until they sink their teeth into the hindquarters of a moose. Dogs are not wolves. No one who looks at a Chihuahua, for instance, or a bulldog, with its pushed-in snout, can doubt that this is the case. There are also a raft of biological differences: dogs have smaller teeth; smaller, wider heads; and shorter snouts than do wolves of the same size. Wolves come into estrus once a year, as opposed to twice for dogs. Wolves bark much more rarely than dogs, and they play less. And wolves seem to have a shorter socialization window. But with dogs, even after their socialization window is closed, their social identity appears to be fluid and adaptable compared with that of wolves.

But on a deeper level, telling them apart is surprisingly difficult. Stella, with her tail-wagging, goofy amble along the dog parade in Manhattan, seems not at all like a wolf; but when she runs and jumps, the consonance is precise. Genetically, the species are almost identical, to the degree that some scientists question whether dogs should even be designated a separate species. The discoveries behind this determination are remarkably recent. Only in 1993 did Robert Wayne prove conclusively, using mitochondrial DNA, that the dog is descended from the gray wolf, differing by no more than 0.2 percent of its mitochondrial DNA. (The coyote differs by about 4 percent.) "Dogs are grey wolves," he wrote. The discovery—or the confirmation, because it had long been suspected—was the occasion to rename the species from *Canis familiaris* to *Canis lupus.* And the wolf's adaptability, its diffusion, over millennia, in many climate conditions and geographical ranges, may underlie the dog's extraordinary adaptability.

Observing wolves in the wild is incredibly difficult because they move so quickly and so often and are mostly suspicious of interlopers. But observing them in captivity poses its own problems. The consensus understanding from the 1940s until the 1990s was that wolf packs were groups of mostly unrelated individuals that assembled in the winter. Their savage hierarchies, with a complex Greek alphabet of social roles, were thought to be a strict order that the alpha males violently imposed and rigidly enforced, to keep the periphery males in their place. Only one pair bred; the alpha female was thought to prevent, by violence and intimidation, any unauthorized couplings. It was not a nice world, but nature isn't supposed to be nice. Scientists believed that wolf social status was almost an inborn quality, and that subordinate animals would never get a chance to breed. But this consensus view turned out to be all wrong. It had been based on studying captive animals—unrelated wolves thrown together in an enclosure. It was like studying a prison in order to figure out how humans typically behave toward one another.

In the wild, wolves, savage though they are to their prey, are as sweet a family creature as you please. During decades of research in the Canadian Northwest, David Mech, a professor at the University of Minnesota who is often called the Jane Goodall of wild wolves, found that in their own environment, wolves are quite peaceful. "Dominance contests with other wolves are rare, if they exist at all," he wrote. "During my 13 summers observing the Ellesmere Island pack, I saw none." Wolf packs, Mech found, are most often family groups, with young adults hanging around to help raise their brothers and sisters, until such time as they go off to raise their own families. That is, any wolf, theoretically, could become an alpha, just by leaving its parents and starting a family. (In this sense, Cesar Millan might be more accurate if he said "be the daddy" or "the mommy" instead of "be the alpha," although the phrase might not have found its way so deeply into American consciousness.) In fact, it was Mech himself who popularized the term *alpha* in his 1970 book, *Wolves: The Ecology and Behavior of an Endangered Species.* ("I'm very much to blame for the term *alpha*," he said sheepishly in an interview.)

The new view of wolves, which has been refined over the last decade, paints a subtler picture. All the myriad behaviors of dominance and submission are still there, but they are less a rigid set of absolute status rules enforced by violence than a system of etiquette, sublimating any underlying aggressive impulses into a code of conduct that restrains the wolves so completely they almost never burst out into open conflict.

The vocabulary of welcoming and leave-taking that makes the dog fit so neatly into our own homes is also present in wolf society. Here dominance and submission take the form of elaborate, ritualized politeness—bowing and turning away to show deference. At one level, these rituals are about food sharing. Wolves also have an abundance of facial expressions, possible levels of communication and meaning that, beyond the bared teeth, we haven't begun to plumb.

Stella certainly has plenty of expressions and postures that reveal her inner mental states, such as they are—I can read her like a book, although I know that many of my readings are inexact. Her array of distinct whines and growls no doubt correspond to internal states, but they are also, self-evidently, meant to communicate. At this moment, she's lurking behind me, occasionally delivering a quiet but insistent whine, undoubtedly intended (unscientific as this assumption may be) to rouse me from my chair and take her for a walk. She has a fear bark, almost a yip, a little pathetic, and a rich, baritone warning bark. She has a booming, joyous bark, delivered most often to the firehouse next door, which always has a good supply of biscuits.

Wolves' vocalizations are a bit more limited. Their true barks tend to be reserved for situations of defense or conflict—too much noise would get in the way of hunting.

But dogs don't have to face this constraint. Peter Pongracz, a colleague of Miklósi's at Eötvös Loránd University, investigated whether a dog's circumstances—fear, eagerness for a walk, loneliness (as when a dog is tied to a tree)—corresponded to its bark. He found that it is fairly easy to intuit a dog's mental state from its vocalization. The fact that dogs bark in situations in which wolves don't suggests to some scientists that the bark may have evolved in order to communicate with humans—a hypothesis that, in the eyes of others, goes much, much too far.

Given that dogs are descended from wolves, it's entirely natural that they would have a highly developed, richly expressive system relating to resource allocation.

The alpha pair is Mr. and Mrs. Manners, making sure that all their charges get their share of food (although, as usual, when Mr. Manners appears, he gets the most—that's just the way things are), and no one mates, but that's partly because the only available mates are their parents and siblings.

The wolf's savage civility has made it an indispensable human symbol, a doppelgänger species, celebrated in myth for its intelligence and family values and even, in many cultures—think of Romulus and Remus—written into the human story. The scientists I interviewed were focused on discovering what this intelligence might consist of, and what mental mechanisms underlie dog social behaviors. But how different the dog is from the wolf is a hard question precisely because wolves are . . . different. A wolf is a difficult animal—an unscientific observation that happens to be true. With people, they're volatile and unpredictable. You can train a wolf, but what you get at the end is not a dog. Wolves are unpredictable at a level that people wouldn't tolerate in a dog. Handlers have to take precautions, and even so, accidents can happen, even to the most careful.

I'd seen wolves at Wolf Hollow, a little sanctuary in Ipswich, Massachusetts, one frigid November afternoon. As their handlers entered the compound, the wolves got up on their hind legs and put their paws on the handlers' shoulders. Once, when a handler entered too quickly and neglected this ritual, he got a nasty bite on the face—a warning. That's one way wolves police their interactions, gauging their corrections to the offense—and giving ammunition to trainers like Millan.

But once the handlers entered the compound properly, the wolves lolled around on their backs, happy to be scratched by their handlers. The alpha, named Weevil, might not have lasted as an alpha in the wild. He was fat from eating the roadkill deer that neighbors brought in the fall. He was nine and had undergone a serious operation for a tumor on his jaw. When a handler was giving the wolves cheese, Weevil angrily chased a female wolf away with lumbering lunges. She moved off but soon found a spot where Weevil had earlier buried a biscuit for safekeeping. She moved over when he wasn't watching, dug it up, and ate it, then urinated directly in the hole for good measure.

Wolf research, in the wild, can retreat into anecdote, into the unique behaviors of individual animals, easily mythologized. Their supposed strategic gifts—ambushing, relay running, heading off flee-ing prey—suggest impressive cognition and are an important part of their legend, but scientific confirmation for these abilities has proved maddeningly difficult to obtain. The best early work on wolves, by Harry and Martha Frank of the University of Michigan, found that they have a kind of core of instinct, a set of reactions attuned to their environ-ment, and if the environment is tweaked too much—as when they are raised in cages in a group of unrelated animals—their instincts can get out of whack. Behavioral patterns can be brittle in this way—it's the same effect that makes it so difficult to breed wild animals in captivity. Tameness might mean behavioral flexibility, but it also means a certain kind of anything-goes dimness; maybe a tame animal is more accom-modating because it has less going on upstairs. Rather than the ele-gance of a complicated series of behaviors initiated by environmental cues, it has a simpler, rough-and-ready system, one that will work any-where but is missing the refinements of the wild variety. Seen from this perspective, domestication was a devolution; it meant drift, a lack of sharpness, flabby and mentally challenged animals waiting for a hand-out: dependents.

In tests of raw intelligence—means and ends, problem solving—it's long made sense to dog researchers that wolves are brighter than dogs: wolves have more to figure out in their natural environment, being required to find their own food. And they have, accordingly, sub-stantially bigger brains than domestic dogs—between 10 and 30 per-cent bigger. In the early 1980s, Harry and Martha Frank found that a wolf can learn to open a gate after watching a handler open it once, whereas a dog struggles to learn it at all; wolves quickly learn to detour around an obstacle, while dogs do not.

But dogs' remarkable responsiveness to humans complicates this picture. That they look to us to solve their problems is not necessarily a sign of dimness. Because who, or what, is a better problem solver than humans? Dogs look to their human owners or handlers to solve the kinds of problems that wolves solve for themselves—is this unintelligence, or a sensible strategy? And brain size too is not the be-all and end-all. Our brains also got smaller ten to fifteen thousand years ago—right around the time we stopped living purely as hunter-gatherers and moved into villages. (All animals lose brain size and brainpower in the domestication process—just as we did.) Coincidentally or not, that was just about when dogs entered our lives.

Wolves come with a considerable legend of intelligence, foresight, and social skills. But studying their specific talents in their natural environment, as they interact with other wolves and with prey, is surprisingly difficult—a hit-or-miss enterprise at best. They're too mobile, too wary, a long way from Goodall's chimps.

The difficulties of studying wild wolves leave canine researchers no option but to study captives. Besides, in order to understand how dogs treat humans, it's necessary to know how wolves treat humans in similar situations. But the thicket of complicated nature-and-nurture questions that this raises doesn't seem likely to be answered anytime soon.

To use the standard techniques of comparative psychology—used on babies and monkeys—to figure out the cognitive talents of wolves, researchers had to socialize the wolves, but that isn't so easy. The wolf's development window is short—barely five weeks, as opposed to at least sixteen weeks for dogs—meaning that socializing it with humans requires balancing its need for its mother. It's also difficult to hold a wolf's attention, even one raised among people—which makes it a challenge to perform the kinds of social cognition experiments that work with dogs.

How captive wolves should be raised is far from clear. At sanctuaries like Wolf Park in Battleground, Indiana, the largest wolf center in the country, wolves are habituated to trainers and visitors. (It's open to tourists.) But they make no special efforts to make their behaviors conform to that of dogs. They're supposed to be wolves, and to act like them.

Other scientists have tried to better acclimate wolves to people. Starting in 2001, scientists at Eötvös Loránd University in Budapest hand-raised a group of thirteen four- to six-day-old wolves. They took them from their mothers, then for the crucial weeks of their development, they fed them from bottles, walked them on leashes, and raised them as much like dogs as possible. Then at sixteen weeks, they let them live in a pack in an enclosure, visiting them a few times a week. These wolves went down the road a little further toward dogdom. They knew their names, came when called, and paid attention when someone tapped a food bowl. But they didn't get all the way down the road. They were still much less ready to make eye contact with humans than dogs raised in a similar way. In one experiment, dogs and wolves were shown some tasty chicken bits in an enclosure. The dogs quickly looked to the humans to solve their problem—to get it for them—and they looked at the experimenter longer than did wolves. Had the dog, Miklósi and his colleagues wondered, been selected to interact in this way with human caregivers? Or was the wolf simply reluctant to look at another animal's face, reluctant to start a fight?

Wolves, Miklósi and his colleagues argue, have a much harder time treating humans as social partners, no matter how intensively they've been raised. One important reason is that they don't form the same kinds of attachments with their human caregivers as do dogs—in the Strange Situation Test, they behave more or less the same to a stranger as they do toward their caregiver.

Geneticists have also been closing in on the distance between dogs and wolves from the inside. The most tantalizing clue emerged from a massive, multiyear study of canid genomes—dogs, wolves, coyotes, foxes, and jackals—by Robert Wayne and some colleagues, the results of which began to be published in 2010. One place on the genome where dogs separate from wolves is a location that, in humans, is correlated with Williams Syndrome, a condition whose symptoms include cheerfulness; social fearlessness; cute, elfin facial features; and sometimes a degree of mental disability. "This is the so-called party gene," Wayne told me. "Syndrome sufferers are often the life of the party. They're very engaging, and there are always people surrounding them. Essentially, they've lost their fear of contact with other humans."

The smiling, winning guilelessness of Williams Syndrome sufferers is actually very reminiscent of the temperament of dogs. "After the paper was published," Wayne said, "I got several e-mails and phone calls from parents of Williams Syndrome kids, and they essentially said, you know, 'This is like dogs! My kid's so friendly and engaging and so focused on people!'" Williams people also happen to be excellent rote memorizers, with superb concrete intelligence that's sometimes not matched by other cognitive abilities. People with Williams Syndrome are also much freer of racial biases than others—suggesting the kind of welcoming openness that might allow a dog to overlook the fact that, while it has four legs, its best friend has only two.

To a certain kind of wolf scientist, the fact that the dog evolved from it is the least interesting thing about the wolf. Real wolf people didn't care much about dogs. They were the children of unwitting traitors. Who was the dim-witted Squanto who first entered the human camp? It had happened, that couldn't be denied, but it certainly wasn't anything to be celebrated. The dog, in their eyes, was kind of the bastard child—and the less said about it the better.

These associations and emotions complicate canine science. Both animals are partly concealed by cloaks of mythology so multilayered and captivating that it can be hard to see the actual animals underneath. But one thing is clear: the wolf and the dog are on different journeys—albeit both with humans as the travel agents. The wolf is inseparable from its ecology, its wilderness redoubts—you can't have one without the other. The wolves that are being tested today are necessary emissaries, but one can't help but feel they're a bit like the Native Americans whom early colonizers took back to the old country, their headdresses and war paint meaning something very different in the drawing rooms of London than they did in the woods.

But the dog is on our road, walking with us—if not always staying close at heel. Its ecology is the human world, as it has been for millennia. It's primed to respond to us, easily learning, without much special training, our world's basic rules. As it turns out, its very tameness—sometimes allied with savagery—is something we also share.

*Five*

# Leaping Toward Humanity

One of the things that makes life with Stella so natural is the interplay of our attentions. She's not one of those brilliant, telepathic creatures who seem to know what her owner will do before he does. Many of her motives are self-interested, but she's obsessed with me. She carefully monitors my progress around the apartment, mostly to see if I'm tending toward the kitchen or the door. Out on the leash, she'll regularly turn to look in my eyes. It's a minor gift, but magnificent too. And part of my attachment is that I want to help her—give her treats, open the gate, untangle her paw from the leash; it's human, and the most natural thing in the world, if you over-look the fact that she's a dog. This attention is one of the benefits of tameness. She sees me as an ally, not a threat. And that opens the door to other sorts of interactions—paying close attention to the nuances of my behavior, to where I'm looking or walking, to what my hands are doing, can bring her rewards.

The language of gesture, it turns out, is one of the things canine scientists have focused on as a key to the human-canine relationship. One morning in Vienna I met Juliane Kaminski, a researcher at the

Max Planck Institute for Evolutionary Anthropology in Leipzig, one of the world's premier centers of animal cognition research (though its primary object is to reach a better understanding of human evolution). Kaminski was scheduled to speak on the last day of the Canine Science Forum, about dogs' remarkable responsiveness to human cues.

Kaminski is best known for her studies of two dog prodigies, Rico and Betsy, genius word learners who were both border collies—a fact that will please border collie owners everywhere, the tiger moms of the dog world. Borders are commonly taken to be the brightest lights in the dog world. Labs aren't bad by these measures, but I'm just as happy not to have to administer an IQ test to Stella. Kaminski speculates that their remarkable talents, primatelike in their extensiveness, are the result of the collie's being bred as sheep herders, their cognitive equipment refined over generations.

By looking at the qualities dogs developed in adapting to life with humans, Kaminski and her colleagues hope to shed light on how humans evolved to live with each other. Dogs "seem to do something which we cannot find in apes, our closest relatives," she said. "We need to explore the mechanisms of this to understand whether human forms of communication are truly unique." The dog is far from Kaminski's only research interest, or even her central one. She did a study of the gaze-tracking ability of goats, and an extensive study of primates.

Her colleague Michael Tomasello, codirector of the Max Planck Institute, is a frequent collaborator on comparative cognition papers. He is a coauthor, along with Brian Hare, the head of Duke University's Hominoid Psychology Research Group, of some of the most provocative papers in the young field exploring the so-called domestication hypothesis—which holds that the dog, after it entered the human story, underwent a cognitive flowering in social communication and, in order to communicate with people, developed "a whole suite of social communicative talents."

Kaminski is partly on board with this hypothesis. "I think dogs are selected for a certain readiness to receive human communication," she told me later in an e-mail. "Temperament most likely played a role in this but I do not think it's the whole story. I think dogs have been specifically selected to 'understand' human communication. This made them the perfect 'tool' for hunting and herding, etc. . . . all activities for which they need to 'understand' human communication over a distance. Dogs which did not perform well in these tasks, because they did not react, were most likely not selected for breeding."

But Kaminski casts doubt on the more extreme formulations of the hypothesis. "They're saying that you just have this one development, for tameness, and then there's this explosion," she said, shaking her head. She's far from a behaviorist, but she's not about to put the dog in a group with dolphins, either. "There are two extremes," she told me. "We need more research." She believes that dogs have a few unique and surprising skills that are somehow involved in their relations with humans. But what they are, and what kinds of mental states might underlie them, is still to be hammered out.

Kaminski's talk was the centerpiece of the conference's final day. Its title, "Like Infant, Like Dog?" suggested that perhaps the dog didn't just fit neatly into human culture; amid all its sniffing and leg-lifting predilections, it managed to acquire some humanlike communication capabilities. Somehow it started to cross the bridge. For me, anyway, this is the issue that glorifies canine science, that pulls all the other issues along in its wake. Maybe the dog's honorary personhood isn't a happy fantasy. Maybe dogs somehow took on human qualities. Maybe, by luck and design, we made them partly in our own image. But I knew to be suspicious of easy formulations.

"What I want to talk about," Kaminski said, showing a slide of a wide-eyed human infant, "is a very specific human gesture, and that is the pointing gesture." Pointing, as she said, is a triadic communication, involving a sender, a receiver, and an object of shared concern. It's closely related to language development in infants and is used in language acquisition—when, for instance, a baby points to an object, and its mother says the object's name. But in some ways pointing develops before language—a basic tool for learning to share the world. Autistic children, for instance, have a hard time with pointing, an early indicator of the barriers between them and the rest of the world. Triadic communication is also a fairly rare phenomenon in the animal world, and pointing is even rarer still (possibly partly because other animals don't have hands). Chimpanzees, bonobos, and baboons—our closest relatives—use a wide range of hand gestures, but in the wild, they almost never use pointing in the ways that dogs and humans can. But dogs, even young ones, quickly learn to point to obtain hidden food. *This* was interesting. It was even more interesting if you considered, as some tests showed, that wolves have a very hard time learning the same skill.

Ádám Miklósi and Brian Hare both stumbled on this anomalous fact at the same time, in the early 1990s. Hare was an undergraduate at Emory University, working at the Yerkes National Primate Research Center with Michael Tomasello, who in 1994 had just begun teasing out the similarities and differences between chimpanzees and other primates and human babies. His attempt to figure out what kinds of ideas they have in their heads is part of his quest for the evolutionary reasons for human uniqueness. One day Tomasello was remarking on the inability of chimps to understand pointing, and Hare said, with the brashness or brilliant ignorance of a nineteen-year-old, "Well, I think my dog can do that."

And that's how it all started. "He said, 'What do you mean?'" Hare told me. "Everybody thinks their dog can do calculus, you know? And I said, 'Well, I don't know. I play fetch with my dog, and if he loses the ball, I can point to where it goes, and he goes and looks where I point.'"

Tomasello was dubious about this claim, but science has ways of resolving these kinds of disputes. "He said, 'Okay, well, prove me wrong,'" Hare said. "'Let's do an experiment.' So then we started doing experiments, and the first papers used my two pet dogs and my parents' garage."

Hare devised a version of what comparative psychologists call the object choice task—a scientific version of three-card monte, a couple of cups with food hidden in one, making sure that both would smell the same, and a trainer to point out which one contained the food: simple for a baby, nearly impossible for a chimp. Dogs' talents in playing this game would not have surprised most dog owners, but primate researchers were amazed—to the point, in many cases, of disbelief. Dogs were not supposed to be able to accomplish anything like that. They simply didn't have enough brain. "They're not little kids, okay?" Hare told me recently. "They're not doing what little children do. They're incredibly limited. But they have a glimmer, this laser beam intelligence."

Hare tested the partly socialized wolves at Wolf Hollow in Ipswich and found them to be far less skilled at understanding pointing than dogs. He knew the comparison wasn't quite fair, but the results were unambiguous; this seemed to be a skill that dogs had and wolves didn't. Though there was still a lot more research to do, it appeared that the dog doesn't just have a suite of cognitive and social skills borrowed from the wolf, wrapped in a sweeter, cuddlier package. Rather, it actually has new communicative abilities. The experiment undergirds the intimacy between dogs and humans with a scientific foundation.

The dog's remarkable ability, interesting on its own, was just as revealing about our closest relatives. Chimps and gorillas, brilliant though they are, are something of a dead end when it comes to certain kinds of communicative tasks. Not that they don't understand gestures—they use plenty of them. They've passed all the theory-of-mind tests with flying colors, the ones that dogs always fail. They can discern what you're looking at and infer what you're thinking; they can deceive and dissemble, with all those human qualities that make our lives so exciting.

But when it came to picking up an intentional signal like the point, they simply didn't get it. When a chimp or a trainer reached for a treat in a gesture that looked like pointing, they could certainly figure out what that meant and get the food themselves. "They were

seemingly able to infer," wrote Tomasello and his partners, "she wants
to get into that bucket for herself; therefore, there must be something
good in there." They could understand very well the idea in the experimenter's mind. Human-raised chimps will even learn to point at
hidden food, or at a place they want to go.

But there was a crucial difference. What a chimp couldn't understand was why the experimenter would willingly show it food without
going for it himself. Without an element of competition, the chimps
were baffled. Actually, chimpanzee selfishness had been a theme of
primate research for some years. Competition, not cooperation, is the
motivating impulse of the chimp's social world, to such a degree that
scientists have sometimes wondered why they are considered social animals at all. "One hypothesis is that chimpanzees may have some of the
cognitive capacities required, but they lack some of the motivational
aspects," said Kaminski. "They lack the motivation to inform others
about things in the environment if there is nothing in it for them."

By contrast, at one year of age, all human infants easily understand pointing. To conceptualize a toy under a bucket, they don't have
to feel that someone is about to come snatch it away. They seem to
assume, until proven otherwise, that an experimenter is there to be
helpful—they would help her, and she would help them. This assumption opens the door to all sorts of communications that wouldn't otherwise be possible. Tomasello concluded that this difference between
humans and chimps is fundamental. It wasn't necessarily a cognitive
deficit, if-A-then-B, a missing deductive faculty. That, the chimps were
quite good at. It was more a difference in approach, in how they treat
other beings, in what kinds of social assumptions they brought to the
table. The key, for Tomasello, was sharing and helping—humans are
ready to share, to help and be helped.

Dogs were certainly ready to be helped by humans—I think of
Stella staring at the refrigerator, then back at me—but they were not
quite so ready to share, to say the least. Still, the scientists were im-
pressed. "The thing we can't ever forget," Tomasello told me, "and it's

a trivial and obvious point, but dogs aren't doing this with other dogs. They're doing this with us."

The mental mechanism by which this humanlike ability operates is still in dispute. When an infant points, she seems to want to transfer the idea of what she sees into your mind, and this is pretty much what happens. But could a dog really have a theory of mind on the order of chimps and humans—that is, an idea of what another creature might have in its head? With a twelve-month-old baby, or a hungry chimp, that would be the obvious assumption. Some researchers, like Marc Bekoff, have been extrapolating from studies of canine play the idea that dogs might have a glimmer of this kind of understanding, but no scientist fully believed that this was possible, and they still don't. At the other extreme, the behaviorist camp believed that this understanding of pointing, like most of what a dog could accomplish, was mere associative learning—the do-this-and-something-good-will-happen, conditioned response upon which the behaviorist edifice is built.

In 2002 Hare and Tomasello, along with Harvard researcher Michelle Brown and Christina Williamson of Wolf Hollow, published their findings and speculations in a remarkably bold paper in *Science*, the most prestigious American science publication, titled "The Domestication of Social Cognition in Dogs." "Dogs," they wrote, "have been selected for a set of social-cognitive abilities that enable them to communicate with humans in unique ways." They stressed that the understanding of pointing was not something dogs had to learn; it was somehow built in; puppies could do it.

The paper went on to frame the questions that still preoccupy dog scientists. They laid out three different hypotheses for how dogs might have acquired this amazing ability. One possibility was that they simply inherited it from wolves: the Canid Generalization Hypothesis. If that were true, they suggested, wolves should perform as well as dogs in similar tests. But Hare and his colleagues had found that however insightful wolves may be, they were unable to factor in the variable of a handler—they weren't ready to be helped.

The second hypothesis, beloved by behaviorists, was that dogs learn about pointing from their early experiences in human households. This suggested that young dogs would perform poorly, but that was not what Hare and Tomasello found. The understanding of pointing, if not exactly innate, develops quickly and with no training; it seems to be part of the dog's toolkit.

The third hypothesis was the domestication hypothesis—that dogs evolved to respond to human cues in ways that wolves did not. "It is likely," Hare and his colleagues wrote, "that individual dogs were able to use social cues to predict the behavior of humans more flexibly than could their last common wolf ancestor." Socially, Hare and his colleagues were announcing, dogs were prodigies. They didn't evolve the ability to suddenly use language, as Csányi dreamed; rather, dogs somehow evolved a new mental mechanism for communicating with humans that wolves didn't possess: mind reading, as it's called in the comparative cognition world. Somehow, by being involved with humans, the dog underwent a mental flowering. Suddenly the dog was as close to the top of the cognitive heap as it had been just after Darwin.

The paper was explosive. "When the *Science* paper came out," Hare told me, "people were always asking, 'Oh, what does it mean for dog owners?' Nothing!" Hare says, laughing. "They all already know this! It's the scientists that are surprised!"

The scientists were more than surprised. They were jealous, disbelieving, and highly critical, as only academics can be. "How did he get it in there?" one eminent ethologist asked me in heated amazement, nine years later, listing a passel of methodological faults that he thought should have disqualified the paper. And in truth, even a dog sentimentalist could doubt that dogs somehow leaped past chimps in intelligence, albeit in a highly limited way—Stella isn't quite ready for college.

In many ways, the domestication hypothesis was a beginning rather than an end. The mechanism by which it might operate was unspecified. Did dogs have an idea in their mind's eye of what a human was trying to communicate by pointing? No one was ready to go that far. And how had the dog evolved this ability, when our closest animal relatives didn't? Some thought the entire project of attempting to peer inside these limited minds was flawed, that there were simpler, and therefore superior, explanations for these behaviors. But Hare and Miklósi's discoveries catalyzed the field. Even as they tried to extend the reach of their ideas, their peers began devising tests to prove them wrong—which is, it should be said, the way science is supposed to work.

Hare, barely past twenty-five, was thrilled by the paper and the attention it brought. But his closest colleagues, including some eminent primatologists (some of whom were almost a generation older), were politely skeptical. "I don't see why it's so important," anthropologist Richard Wrangham said to Hare one day at Harvard. Then, Hare told me, "I made the mistake of saying out loud that I thought that the *Science* paper might be the first evidence for a social cognitive adaptation."

Dangerous words. "I don't believe you," said Wrangham. No one had concrete evidence for a social cognitive adaptation, although large segments of the evolutionary anthropology world assumed they must have occurred.

Wrangham said that, in order to convince him, Hare would have to test an old family of Siberian silver foxes. Wild foxes tend to be solitary, and they're deeply fearful of humans—which makes them hard to raise for their fur. So in 1959, at a farm near Novosibirsk, a scientist named Dimitry Belyaev began breeding one group of silver foxes selected for tameness, and another group randomly. It turned out to be the most important canine experiment after Pavlov. Some of the foxes, while becoming incredibly tame, also developed a whole suite of other doglike qualities: floppy ears, piebald coats, and star-shaped white blazes on their foreheads. Some of the females even went into heat biannually rather than annually—just as happened when the dog evolved from the wolf. Newborns opened their eyes earlier and had a longer socialization period. The Siberian fox study suggested an all-purpose mechanism for canine evolution. Selecting for tameness—an event that must have happened at some point in dog history—seemed to give rise to many of the qualities that, visually and behaviorally, separate the dog from the wolf.

Testing these foxes would provide new perspective on the dog's special talent. Hare, confident of his own hypothesis, was sure they wouldn't pass the pointing test, since they hadn't had the generations of selection for those talents that the dog had. Wrangham had suggested he send a student, but Hare decided to go himself. He went to Siberia for a six-week stint and found Belyaev's foxes to be as tame as could be, but with certain problems. "When you pick the foxes up, the unfortunate thing is they pee for joy! I mean, they are just obsessed with you. They just want more than anything in the world for you to touch and hold them. Now, this is also a fox that has never been held by a person!"

The Siberian foxes were difficult subjects. Unlike dogs, they like to eat only when it's time to eat, so there was only a brief window during which Hare could conduct the experiment using treats hidden in cups. So he adjusted the procedure, using various toys the foxes seemed obsessed with, and accounted for the shyness of the control foxes.

Hare fully expected both groups of foxes to fail the object choice task. Dogs, he hypothesized, had been selected specifically for social cognition—for understanding a gesture like the point. But nothing so refined had happened to these foxes—they'd been bred simply for their slavishness. "They didn't select for any kind of social problem solving," said Hare. "It was just approach or avoidance of humans. Why would they have developed this new cognitive faculty?"

But to his surprise, the tame foxes seem to have developed their skill at the object choice task—understanding a human point—along with their piebald coats. As a result of the fox experiment, the domestication hypothesis needed major revisions. For Hare, the notion of the cognitive adaptation, the new faculty, was now out the window. It seemed that tameness itself enabled the foxes to use an existing cognitive skill to interact with the humans they had become so fond of. This new, simpler formulation had many virtues. It showed how complex behaviors could arise quickly—within a generation or two—and from relatively simple mutations. It also filled in the picture of neoteny as a process that could change the course of a species, as it had with the wolf and the dog—and may have done with humans.

"Actually," Hare told me, "what you're seeing in terms of the problem-solving skills in dogs—if they're really, truly more skillful or flexible than wolves—is just the by-product of a temperamental shift that has happened as a result of selection against aggression. Now, I said that as if it's a bad thing. It's not a bad thing. It's totally exciting. That's why I immediately embraced the finding and was happy to be wrong, because it's actually way cooler!

"You can't have, genomically, a cheaper change than a temperamental one," Hare told me. "You shift a little bit of a regulatory gene in control of how androgens are expressed, or the serotonin transporter gene, and you have this cascading effect. And it's totally cheap! It's a cheap evolutionary trick, and you get a huge benefit."

This newest version of the domestication hypothesis posits that humans did not necessarily select dogs to breed based on their attention and skill at responding to human cues. Rather, the tamest and least situationally aggressive dogs somehow had those qualities built in. In the human environment, the least aggressive, friendliest wolves, or at least the ones that didn't take off when people came near, must have outcompeted their wilder siblings. Then the breeding process got to work, selecting in some cases for especially intelligent and responsive creatures—cue the self-satisfied murmurs of border collie fanciers—or, much later, for dogs with freakily short legs, or flattened faces, or bulging eyes.

As insightful as it is about dogs, Hare's tameness finding is most remarkable as a window onto the talents (and lack thereof) of chimpanzees—and, by extension, of humans. It shows the dog to be, in this respect, more humanlike than the chimp. For an explanation, Hare looked to experiments where chimps have to cooperate. He describes a classic cooperation experiment in which a pair of chimps have to pull on opposite ends of a rope in order to receive a reward.

But due to their competitiveness and aggression, many of these animal Einsteins fail to solve the problem. In the chimp universe, you can't get there from here. An alpha chimp will simply take a lesser chimp's food, and the weaker one has no incentive to cooperate. No one gets a banana. The only chimp pairs that successfully solve the problem are ones that can eat together without warring at the same food dish—the tamest sort of chimps.

These kinds of experiments showed that the first step to human-like cooperation is lack of aggression—tameness. And as with pointing, to understand that a human, or indeed another chimp, is showing its food, a chimp has to first pay attention to the human; and it also has to believe that a human would show it food, that a person would try to help. To a dog, this understanding is almost second nature. And an infant of a certain age is programmed to believe that another human will help; it's our most human of instincts.

Hare, Tomasello, and other colleagues built on this idea—dogs' success, having evolved in a human environment, and chimps' lack of success—with speculations about how humans might have evolved, or at least which qualities predisposed them to begin evolving. Tomasello has been working for the better part of two decades on a theory of the beginnings of human communication—the underpinnings of language. As he and Hare were compiling their research on dogs, Tomasello was forming his studies into a comprehensive theory of how animal minds might have evolved to become our minds. Cooperation and paying attention are at the center of this theory. In terms of the dog, a cooperative attitude makes the task seem simpler, Tomasello told me. "So we shifted from thinking about it in a cognitive way to thinking about it in a more cooperative way."

This cooperation insight bolstered their theories about how human communication might have evolved. The chasm between chimps' highly limited vocabulary of howls and grunts and human language has long been considered a mystery, nearly unbridgeable. How could we have leaped across it? But for Tomasello, the language of gesture is a kind of missing link, possibly explaining how we might have crossed the chasm. And his study of the dog helped him make the connection.

Based on his observations and research into the ways babies and animals communicate, Tomasello hypothesizes that gestures like pointing are at the core of language, and that the basic communicative act consists of two individuals holding the same idea—*banana!*—in their heads at the same time, each knowing that the other knows. This is what Tomasello calls "shared intentionality," and his theory proposes it as the basic building block of language. Gesture is crucial—it's a kind of protolanguage. Dogs don't have the brainpower to get all the way to shared intentionality—Kaminski stresses that dogs understand pointing as a kind of command. But they seem to have some of the necessary equipment: responsiveness, dependence, willingness to trust and be helped—qualities that reflect our own talents.

Stella led me to this most basic of human mysteries—what makes us different from the animals, and how we could have become that way. She even tried to sneak into the party, populated by the brightest animal minds in the world. Unfortunately, she had to wait in the vestibule—what looked like higher understanding was actually quite a bit simpler. But still, I felt she'd come a long way, given where she'd started.

## Six

# Dumb Animals

Some scientists are skeptical as to how far the dog has really come. They argue that the new view of the dog is wish fulfillment masquerading as science. They think dogs are simpler creatures, not humanlike at all, and not the lesser for it. Dogs are glorious animals, they say, who've found a niche in the world we made—but that doesn't mean we should see them as people.

The problem with the dog cognition research, said Ray Coppinger, "is that people want to believe it. They want to give dogs something special. And no one has even come close to showing that they're different from any other mammal."

Coppinger is a gruff, lanky man in his seventies, the flinty New Englander of legend. We were sitting in his western Massachusetts kitchen, much of which he'd built himself. Coppinger used to race sled dogs—at one point, he told me, he had more than a hundred dogs on his property. Now that he's always traveling from conference to conference, he has only one: a plump little weiner dog. The dog came out to greet me when I drove up and swiftly rolled onto his back for a scratch. It made its way into the kitchen, where Coppinger and I were having a sandwich. The dog coughed loudly a couple of times. "Oh," said Coppinger, with broad sarcasm, "he evolved that coughing behavior to communicate to me that something was wrong."

Coppinger is one of the dog world's great men, a pioneer in the field, who began his work with dogs in the late 1960s, and a beloved figure, if a somewhat cantankerous one. Once, greeting him at a conference, Brian Hare gave Coppinger a friendly hug. Coppinger said, "That was weird—what did you do that for?" A generational difference. Before his book *Dogs*, written with his wife, Lorna, was published, pet keeping had been generally accepted as the mechanism by which dogs had evolved from wolves. Pet keeping looks a lot like how we interact with our dogs today, involving a lot of effort and planning and management through leashes and even cages. In Coppinger's view, Pleistocene breeders would have been hard-pressed to guide the development of the dog, given wolves' leisurely cycles of breeding and the considerable time it would take for selectively bred qualities to appear in pups, not to mention those early humans' own forty-year lifespan. Meanwhile one had to control the wolves, prevent unauthorized matings, and wait for worthwhile variations to appear, a process that can happen at a geologic pace—all the while worrying about how to get fed. Coppinger calls this artificial-selection model of dog evolution the Pinocchio hypothesis, for its wish-fulfillment overtones.

But Coppinger's insight was to see the process as the result of a new ecological niche. "For simplicity," he wrote, "we'll call that niche the town dump." The wolves that were best able to take advantage of humans—and of the human leavings that were filling up the world—shared one crucial characteristic, according to Coppinger. They were less afraid of humans than their brethren; their flight distance was shorter. This quality, essentially, erected a physical barrier—a mountain range, or an ocean—between the wolf populations. The less fearful wolves bred with one another, rather than with their wilder cousins. The dog, essentially, domesticated itself. Coppinger's theory drew heavily on his knowledge of Belyaev's silver foxes, namely, the way selection for a single trait was apparently accompanied by a cascade of other modifications—the floppy ears, piebald coats, and smaller heads and teeth—that we now associate with dogs.

In a rich new niche, animals that breed as swiftly as possible have an advantage because they leave the most offspring—which means that accelerated estrus, as happened between the wolf and the dog, could be selected for. The niche helped accelerate the neoteny in wolves, which in turn helped create the friendly, multicolored creatures that we were happier to spend time with. It was a fortunate accident.

Coppinger's version of dog domestication is especially parsimonious—and not always flattering to the dog. Dogs are less cautious, less fearful of humans, than wolves, in his view—Hare and his colleagues agree with this—but Coppinger vigorously disputes the idea that the dog's development had anything to do with communication with humans. In fact, he believes dogs probably got dumber in their evolution. The dog might have gotten its smaller head to ease access to narrow places, in order to ferret whatever meager nourishment might be lurking there. It developed only as much brain as it needed—a brain is expensive to support, and difficult to feed on a diet of garbage. Because the dog didn't have to hunt anymore, some of its cognitive machinery could have gradually been decommissioned.

So, in this theory, dogs are essentially small, lazy, slightly dim wolves. And, significantly, the mutuality that seems so evident in people's current relationship with dogs—in which dogs look to humans to solve their problems—is largely absent. He sees dogs at dumps in Mexico or foraging on the streets of Madagascar as the direct, virtually unchanged descendants of the original dogs: they need humans for trash but not much else. Whereas others suggest that the relationship is mutual, Coppinger doesn't think that, especially at first, dogs provided any benefit. The dog, like a pigeon or a rat, was just there.

Coppinger's theory of the dog's origins has supplanted the pet-keeping theory in large swaths of the dog world. It's now the most widely accepted view of dog origins, at least in outline. But while it informs many scientists' thinking, there are enormous areas of disagreement within it. Coppinger is dismissive to the point of contempt about even the idea of social-communicative adaptation: what humans gave to the dog, primarily, was trash. His ideas have a quiver of corollaries in the modern dog world. The village dog, far from a mongrel, is the ur-dog, "the original non-wolf," wrote Coppinger, from which all other breeds have been shaped. Pet keeping followed inevitably, and possibly in some cases selection for behavioral excellence. Dogs that guard sheep and those that herd have had their instincts revised in very different ways—but more often, he speculates, color was the determining factor in deciding which dogs got to breed.

As for the whole alpha business, Coppinger doesn't believe a word of it. If you roll a village dog onto its back, Cesar Millan style, it won't have a clue what you're trying to do. His experience with village dogs suggests that they're semisolitary, not pack animals. The wolf is adapted to life in the wild; the dog is adapted to life in the dump. Far from being a behaviorist, Coppinger also dismisses the tenet that dogs do what they do in order to get humans to give them food. His sled dogs, for instance, were not running because someone was dangling a steak in front of the sled. To Coppinger, behaviors are shaped instincts, things that, like courtship or play for humans, simply feel good.

Coppinger began life as a city boy, in Boston. When his mother wanted to remarry and move into the man's house in the countryside, Coppinger demanded a dog as the price for his consent to the union. His mother agreed. The dog became his companion on his forays in the woods around their new rural home, but his stepfather wouldn't permit the dog in his house.

Which was fine with Coppinger. In the 1940s Boston neighborhoods of his childhood, dogs were a relative novelty. But after the war, with the burgeoning of suburbs and Lassie on television, that quickly changed. The mythology of the purebred dog came to dominate, along with legends of how ancient breeders had carefully selected them in order to do man's work. Purebreds rose as marks of status, and kept rising, to a place Coppinger didn't think that they belonged. It wasn't good for them. He talked to me about dogs rescued from Puerto Rico—from their lives as village dogs—and brought to Florida, put on leashes, and kept in living rooms. What kind of life is that for a dog? he asked—not that a dog's happiness is Coppinger's first priority. For him, the dog does not merit certain forms of human consideration—they are animals. In fact, Coppinger looks askance at the whole honorary-human business. "I have a bumper sticker my wife won't let me put on my car," he reported with a grin. "It says, 'What is this country coming to if a man can't shoot his own dog?'" He scanned my face for a reaction.

Back in the 1970s, Coppinger was one of very few scientists studying dogs for their own sake (as opposed to using them in experiments). No one would fund his research—he was lonely in the field for a long time. "If you tried to do work with dogs, they would look at you and say, 'Why don't you work with a real animal.' They said, 'Go over to animal science.' But animal science can't teach you anything about dogs because you can't eat them. And vet school wouldn't teach you anything about behavior." Now the field is much more crowded, but Coppinger is no happier, at least not openly. "The problem with the Hungarians and Brian Hare and so forth is that the very characteristics that they're saying the dog has, they can't define. When I came up as a behavioral scientist, I was taught that you couldn't give animals human characteristics because you couldn't test for them."

Coppinger enumerated various problems he saw in Hare's experiments with dogs, wolves, and chimps, speaking in a rush, as if he'd thought about it a lot. "The chimpanzee is in a cage, the dog's outside the cage. The dog's been socialized with people, the chimpanzee, you don't know."

But he reserved special opprobrium for Peter Pongracz's barking study. "The idea that barking may have evolved to communicate with humans is just going too far with the argument," he said. He pointed outside, into his yard. "I can listen to the crows out there and say, 'I bet there's an owl or a hawk.' Barking didn't evolve so a dog could communicate with humans."

Coppinger's central mission is to rain on this cheerful dog parade. "I know there are isolated examples of dogs doing remarkable and uncharacteristic tasks," he told me. "But many who love their dogs impart supercanine abilities to them, letting their imaginations overrule their observations."

Talking to Coppinger reminded me of what a tiny world the dog people, including their ethologist and anthropologist colleagues, comprise. He knows Richard Wrangham, who helped guide Hare's early study—"we're thick as thieves." Coppinger had actually been one of the evaluators of Hare's Ph.D. defense at Harvard. Over the years, he'd invited Hare to study wolves together, but Hare had always been too busy. Now the *Science* paper and its various repercussions had made it difficult for them to be close colleagues, at least from Coppinger's side. Not from Hare's. "I'm, like, the hugest fan of Ray's ever," he told me. "I love Ray. He's just fantastic." Coppinger's idea about the temperamental variations between the domesticated and control foxes had, in fact, partly inspired Hare's fruitful revisions of the domestication hypothesis. The two men had dinner with a mutual student a couple of years ago. "He was asking questions in a very critical way," Hare said, "and I said, 'Ray, I'm fine with that.'"

As much as anyone in the dog world, Ray Coppinger is a moralist. He has strong ideas about the proper order of the dog world, partly based on his scientific knowledge of dogs' fundamental nature. We should, he believes, treat animals as what they are, not as what we hope or fantasize them to be. Coddling them and treating them like humans misses the point and worse. Dogs should be allowed to be the natural creatures they are. We should delight in their magnificent physical abilities, without trying to turn them into honorary humans.

On the staircase leading down to Coppinger's office was a poster of the 1971 New England Dog Sled championship. "The winner from the previous year got to have his picture on the poster," he said proudly. And there was Ray Coppinger, a rakish twentysomething fellow with big mutton-chop sideburns and a black cap, his face contorted in an ecstatic grimace. "Best sport there was," he said with feeling. Before dog sledding, he had been studying butterflies, but one thing led to another. He followed the dogs, deeper and deeper into the life he has now. And his dogs pursued their own excellence too. Sentiment didn't enter into it. "What I wanted to do was win," he told me. "I'd do anything to have great dogs." If you're a scientist or a dog-sled racer, you can't let yourself be distracted by sentiment.

He led me outside toward a pine grove behind the house. There, amid the forest clutter, were the archaeological remains of Ray Coppinger's glorious youth, where he had kept his dogs in his dog racing days. His dogs lived in very unusual dog houses. Coppinger would mound sand in a pit, then pour concrete over it, making a kind of igloo structure, with a dog dish molded into the top of the igloo. And here they are still, half-buried, partly filled with forest debris, like pyramids that explorers might find in the Yucatán. In Coppinger's prime as a sled man, he had some fifty dogs at a time. What a din there must have been. It's a lost city of dog, from a world that's not coming back anytime soon.

For others besides Coppinger, the real question is not how smart dogs are but how dim. Even dog lovers sometimes think like this. I'm susceptible to this thinking from time to time, as when Stella positions herself at the side of the door where the hinge is, when she's seen it open on the other side a thousand times. And for decades, the main thrust of animal research—behaviorism and its cousins—was devoted to the proposition that dogs and their mammalian brethren are very simple-minded indeed. It was somewhere between an assumption and a hypothesis. The impulse to reduce behavior to a set of simple rules was powerful. The chimp, along with the other great apes, got something of a pass, but in general the entire field of cognitive ethology was considered highly suspect—even though it had been developing for the last four decades. In the minds of behaviorists, cognitive theorists were chasing ghosts.

Behaviorists are much fewer today than in their heyday in the 1940s, but they remain as fervent as ever. In their worldview, the domestication hypothesis is a major irritant, smacking of the kind of sentimentalism that science has tried for the past 130 years to expunge from its laboratories.

The other very vocal intellectual opponent of Hare and his colleagues is University of Florida researcher Clive Wynne. Wynne got his Ph.D. at Edinburgh, working with pigeons. Then he spent time in Australia, working with marsupials. He came to the University of Florida in 2002. Bored with pigeons and looking for "something a bit more colorful to work with," he established a dog lab, the same year Hare and Tomasello published their paper in *Science*. He's been challenging their work ever since. "I've become such a skeptic of the work of Brian Hare and the Budapest group that people think I must have come into this with a negative prejudice, but the skepticism comes from research that we've done."

Debunking the idea that the dog somehow acquired special talents for social cognition became the defining focus of his work. To a behaviorist, it raised a huge red flag, and he's prosecuted the case avidly. "Brian Hare and his group argued that the dog, during the period that it became a domestic animal, developed special mind-reading skills," he told me. "They argued that dogs have the special ability, a unique ability, to understand what people are up to. I don't deny that the dog is different than the wolf. The pet dog that you have in your home, I don't deny for a moment that it has an exquisite degree of sensitivity to its owner that you wouldn't easily find in any other animal.

But I don't believe that the two things are tightly linked. I don't think that in the process of domestication that dog acquired special brain-power."

Wynne invoked Lorenz's 1935 study of goslings—thinking Lorenz was their mother, the baby geese followed him around—the foundational research of all ethology. Wynne told me that the dog's unusual responsiveness to humans was essentially analogous to the greylag goose's fixation on the mother. "The first thing the dog has to do," he said, "is become imprinted on you." In his formulation, the crucial difference between dogs and wolves is the dog's long, neotenized period of socialization, which allows them to bond with humans in ways that wolves can't. "In the relatively short period of time in which the wolf puppy can answer life's abiding question, 'Who are my kind,' you really have to cram maximum exposure to a human being onto the wolf pup if it's to learn that humans are decent social companions." Once a dog has imprinted on humans, associative learning can begin. There is no mystery here. The dog's human affiliation is, at its essence, instinct, activated by learning. "The dog makes the connections between your actions and things that matter to the dog by learning."

The notion that a pet dog pays special attention to its owner and learns to use cues like pointing is absolutely unsurprising to Wynne. "The dog is in your home," he said. "The dog is dependent on you for its whole life. It has nothing to do but watch you. You provide for all of its important needs. It's a basic, simple form of learning." *Press lever, get food:* not so different from a rat or a pigeon. In this view, Hare and Miklósi's brand of canine science seems like a lot of wasted effort.

Comparative psychologists see the mind as a toolbox with a whole range of particularized modules—some of them fairly complex and specialized—that fit together in specific ways. By contrast, behaviorists like Wynne see it more as a Lego set. Their aim is to break complex behaviors down as if they were Lego constructions, to see how they're linked, finally getting down to a pile of neat blocks. "I believe that the essence of science is to analyze something that looks complicated into

its simpler parts," he told me. "Take a behavior like an animal following a human point. I think it can be disassembled so that you see
that it's basically a form of associative conditioning."

The two groups have fired salvos back and forth over the last few
years, critique and response and responses to responses on a wide
range of issues. As I read these papers, with their dizzying array of vari-
ables and alternate interpretations of data, the science seems murky
indeed.

Wynne's papers, written with a younger colleague, Monique Udell,
sometimes seemed to have a scolding tone: *Dogs are not human, you silly
scientists.* "Humans and dogs do not visually signal with many of the
same body parts. Humans do not possess tails or substantial amounts
of hair on the back of their necks, nor do they signal with the position
of their ears. Dogs do not signal with their forepaws or by use of an
elaborate semantic vocal language."

Furthermore, these phenomena have perfectly serviceable explanations, ones that twentieth-century scientists spent years proving
and that are now being tossed out by the rising band of sentimentalists.
It's not easy to be a behaviorist in the second decade of the twenty-
first century. Even Wynne seemed a bit sheepish about claiming B. F.
Skinner as a forebear. Wynne stressed his intellectual allegiance to
Niko Tinbergen, the father (with Lorenz) of ethology as it's currently
practiced.

Preparing for my talk with Wynne, I came across a paper in which
he argued against using evolutionary hypotheses in animal research. I
found this perplexing. Didn't this make him a creationist? Wasn't every
self-respecting scientist a Darwinian? When I asked Wynne, he has-
tened to assure me he hadn't discounted Darwin. Rather, he believed
that those speculations inevitably distort what scientists are analyzing,
causing them to see billowing mysticisms like consciousness and superpowerful mental tools by analogy with our own brains, when what is
really going on is quite simple. *"Okay, humans have this particular mental
instinct,"* he said, mimicking his intellectual opposition. *"Let's go and see*

*if our closest relatives have it, then go and follow the natural history of it.* It just seems to me to be naïve."

Underlying this naïveté, in Wynne's view, is anthropomorphism, that tendency to start with human capabilities and trace them back. Scientists like Wynne consider anthropomorphism to be imaginative rather than factual, nothing more than a metaphor. "To me it's not science," he told me. "It's just a lay understanding." And for at least a century, one of science's prime directives has been to rigorously scrub away any hint of lay understandings, lest they infect a laboratory's findings.

For two years in the 1940s, researchers at Atlanta's Yerkes National Primate Research Center tried to record the activities and behaviors of their chimpanzee inmates without resorting to anthropomorphism, to describe them objectively. What they got was, essentially, hieroglyphics: "an almost endless series of specific acts in which no order or meaning could be found," wrote psychobiologist Donald Hebb in a famous 1946 paper on chimpanzee emotion. Meanwhile the chimps' caretakers had done what comes naturally, describing the behaviors like a soap opera: Bimba is friendly but quick-tempered; Pati hates men (and who wouldn't, kept in a cage most of the time). Anthropomorphism, the language of intentions and all manner of unprovable mentalisms, the language I use with Stella, could provide a kind of Rosetta Stone. "By the use of frankly anthropomorphic concepts of emotion and attitude," wrote Hebb, "one could quickly and easily describe the peculiarities of individual animals." Behaviorism has its uses, and there are many ways of thinking about animals, but whatever its flaws as a scientific tool, anthropomorphism works.

## Seven

# Darwin's Muse

It turns out that, in my imputation of all manner of motives and family feelings to Stella, I have an unlikely forebear. To Charles Darwin, anthropomorphism came as naturally as breathing. And his close observation of his dogs played a surprisingly central role in his work. The Galápagos finches have gotten most of the attention, but dogs were just as important to Darwin's scientific enterprise. The work of scientists like Brian Hare, Michael Tomasello, and Juliane Kaminski, and before them Jane Goodall, represents a return to Darwin's approach. The casual anthropomorphism has been carefully policed, but the notion that dogs, in their uncanny suitability for life with people, have much to teach us comes directly from Darwin.

In Darwin's domestic life, from childhood to old age, dogs were a constant, irreplaceable presence. His sisters liked to tease him that he preferred dogs to people. He doted on them, sentimentalized them, treated them as family members. When he was a dreamy, distracted boy, just beginning to order his speculations about the natural world, dogs were always in the picture, creatures of both the human and the natural world. Dogs were his companions on his first voyages, through the fields and at shooting clubs around the Mount, the family estate in Shrewsbury in the English Midlands. Darwin was an obsessive hunter, keeping a piece of string that he knotted in order to count the birds he shot.

Darwin's concerned father took him out of prep school and sent him to the University of Edinburgh to study medicine, hoping to break him of this obsession, but his sisters sent him regular reports of the canine goings-on. In his absence, the dogs were "pictures of Melancholy and are really grateful for any notice, from anybody," wrote his sister Susan. "Mrs Shelah condescends to pay me much more attention than when you were at home. She does not get much exercise beyond her daily walk into town & a little romping with any odd apple which she entreats me to throw down the bank for her to pick up."

Poor little Spark. She had been Charles's favorite, a black and white terrier—"Little Black Nose," he called her. But with Charles away, the family sent Spark to Darwin's eldest sister Marianne's house in Overton. The momentousness of this event is captured in the tone of his sister's letter: "I must now give you a piece of news about your favorite child, which I am afraid will prove a blow to you; i.e. that Spark is gone to Overton; at least till your return next summer, as they were in want of a watch dog. . . . I am afraid this intelligence will be a shock to all your nerves."

Not as much as the letter to come. Marianne Parker wrote Charles in February 1826 to tell him that Spark had gone missing for two weeks. Finally found at a neighbor's house, she was pregnant. She later died giving birth to a litter of pups. "You cannot think how sorry we have all been about it," Parker wrote. "Every body in the house had got so fond of her, & she was such a nice little Dog."

At Edinburgh, Darwin proved an indifferent student, and his father pulled him out of school again, scolding him harshly: "You care for nothing but shooting, dogs, and rat catching, and you will be a disgrace to yourself and all your family." But what looked to his father like idleness was actually the beginnings of Charles's data gathering. From hunting, he developed keen observational habits, and the fields he walked were an endlessly rich resource for studying the habits of his favorite game birds. Now he increasingly turned these skills to other purposes. His friend and second cousin William Fox introduced him to entomology. And his dogs, more than mere helpers in killing birds, became a focus of his youthful imaginings in their own right.

In the 1820s, as Darwin approached adulthood, the British cult of the dog was at its height. The dog was considered an emblem of civility, and appreciation of dogs was the mark of a gentleman. British dogs' moral virtues—loyalty, selflessness, service—were thought to be of the highest order, superior to those of any other animal (the horse was just below the top rung of the ladder) and superior to those exhibited by people of other classes and races. The excellence of British dogs was thought to be evidence of Englishmen's own excellence, reflecting the universal civilizing effect of British culture.

In 1808, when his Newfoundland, Boatswain, died from rabies, Lord Byron had provided the dog cult's manifesto:

> [He] possessed Beauty without Vanity,
> Strength without Insolence,
> Courage without Ferocity,
> and all the virtues of Man without his Vices.

Darwin's sojourn on the *Beagle*, from 1831 to 1836, marked his transition from child to scientist. In his new life, the role of his canine friends expanded. One of the first things he did upon returning from his five-year voyage was to conduct an experiment on one of his dogs. "I had a dog who was savage and averse to all strangers," he wrote in *The Descent of Man*, "and I purposely tried his memory after an absence of five years and two days. I went near the stable where he lived, and shouted to him in my old manner. He showed no joy, but instantly followed me out walking and obeyed me, as if I'd parted only a half an hour before."

Part of Darwin's method was to correspond with anyone and everyone in hopes of finding new information that could prove or disprove his ideas. He did not believe everything he heard from his many correspondents, but these sentiments he imbibed more or less uncritically, and the notion that the dog was a moral creature—sharing many important qualities with human beings—never left him. It became an all-purpose metaphor, one he often applied to himself in his letters. "My dear Fox," he wrote to his entomologist friend, "I have been a neglectful dog."

Darwin, an intellectual omnivore, did not quarantine scientific speculation from the rest of his life. His preposterous laboratory had skins and bones and barnacles flying in from everywhere, orchids in the hothouse, worms in garden boxes. What a house it must have been! But the dog, being the animal closest at hand, was the one he studied most closely. "I have somewhere, I am almost certain, the head of a Chinese Dog," Darwin wrote one of his friends. "Would you like to have this? if so (always supposing that I can find it) shall I send it you direct, or have it left anywhere in London." Darwin, his enthusiasm aroused, made another, more unusual offer, before seemingly realizing that he may have overpromised. "I have alive a German Spitz Dog, very pure bred; if it shd. die, shd. I send you the carcase? but as it is young, probably it will live long.—"

Darwin notebooks M and N, written mostly in the 1830s, contain his most far-reaching speculations about humans' animal origins, the ones that later formed the basis of *The Descent of Man*, and the dog plays a central role. He was constantly on the lookout for similarities. "I have seen a dog doing what he ought not to do, & looking ashamed of himself," he wrote, an observation that's been much discussed of late. "Squib at Maer, used to betray himself by looking ashamed before it was known he had been on the table,—guilty conscience.—Not probable in Squib's case any direct fear."

Darwin believed dogs had a full complement of humanlike emotions. "Dogs laughs for joy," he wrote in his notebook, "so does dog bark, (not shout) when opening his mouth in romps, so he smiles." He marveled at how, when his dog Nina was taken away from Shrewsbury, she wasted away—then regained her health when she was returned home. "What remarkable affection to a place," he wrote. "How like strong feelings of man."

Darwin was also comfortable ascribing certain powers of reason to his canine friends. In the margins of his copy of John Abercrombie's *Inquiries Concerning the Intellectual Powers and the Investigation of Truth* (1838), Darwin observed that dogs, too, reason by analogy—a hat signifies a walk.

His dogs' devotion to him was not just a matter of treacly sentimentality, to be set aside when he turned to his serious studies. It was a subject for scientific observation, a fact like any other fact. Darwin carried a long, multifaceted discussion about dogs with his friend the geologist Charles Lyell, whose work on the great age of the earth had inspired Darwin's own theory. "To give one infinitely little criticism; I demur to your saying—p.17. that animals are governed only by selfish motives.—look at the maternal instincts & still more at the social instincts. How unselfish is a Dog!" he wrote in response to one of Lyell's books. "To me it seems as clear that we have a conscience as that the lower animals have a social instinct: indeed I believe they are nearly the same."

Not that he thought dogs and humans were on the same plane, or even the same evolutionary line. Evolution would have played a part. "Dogs conscience would not have been same with mans," he wrote in his notebook, "because original instincts different." But underneath, Darwin saw a huge commonality; evolution had built both of them for living socially; they had converged.

Darwin even suggested that the origin of property could be glimpsed in the passion of a dog for its bone. And "with respect to free will," he wrote, "seeing a puppy playing cannot doubt that they have free will. Free will is to mind, what chance is to matter." Dogs dream, he thought, replaying old memories—they have a past, which meant some kind of sense of time.

The dog's domestication had been an unalloyed boon to the canine race. "Dog gained in moral qualities, affection and trustworthiness," he wrote in a letter, "and probably in general intelligence." While wolves and jackals seldom barked, dogs had developed an extensive vocal repertoire. "It is a more remarkable fact that the dog, since being domesticated, has learned to bark in four or five distinct tones," he wrote in *The Descent of Man*. The implication, not quite stated so bluntly is that the dog had learned to communicate. "With the domesticated dog," he continued, "we have the bark of eagerness, as in the chase; that of anger; the yelping or howling bark of despair, as when shut up; that of joy, as when starting on a walk with his master; and the very distinct one of demand or supplication, as when wishing for a door or window to be opened."

These are the kinds of speculations, complete with anthropomorphic descriptions of internal emotions, that drive behaviorists mad. How could Darwin know these things for certain? He just knew—he had no other means or vocabulary for expressing his observations, and certainly no scientific tradition to violate. And though he had developed these ideas soon after he returned from the Galápagos, he purposely left them out of *On the Origin of Species* because the notion of humans' relation to animals was simply too controversial. To suggest that human creation was not unique violated the popular understanding of the time and the formal position of the Anglican Church.

Darwin was under no illusions as to who our closest relatives were. "He who understands baboons would do more towards metaphysics than Locke," he wrote in one of his notebooks. But with the rise of empire, Britons' growing familiarity with great apes from Africa and South America made evolution a difficult proposition for them to swallow. The apes that made it to London were lauded for their intelligence and sometimes dressed in human clothes and given forks and spoons (though the cold climate didn't agree with them; they usually died after a season or two). But the notion of being related to such an un-civilized creature was nevertheless frightening to the gentlefolk—even worse than being related to the Tierra del Fuegans or the Hottentots.

When Darwin eventually published his ideas in *The Descent of Man* and *The Expression of Emotions in Man and Animals,* the dog was an im-portant ally. His readers, scandalized by the prospect of descent from apes, found the dog a much more comfortable cousin. For the Victori-ans, as for ourselves, dogs brought up simple associations of home and hearth and the ties that bind, an antidote to the tensions of the city. "I think on consideration I had almost rather have a dog for an ancestor than even a ring tailed monkey, at any rate they have more attachment, more sense, and nearly as much morality as a good many of our la-bourer," wrote Darwin's frequent correspondent John Brodie-Innes.

"I have never been able to discover in any of the simian tribe a single human quality," wrote the prolific American creationist Orestes Brownson in a broadside against Darwin's *Origin.* "The dog is certainly far ahead of the monkey in moral qualities, in affection for his master and fidelity to him, and so is the horse when kindly treated." While the dog didn't quite convert Brownson, his view was one that Darwin's au-dience could understand.

The dog also figures in perhaps the most surprising image in all of Darwin's work, a breathtaking leap from the most ordinary of situa-tions to the deepest possible questions. "My dog, a full-grown and very sensible animal, was lying on the lawn during a very hot and still day; but at a little distance, a slight breeze occasionally moved an open para-sol, which would have been wholly disregarded by the dog had anyone stood near it. As it was, every time the parasol slightly moved, the dog growled fiercely and barked. He must, I think, have reasoned to him-self in a rapid and unconscious manner that movement of any kind without any apparent cause indicated the presence of some strange living agent, and no stranger had the right to be on his territory."

Then he takes another step: "the belief in spiritual agencies would easily pass into the belief in the existence of one or more Gods." The progression is vertiginous—from a dog on a lawn, growling cluelessly at an umbrella, all the way to God. It wasn't that the dog saw God there, but slowly, in the same way a light-sensitive cell becomes an eye, or an arm becomes a wing, something might develop from these seeds. That impulse to impute a living thing inside the parasol gave evolution a structure, something to build upon. The dog didn't see God, but it saw *something*. And in untold future generations, that something might be filled in, elaborated upon. In the workings of evolution, the original impulse might become something completely different. The dog, in Darwin's eyes, had not come all the way on the trip that humans had embarked on, but now we were traveling the same path. And the dog on the lawn also said much about Darwin himself, and his methods: that sudden flash on a dreamy afternoon. It was the method of the gentleman. Not everyone could do science this way.

In Darwin's time, the dog was at the pinnacle of animal intelligence and morality, and it did not immediately descend. Darwin's carefully chosen disciple and heir, the young Canadian evolutionist George John Romanes, began to systematize and quantify Darwin's looser formulations in his 1880s books, *Animal Intelligence* and *Mental Evolution in Animals*, which included as an appendix a chapter on mental evolution that Darwin had prepared for *Origin*, then decided to leave out. They are wonderful books of animal stories, and also towering icons of the Victorian mind, in all its excellence and shortcomings. Romanes made several notable insights into his mentor's theories; he was among the first to perceive that Darwin had not fully come to grips with how species are actually differentiated, an issue that's been contested ever since.

But his role in the debate over animal intelligence is more problematic. Romanes practiced the Darwinian scientific method of corresponding with anyone and everyone in hopes of finding new information that could prove or disprove one's ideas. But that method needed a genius like Darwin to operate it. While Darwin had used dog anecdotes only sparingly in his work, Romanes's *Animal Intelligence* is as full of them as any Victorian pet compendium. A Dr. Rae, in Orkney, had reported that a certain dog could calculate the tides—an ability confirmed by the talents of an excellent retriever belonging to Mr. Percival Fothergill. Another correspondent wrote of Nero, "a highly intelligent animal" of "Norwegian birth," who traveled between his master's estates by train. "If Nero did not make use of abstract reasoning," writes his master, "we might as well give up use of the term."

Romanes believed that dogs were not necessarily the smartest of animals: "monkeys certainly surpass all other animals in the scope of their rational faculties." Even cats had an edge on dogs when it came to certain puzzles like latch opening. But dogs excelled in the variety and refinement of their emotions. "The emotional life of the dog," he wrote, "is highly developed, more highly, indeed, than any other animal." (The elephant, so familiar from the Raj, ranked close behind.) Dogs felt pride, a sense of dignity, self-respect, a sense of justice, and jealousy. (In an odd omission, given its presence in every other account of dogs' cognitive equipment, he didn't mention guilt.) Most of these qualities were so obviously manifested, he thought, that he needed only to provide one or two confirming examples. Romanes also observed a faculty that he called "the emotion of the ludicrous," expanding on Darwin's observation in *The Descent of Man* that dogs have a sense of humor.

For a dog person, Romanes's *Animal Intelligence* makes for delightful reading. It reminded me of Csányi's *If Dogs Could Talk,* with its procession of canine wizards, solving puzzles in novel ways, worthy of all the attention lavished on them. One needn't even necessarily discount these anecdotes—even so unreasoning and exuberant a creature as Stella seems aware, at times, of the movement of the tides if she's crossing a stream. But those stories seem a long way from science, even as Darwin understood it. Rather than challenging any orthodoxies, Romanes's work in this area merely confirmed what everyone of his class and background knew: his dog was a very smart and civilized creature indeed—and why wouldn't he be? In keeping with the British upper class's pride in its own distinctive accomplishments, Romanes believed that these emotions flowered only in the proper civilizing circumstances.

As Romanes was preparing his book, the scientific method was entering its adolescence. The project became not just to persuade the public of its validity but actually to prove it. The theory of evolution, in the decades after publication of *On the Origin of Species* in 1859, became widely accepted, but the underlying edifice of animal intelligence was not solidly anchored in science.

C. Lloyd Morgan, a mining chemist and psychologist, was the first to show how fragile was the evolutionary argument for animal intelligence. His book *Animal Life and Intelligence,* published in 1891, announced in the politest of terms that he would take issue with Romanes's ideas. Culturally, Lloyd Morgan was a man much like Darwin and Romanes, and his book draws on their gentlemanly traditions while containing startling intimations of the birth of a new science. He investigated the maddening complexities of interpreting dog behavior—and used Romanes's own techniques against him. The book is filled with extravagant praise for the intelligence and perspicacity of Darwin's protégé, but its close reading and reinterpretation of Romanes's anecdotes are devastating. "There can be no question that the quality of eatability," he wrote, "is built in by the dog into a great number of his constructs. But I question whether this quality can be isolated by the dog, and can exist in his mind divorced from the eatables which suggest it." Where was the evidence for these mental qualities? he asked.

Morgan was a skeptic rather than a denier. He was careful to allow for the possibility that new evidence might overturn his doubts. But he challenged Romanes's interpretation of, for example, a dog's supposed effort to lift a latch. Romanes had written: "Whenever he wanted to go out the fox terrier raised the latch with the back of his head, and thus released the gate, which swung open." Brilliant, you say? Well, maybe not, said Morgan. In looking out through the gate, the dog happened to bump the latch, and presto, he was free: it opened by luck, not by insight. "In this case the lifting of the latch was unquestionably hit on by accident, and the trick was only rendered habitual by repeated association in the same situation of the chance act and the happy escape." Morgan's analysis is strikingly Darwinian—a chance occurrence that is then embedded and reinforced by a positive outcome, then gradually builds into magnificent edifices of complex behaviors. But in other ways, Morgan tends in the opposite direction from Darwin and Romanes: the passage begins to remove mentalism from the animal mind.

Morgan's most lasting contribution was not an insight but a rule, now known as Morgan's Canon, still a potent force in the life sciences. "In no case," he wrote, "is an animal activity to be interpreted in terms of higher psychological processes, if it can be interpreted in terms of processes which stand lower in the scale of psychological evolution and development." In other words, we must not read mental complexity into animal behavior, even where it might seem apt. Elsewhere, Morgan cautioned against the casual anthropomorphism of Darwin and Romanes. What might seem obvious to the ordinary dog person was not necessarily true: "If, on the perusal of familiar anecdotes, we also credit [dogs] with jealousy, envy, emulation, pride, resentment, cruelty, deceitfulness and other more complex emotional states, we must remember that every one of these as we know them is essentially human."

After Morgan, the laboratory became the place to study animal behavior. (A few eccentric Englishmen got up at ungodly hours and endured terrible British weather to watch birds, but they were the exceptions. Modern ethology would not begin in earnest for another four decades or so.) The cherished kinds of dog stories that had done so much for the new science of animal behavior were left to dog people. Scientists were professionals, and after Morgan their amour propre was bound up with a rejection of sentiments that Darwin took for granted. In the lab, the dog became not a marvelously multifaceted social creature but more like the pigeon and the rat—just another animal. The dog's lives in the home and in the laboratory were bifurcated, not to be reconnected for another century or so. As a result, the science became purer, but its view of animals, in its extreme fastidiousness, was somehow incomplete.

The Victorian idea of animal intelligence was finally smothered in Edward Thorndike's puzzle boxes, crudely hammered together from chicken wire and scrap lumber. Thorndike was a severe fellow, to say the least. His father was an itinerant Methodist minister in New England, and while Edward doesn't seem to have inherited his father's religious ideas, the stern moralism is unmistakable. A lecture by Morgan at Harvard may have pollinated Thorndike's burgeoning research interests. Far from an animal lover, he entered the field, he wrote, "because I thought I could do better than had been done." While he agreed with Morgan's analyses, he also believed he had not gone far enough. He exhibited no gentlemanly politeness whatsoever in his rejection of Romanes. His research began in the last years of the nineteenth century. Beginning with chickens, he moved on to cats, and then to dogs. To keep them motivated, Thorndike kept the animals in a state of "utter hunger," a phrase that he was later said to have regretted.

Thorndike began with the assumption that animals can learn by imitation, but was surprised to find that when one dog watched another dog perform an action that earned it a much-desired reward, the observation had no measurable influence on the first dog's performance; it learned slowly, by trial and error, just as Morgan had found. Over time he came to have an even lower opinion of dogs' intelligence—not to mention of the scientists who had committed those earlier errors. Thorndike knew he was throwing bombs at the establishment and delighted in it. He referred to Romanes and his colleagues as "the anecdote school," and he sneered that an animal psychology built on such observations was "like an anatomy built on the observation of dime-museum freaks." Romanes and his colleagues, he said, "have looked for the intelligent and unusual and neglected the stupid and normal."

He paid no attention to the canine social graces that had so captivated Darwin and the Victorians and that even Morgan had paid lip service. Animals weren't quite Cartesian machines, devoid of consciousness, but they were pretty simple. For Thorndike, measurement became its own kind of religion—and what couldn't be measured, even what was difficult to measure, couldn't be true.

Given his low opinion of the animal mind, his speculation on their mental lives is strangely evocative and poetic. "Sometimes one gets this animal consciousness while in swimming, for example. One feels the water, the sky, the birds above, but with no thoughts about them or memories of how they looked at other times, or aesthetic judgments about their beauty; one feels no ideas about what movements he will make, but feels himself to make them, feels his body throughout. Self-consciousness dies away. Social consciousness dies away. The meanings, and values, and connections of things die away. One feels sense impressions, has impulses, feels the movements he makes; that is all." This meditation sounds like fun—dim and unformed maybe, but not at all unpleasant. It's kind of an opium-den vision of the animal mind—and one hopes his hungry, caged animals felt that way.

As Thorndike was hammering together his puzzle boxes, Ivan Petrovich Pavlov, also the son of a hinterlands religious man—a village priest, outside Moscow—was beginning to study "psychic secretions." Having studied the gastric systems of dogs for a decade or more, he was already middle-aged. Punctual, disciplined, and ascetic to the point of near madness, he was also surprisingly warm-hearted.

In his most famous experiments, Pavlov surgically isolated salivary glands so their output could be measured after the animal was presented with various stimuli. Pavlov's temples of pleasure and pain—

food and electric shocks and gastric juices collected in surgically created fistula, all set in motion by the sound of a ringing bell or a metronome or a tuning fork—are infamous images of captivity and thoroughgoing manipulation. (The laboratory paid some of its expenses by selling the gastric juice he collected from his dogs, which, amazingly, was a health craze in Moscow at the time.)

The idea was that scientists could reduce to simple laws much that went on in a dog's mind—and if they could get into a dog's mind, could a human's mind be far behind? It was Pavlov and his students who began using locutions like "freedom instinct" that reduce our noblest aspirations to mere mechanisms, subject to scientific and political tweaking.

In fact, Pavlov, for all his oddball grandeur, was far from a monster. His laboratory itself was a kind of collectivist experiment, where credit was shared much more freely than at other enterprises of its kind. Later in his career he was so renowned that even Stalin couldn't mess with him. Unlike many scientists, who prided themselves on their stoicism in the face of animal pain, Pavlov tried to ensure that his animals didn't suffer and could live somewhat normal lives—partly, but not only, out of concern for their welfare. (He felt that vivisections leading to an animal's death were liable to provide distorted results— and he also disliked the sight of blood.) He performed surgeries in a state-of-the-art operating room, possibly the first devoted solely to animals, with anesthesia. Plenty of dogs died as he perfected his surgeries, but the ones that lived were named, loved, and treated—as much as possible—like family members, even appearing in eerily cheerful group photographs as bright-eyed and eager, maimed though they were. Pavlov rationalized his dog work by saying, "The dog, man's helper from prehistoric times, may justly be offered as a sacrifice with science, but this should always be done without unnecessary suffering."

Thorndike's and Pavlov's ideas were remarkably powerful, breaking down previously indestructible barriers, clarifying questions, simplifying everything. They closed the loop, leaving out the murkiness of mentalism, giving science something it could measure. Pavlov's experiments with visual stimuli followed by salivation provided a powerful metaphor for the simple workings of animal minds: the linkage didn't have to be mediated by anything so refined as an idea. The mind of a dog, in this view, is a mechanism, and all of our everyday anthropomorphisms—*Stella wants, Stella is sad*—are mirages. In the decades after his death, Darwin's views on the animal mind seemed to have vanished entirely. But that too turned out to be an illusion.

*Eight*

# The Mind Returns

Banishing intelligence from the minds of animals placed humans back on our old pedestal: we had it, and animals didn't. But B. F. Skinner had big ideas, dreaming of becoming another Darwin, of explaining animal behavior with one simple, superpowerful principle. He expanded the simple structures described by Thorndike and Pavlov into whole chains of complex behaviors, building up toward something that looked like how creatures behaved. And he didn't stop where Thorndike and Morgan had, putting animals in their place and letting humans have their self-evidently magnificent world. He wanted to abolish mentalism from the human world too. So much pain, neurosis, and complexity—if it could be reduced to its basic building blocks and rebuilt, that would be progress: the good society would be understood to be a well-trained society, where desirable behaviors were reinforced and undesirable ones mostly ignored. Skinner thought punishment, as a response to undesirable behaviors, created too much feedback. Subjects, human or animal, tended to focus on avoiding the punishment rather than avoiding the behavior that caused it. (Long after his scientific reign was over, Skinner played a role in abolishing corporal punishment from the California public schools.)

With his self-invented scientific vocabulary and array of newfangled devices (most notably the Skinner box), Skinner was a figure of fear and fascination, an eccentric who seemed, for a while, to hold the future of the world in his hands. It all seemed so easy. Skinner's insight was that we'd anthropomorphized ourselves, imagining we were human beings when in fact we were only a series of connections. We could achieve contentment and perfection if we freed ourselves from the myths. Mentalism, having been banished from the lower animals, was now about to be cast out of our brains too, in favor of a cleaner, more orderly, much less mystical regime.

Skinner's attempt to reduce the complexities of language to a series of conditioned responses in his 1957 book, *Verbal Behavior*, was as odd and radical as anything he ever did. Skinner believed that language was no different from everything else we learned—and learned in the same way, built from the ground up by association.

It was an audacious theory—and Skinner's orderly white city, and his fame, made him a very big target. Noam Chomsky, a young linguist at MIT, picked it apart in a 1959 review in the journal *Language* with the kind of savagery that only a young man can muster. The mind didn't function like a Lego set, he averred, building complex structures out of simple parts. It was complex, and the complex didn't always resolve or break down to the simple. Language was probably in some sense "an inborn structure," Chomsky wrote, not merely the product of experience and differential reinforcement.

Skinner, accustomed to rewriting the rules of nature to make them so obvious that even a child—or a dog—could understand them, didn't know quite how to respond to this young person's tantrum. The best way to deal with it was neither to punish it nor to reinforce it but to ignore it. But in the absence of a response, a new movement grew. The cognitive revolution, as it was later called, posited that the behaviorists, by defining psychology as the science of behavior, had made an elementary error: Chomsky said it was as if physics had been defined as the science of meter reading. The mental machine had to have been built somehow. Something was happening in there that was worth studying, a notion partly inspired by the nascent field of computing. The cognitive revolution was the beginning of the end of the blank slate, and it also reintroduced a host of Darwinian questions about how that mental machinery might have evolved. And eventually, it gave animals back their minds. Their minds did have systems: for solving problems, for mapping landscapes, for distinguishing friends from enemies, for figuring out what other animals' behavior means.

Chomsky himself didn't follow all these threads. In his view, language, the basis of our reason and humanity, is so complicated and irreducible that animal minds, even those of our closest relatives, are of little use in explaining it. Chomsky was always cagey about the evolutionary history of this marvelous faculty. "In the case of such systems as language or wings," Chomsky wrote in 1988, "it is not easy even to imagine a course of selection that might have given rise to them."

It was as if an obelisk had been set down to change the minds of the monkeys, from who knows where. The arrival of language, to borrow a term from physics, was a kind of singularity: what came before couldn't explain what came after. Some deep laws of organization had somehow been activated, Chomsky sometimes suggested—but even asking how it began seemed a kind of sacrilege. The name he gave this faculty, "unbounded merge," has a mystical tinge, a sense of awe in the presence of the infinite—not God, but a force that we may never comprehend.

The question of language evolution is still at the center of the debate over Darwin's ideas. And it's this idea of Chomsky's—that what came before can't explain what came after, and that humans are at an absolute distance from animals—that scientists like Hare and Tomasello are now contesting. Language, Tomasello argues, is built partly upon something as basic as shared intentionality—a simple enough step, rather than some unknowable inheritance. But the notion that the mind contains inborn structures—that the brain is a toolbox, not a simple machine—is what everyone but the behaviorists share at this point.

. . .

I n 1959, as Chomsky was publishing his broadside against Skinner, Jane Goodall was preparing to go to Gombe, in Tanzania, to do the work that made her famous. As it happened, the death of a beloved dog had devastated her, and also allowed her to pull up stakes. A wealthy, lonely girl with a glamorous race-car-driving father, Goodall lived during and after World War II at The Birches, her parents' home in Bournemouth, England. She'd always dreamed of studying animals, though "studying" is perhaps too dry a term. "I wanted to talk to the animals, like Doctor Doolittle," she wrote. And for Goodall, as for Darwin, the dog was a gateway into nature. The dog in question was a black spaniel with a splash of white on his chest, named Rusty—"the little black man," she called him, along with "black angel," "black devil," and "pig."

Rusty was one of those canine prodigies who cause people to question their assumptions about how smart an animal can be. The owner of a local sweetshop had enlisted Goodall to care for a gorgeous but somewhat dim collie named Budleigh, but Rusty, who lived in a local hotel, barged in. He quickly learned the tricks Goodall had been laboriously trying to teach Bud, then added refinements, flipping the treats up on his nose. He would lie down and die on command, and climb a ladder. Goodall claims that he loved to be dressed up but disliked being laughed at. She wrote in *My Life with the Chimpanzees* that Rusty was "the only dog I've ever met who had a sense of justice."

Rusty's humanlike qualities catalyzed Goodall's research: "Rusty, and a series of cats, and assorted guinea pigs and golden hamsters had taught me well. They had made it abundantly clear that animals had personalities, could reason and solve problems, had emotions—I thus felt no hesitation in ascribing these qualities to the chimpanzees."

Lacking scientific training, Goodall thought anthropomorphism was the only possible approach—she'd already practiced on the dog. By the time she met Louis Leakey, who signed her up to investigate the chimpanzees of Gombe, Tanzania, her mind had been largely unsullied by modern science—she hadn't even been to college. She was adventurous, passionate, and empathetic, and she got into much scientific trouble for her methods. She famously named the chimps, allowing a host of other anthropomorphisms to flow in, yet managed to lift the curtain on a long-hidden world. The chimpanzees' tool use was the groundbreaking headline, and Goodall's detailed observations greatly advanced the ethology of the chimps. But a lot of the power of her work lies in the richly detailed, almost novelistic account of chimp society: chimps rise and fall in their social group, nurse their children, and devise new strategies to conquer territory.

When Goodall arrived triumphantly at Cambridge, having discovered chimpanzee tool use and decisively changed the way science (indeed, everyone) sees the relationship between humans and our closest relatives, the scientists eagerly accepted most of her findings. But they were unwilling to fully accept her methods, castigating her for discussing chimpanzee minds, emotions, and personalities. Far from being sheepish about her anthropomorphisms, she knew they were central to her methods. "Fortunately," she wrote, "I had had a marvelous teacher in animal behavior throughout my childhood. So I ignored the admonitions of Science." The teacher was her little dog Rusty.

Goodall revolutionized ethology, in its practice and its subjects, but also in the people who were attracted to it. With her lush *National Geographic* spreads and her glamorous multicontinental life, she made science safe for animal lovers. She was the twentieth-century equivalent of a nineteenth-century explorer. And just as for Darwin, a dog had helped her along the path to discovery. Goodall, now the grand dame of anthropology as well as an important advocate for animals, both wild and domestic, made anthropomorphism less problematic by showing how it could catalyze real insights that simply couldn't have occurred any other way.

Anthropomorphism is not only a strategy for generating scientific hypotheses. If you take seriously, as Goodall did, the notion that dogs or chimps are creatures something like ourselves—with emotions and interests and family feelings—you open the door to moral questions. "When I'm thinking about some forest being logged, and the bush meat trade," she told *National Geographic* in 2003, "it isn't just a population of chimps that's going. It's individuals . . . I can't separate the loss of a population from the harm to individuals."

Goodall's impulse to think of animals as individuals led her to a new scientific understanding—which led her back to a different kind of commitment. The imputation of higher mental processes led to new political imperatives. Animals are not only worthy of study—they are worthy of human concern and even of humanlike treatment. Again, a dog—an honorary human—had pushed this door open.

G oodall's ideas have gone forth and multiplied. Brian Hare, who is now near the center of research into the psychology of dogs and primates, is one of the many scientists inspired by Jane Goodall. Part of it was the glamour of her jungle life—he saw a documentary about her at the age of nine, and his path was set. And her intuitive sense, so much like Darwin's, of the continuities between humans and animals still underlies his work.

One late fall afternoon I followed the signs to Hare's Dog Cognition Lab—in an out-of-way corner of the biological sciences building at Duke—to watch him and his students investigate the mysteries of the animal mind. The brain of the day belonged to a little brown and black dachshund named Cooper. Cooper arrived in a burst of energy—his tail propellering, his shiny-marble eyes darting around, looking for something interesting to do—followed by his owners, a local couple with a teenage daughter. They sat on chairs at one end of the room as Cooper leaped up onto laps, then leaped off, then back up, every action accompanied by a chorus unusual for a science lab: "Oh, Cooper, Cooper, you're such a sweetie. Cooper, look how cute you are."

Cooper does happen to be rather cute—but every dog that's brought in receives more or less the same treatment, no matter how homely. The lab gets stacks of correspondence from people who believe their dogs are prodigies—"he thinks he's a human" is a typical remark—recounting their miraculous feats of intelligence, practically begging for them to be tested.

Hare and his students are working on the influence of trust on learning. The research builds on earlier experiments, trying to see how the kind of social bonding that Ádám Miklósi and his colleagues detected might affect dog-human communication. One experiment involves a researcher sitting down with and cuddling a dog for twenty minutes—the time required for oxytocin (the bonding hormone) to be released into the dog's system—after which various cognitive talents are tested for. The idea is to measure how the dog's social impulses, down to the chemical level, interact with its cognitive ones.

Hare, now a thirty-six-year-old assistant professor, is somewhere between schoolboy and rock star, slim in black dress pants, with a luxuriant shock of unruly brown hair. He spends part of every year at primate sanctuaries in Africa and visiting other animal laboratories—when I saw him, he'd just returned from Japan, where they raise chimpanzees in family situations and are therefore able to perform procedures that would be dangerous or even impossible in American laboratories without anesthesia—he'd been amazed to watch an expectant chimpanzee mother receive ultrasound. Hare's wife, Vanessa Wood, an author and fellow researcher, has an office at Duke. She's in the last months of pregnancy—a new primate to study in the Hare household. Both of them have the enthusiasm and welcoming mien of people who really love their work.

Hare's research is devoted to studying the cognitive machinery at play in the dog's relationship with humans: to mapping out the various systems in the dog's cognitive abilities, and discerning how they acquire knowledge from their human companions. Domestication, in Hare's view, enabled some form of communication between the species. But the mechanisms by which it occurs are as yet very poorly understood, and that's what he's trying to tease out. "The question is, if they trust you in one context, do they trust you in another?" Hare asked. "And how quickly do they form a trusting relationship? Is there individual variance in how they form a trusting relationship?" In contrast to, say, Thorndike's boxes, which bring to mind a medieval jail, the study space in Hare's lab, the size of a modest Manhattan one-bedroom, feels merely minimalist and modern, with nothing to distract the dog. "We test the dog with two strangers," said Hare. "One of the strangers has interacted with the dog for twenty minutes in a playful way. Or one of the strangers has already pointed, reliably, to the dog, on eighteen trials. And then we test the dog again, and we want to know if you pat them and play with them, does that then make them trust you in the next session?"

Cooper was being tested for his skills in social learning, with what's known as the color cookie test. Hare and the students watched Cooper choose which of several brightly colored treats to eat based on the way a student handler, Katie Patellos, had reacted to it—in short, whether the dog learned by watching. His owners held him in front of them, and he watched as Patellos pretended to take a bite out of a particularly tasty morsel. "Mmm." Cooper rushed in to vacuum it up. "Good dog, Cooper!"

The test is based on a study done with rhesus macaques in Cayo Santiago, off Puerto Rico. The macaques were found to have a strong inclination to base their choices on how a human handler had reacted to a particular treat. The dogs, however, aren't showing quite as strong an effect.

Cooper ran through the test a couple of times, showing his cognitive gifts, but then made an error, taking a treat that Patellos didn't show a preference for. There was laughter and praise anyway, the same explosion of mirth: no judgments here. Next, Patellos ran through variations intended to tease out details of what the dog might be perceiving; instead of pantomiming taking a tasty bite, she scratched her ear. Then, Patellos put a couple of small boxes in front of her, stuck her hand into one of them, and acted as if something in the box had bitten her. Cooper rushed up and tentatively stuck his snout in, trying to find what mysterious creature had caused his friend such pain. A bold dog. Most dogs in this situation come to the handler first and only then begin to explore the dangerous box; the most timid dogs won't even go near it.

Finished with his tests, Cooper proudly bustled out of the building, family trailing behind, and Hare and I retreated to his office down the hall to talk about what he and his team had been learning. The lab's first finding was a further refinement of his work on pointing. "You have two individuals point at the same time," he said. "So now you have ambiguous information, and there are two locations where food may be. Well, where do you go? One of those individuals is your owner, and one of them is somebody you've never met before. It's just some guy who's standing in the room and pointing. So who do they follow? Well, it ends up they follow their owner significantly more than the stranger, but they use the stranger's gesture if the owner isn't there giving one."

But while the dogs prefer to follow their owners' points to those of a stranger, Hare and his colleagues found that they have no preference between taking food from their owners or from a stranger. "Basically, the finding was, dogs will take candy from strangers, but not directions," Hare said.

Hare intends to adapt these experimental protocols into techniques to evaluate and train service dogs. But again, he's trying to understand human cooperation. To Hare, chimps and bonobos are analogous to dogs and wolves. Bonobos are tamer, more ready to form bonds, though their methods of doing so might not work in polite society. "They're incredibly tolerant," Hare told me. "And what that means is, I don't get that upset if you eat food with me. If we were chimps, we could not sit here with this Diet Coke. We would have already had a big fight, and somebody would have had both of these Cokes. If we were bonobos, we wouldn't have had a fight. Unfortunately, we would have had to rub our genitals together—but we would have shared the Cokes."

Hare's point is that the process by which bonobos and chimps diverged in evolutionary history is analogous to that of dogs and wolves. "Bonobos are juvenilized," Hare said. "They've been naturally domesticated. They're less aggressive, and if you look at the morphology, they have smaller crania, they're more gracile, and they even have lack of pigmentation on their lips."

Because cognitive qualities are not preserved in the archaeological record (at least until tools, and then art, entered the picture), scientists like Hare and Tomasello can make inferences about the past only by triangulating from similar species—and chimps and bonobos are as close as we're likely to get to our ancient forebears. "We don't know what the last common ancestor of bonobos and chimps was like," he said. "We have no clue. We have not a single fossil. We have nothing to go on. So with no physical evidence, all we can do is make a deductive argument."

Dogs, by analogy, are helping Hare and other scientists tease out the conditions by which humans may have evolved. Hare has suggested, essentially, that humans domesticated themselves—opening the door to language, and to our cooperative talents that hugely magnify our intelligence. For me, the science suggested simpler lessons. It wasn't that I had come to see Stella as some sort of cognitive prodigy, a black-furred, unspeaking savant. It was more that, knowing more about how she may have been built for this relationship, our mutuality came into focus. Both of us were tame (if neither quite tame enough, sometimes). We had plenty of similar interests and some of the same needs. The research had begun to clarify the space where we coexisted. It made sense that she was my friend. Tameness is the price of admission into human culture, and as it was for Darwin, the dog's social abilities too are most revealing in this context. "The thing about the dog," said Hare, "is it got us here."

*Nine*

# The Wolves That Came in from the Cold

Wolves became dogs because, in prehistory, they were engaged in the same kinds of activities as humans, and in their shared interests, the two species forged a brotherhood. Much as Charles Darwin, Jane Goodall, and Brian Hare did with dogs, the earliest humans probably understood wolves as creatures much like themselves: gregariously social, nurturing, cooperative, and deadly. Before humans came along, the gray wolf was the most successful, adaptable, and widespread predator in the world. Long before dogs enter the archaeological record, there's clear evidence of a sense of kinship between man and wolf: wolf teeth were highly desirable ornaments for early humans, much more prevalent than other such ornaments. At a site in Bulgaria, archaeologists discovered perforated wolf teeth that were dated as forty-three thousand years old, placing them near the beginning of human art making. And at one site in France, canid teeth make up two-thirds of the ones that are perforated for ornaments, even though animals were much more common. Scholars like Randall White at New York University believe that ornaments of this kind have a tribal significance—which would make these earliest humans The People of the Wolf.

That this sense of kinship developed is not surprising. In Europe, early humans and wolves derived their sustenance in exactly the same way: by cooperative hunting, killing large animals, a pastoralism red in tooth and claw. Wolfgang Schleidt, a German anthropologist and student of Konrad Lorenz, went so far as to theorize in a 2003 paper (with highly limited evidence, as happens with much theorizing about the culture of early humans) that humans learned how to herd and kill from wolves, some of which then adapted to life with humans—a possible example of coevolution, and an origin story that glorifies both species.

Just how this adaptation occurred may never be known with certainty. Did a bold wolf wander near a human campsite hoping for a cast-off, then stick around? Or could the dogs' ancestors have been orphaned wolf pups, brought into the early humans' shelters, raised without fear, and bred from there? That's the view of scientist James Serpell (whom we met in chapter 2), who studies the pet-keeping habits of hunter-gatherers. Only a few years ago that was the consensus view of dog evolution, but since Ray Coppinger's early work (in chapter 6), it has become much more controversial.

In the late 1990s, Robert Wayne analyzed the DNA of 142 dogs (of several different breeds) and a similar number of wolves and calculated that the two species had diverged as much as 135,000 years ago. This early date would suggest that humans had an animal ally during the crucial years in which they moved out of Africa into Europe, started making art, and decisively defeated the Neanderthals. To some dog lovers, that is the most beautiful story of dogs' possible origins: present at the creation of modern humans. Some archaeologists have even suggested that the early dogs played a role in vanquishing the Neanderthals, who controlled Europe before more evolved humans arrived. But the scanty archaeological record, which reveals no physical evidence of the presence of dogs at that early date—or indeed for the next 100,000 years—brought Wayne's date quickly into question.

More recently a confident young Swedish scientist named Peter Savolainen did a more extensive study using mitochondrial DNA from the hair of 650 dogs from around the world. Savolainen found that domestication events may have taken place as recently as fifteen thousand years ago, a date that fits better with the most securely dated archaeological evidence. He also found that the most genetic variation appears in East Asia, suggesting that the dog probably originated there. Based on his own extensive study of nuclear DNA, Robert Wayne hypothesizes that dogs originated in the Middle East. But both scientists agree that domestication did not take place multiple times—probably just a few hundred wolf individuals were involved.

The archaeological record is extremely sparse, in part because early archaeologists weren't particularly interested in dog skeletons. Many specimens have probably been lost. More recently, with growing interest in the dog as an important part of human culture, dog archaeology has become its own subspecialty. Still, it's hard to get the picture into focus, not least because dog and wolf skeletons—and skeleton fragments—are difficult to differentiate. In Goyet Cave in Belgium, a full canid skull discovered in the Victorian era was recently reexamined. It was found to be wider and shorter than a wolf skull in such a way that could be characteristic of a dog, and it has been dated to more than thirty thousand years ago. Mietje Germonpré, the Royal Belgian Institute paleontologist who made the identification, is the leading archaeological advocate for an early date of dog domestication. He's speculated that the mammoth hunters who occupied the cave at that point in history may have used German-shepherd-size animals to haul their kills. But most archaeological hypotheses are only speculative— it's almost impossible to reconstruct a way of life based on a scatter of bone. The skull could be an intermediate form between dogs and wolves—and scientists like Bob Wayne believe that the dog must have

evolved for millennia before the first securely identified remains appeared, dated to about fourteen thousand years ago. Other, skeptical
archaeologists posit that the skull actually belonged to an immature
wolf.

Chauvet Cave in southern France (which also features a gallery of
animal portraits), contains a remarkably well-preserved set of child's
footprints, carbon-dated at some twenty-six thousand years old. The
prints are intertwined with those of a wolf, or possibly a dog, judging
by the shortness of one of the digits on its front paw. So far the animal's prints have been found only on top of the child's, suggesting that
the wolf—or dog—came afterward. If one of the animal's prints were
to be found under the child's, it would provide a simple, elegant archaeological proof that the two had walked together. It's a beautiful
image, a child and his best friend making their way through a dark
place by torchlight, but thus far no such print has been found, and it
remains just a dog lover's dream.

It took a few more millennia, comprising the ice age, for dogs to
appear conclusively in the fossil record. One might imagine that, if they
had been around, dogs would appear in the spectacular menagerie on
the walls of the famous Lascaux caverns, also in France, which are
about 17,500 years old. The images represent a warming world, and the
flowering of a vibrant new civilization. But there are no dog pictures in
Lascaux, nor in Altamira, a cave with similar wall art in northern Spain.
These encyclopedic depictions of large fauna show only a few images of
wolves. But the caves feature no images of humans, either—leading
some historians to speculate that humans and dogs were considered
somehow separate from other, wilder animals.

The first dog that's indisputably a dog, according to canine
archaeologist Darcy Morey, a researcher at Radford University in
Virginia, entered the archaeological record about fourteen thousand
years ago (though fragments that may be somewhat earlier, on the order
of fifteen thousand years ago, have been found in Russia and Switzer-

land). In the 1920s, in what is now the suburb of Bonn-Oberkassel, on the right bank the Rhine, quarry workers uncovered a grave containing the skeletons of a woman of twenty-five, a man of fifty, and a dog. This May-December couple—and their pet—are, according to standard classifications, the Magdalenians of legend, relatives of the people who created the caves at Lascaux. In archaeological terms, this makes the first dog a late Magdalenian artifact—contemplated and even shaped by the same splendid imaginations. These Magdalenians were hunters of the steppes, although at the time of the burial, horses might have been a more important part of their diet. The ice age was over, and the creators of Lascaux had multiplied and spread out over the land where the glaciers had been. Europe at that time was a subarctic expanse, with sparse stands of trees around the rivers and vast herds of game, reindeer, horse, and auroch—many more species than exist in similarly harsh environments today. There were bear, hare, and foxes, the bones of which appear in large numbers in the archaeological record and which, given their scrawny physiques, must have been hunted for their fur.

The Magdalenians had this world to themselves: Neanderthals had disappeared by 28,500 years ago. Neanderthal life was difficult. Without the intellectual wherewithal to stitch fur into garments, the Neanderthals had a hard time of it. And without the flashes of insight that allowed early humans to manipulate their environment, Neanderthals had to work tirelessly just to survive. It was a race of linebackers, women and children too, with massively muscled arms and torsos. Their skeletons show signs of extreme wear—stress fractures and healed injuries that seem to indicate that they hunted in close quarters with their prey, and that their lives were ones of constant toil. The condition of their remains also suggests that they cared for elders long past the point where they could make a contribution to their community's livelihood. And apparently they had no dogs.

There is something poignant in the Neanderthal story. They came first and worked so hard, yet they were supplanted by a race to which things came easily, almost. Modern humans substituted cleverness for physical power. The Neanderthals made tools and fires and buried their dead, but they didn't make art, and they didn't seem to have the predictive capacities that would later revolutionize hunting.

In Europe, the Magdalenian period was a golden age. Game was abundant, and the arsenal of weapons and strategies for killing it—the battue, the drive line, the surround—was ever growing. As the glaciers retreated, the nomadic Magdalenians moved north from their redoubts in modern-day France and Spain into present-day Germany, Denmark, and England, following the reindeer herd. It was the era of industrial hunting. Humans had developed the gift of predicting where the animals would appear each season and how they would behave. They used valleys and rivers to funnel and channel their prey, apparently driving them off cliffs in large numbers. The Magdalenians were ingenious hunters, with a sophisticated array of battlefield tactics and tools. They had atlatls, some of ivory with beautifully carved handles, possibly bows, traps, and an array of stone and bone tools. They may have also hunted with nets. They stored their kills against the lean seasons to come by drying the meat and saving the fat.

The part played by dogs in this prehistoric abbatoir is still murky. But in many respects, the environment seems ideal for a dog—and dogs are highly effective hunting companions in modern hunter-gatherer cultures. Excellent as the Magdalenians' weapons were, they were as likely to wound as to kill—giving dogs an opportunity to be useful. Dogs' wolfish, violent hunting methods—surrounding the prey, some dogs grabbing noses while others attacked haunches—would certainly have helped take down the large animals that the Magdalenians depended upon. In the 1980s British archaeologist Juliet Clutton-Brock hypothesized that dogs catalyzed an advance in hunting technique: Magdalenians used arrows that could wound but not kill, while dogs tracked down the wounded. Clutton-Brock gathered much of her evidence at Star Carr, a third of the way up England's east coast, another frontier that the Magdalenians reached in the millennia after the ice receded; it's dated at about eleven thousand years ago. At Star Carr, digs have uncovered dog bones and microlith arrowheads aplenty. The dog didn't have to be particularly obedient to assist in these hunting efforts, although obedience would have helped. Analogs of hunter-gatherers using dogs this way are plentiful.

It's not a coincidence, given the close relationship between dogs and humans, and the dog's gift for exploring places their masters wouldn't think of going—that several of these ancient sites were sniffed out by dogs. Lascaux was discovered when a dog named Robot went walking in the woods with four teenagers. Robot chased a rabbit into a hole that opened out into a cavern full of mysterious and magnificent cave art. Altamira, another great Magdalenian temple, was discovered in 1868 by a hunter whose dog had gotten trapped in a pile of rocks. A few years later another local Spanish man, an amateur archaeologist, returned to that cave with his daughter and noticed the drawings. "Look, Daddy," the little girl said, pointing at the elegant forms on the wall. "Oxen."

Another place to look for the origin of the dog is the human brain. After about fifty thousand years ago, something seems to have happened in early humans that underlay our amazing success at hunting and art making, as well as, eventually, all our cultural practices; that's when we became humans. And besides making art and learning to kill with abandon, early humans also prepared us to domesticate the dog. The British anthropologist Steven Mithen has posited that early humans' various cognitive modules—their natural history intelligence, their technical intelligence, and their social intelligence, which had previously operated more or less independently—were linked by a new, recombinant faculty. Early humanlike creatures, our predecessors and the Neanderthals, could kill large animals but not in great numbers. Their limited tools seemed to leave fish and birds largely out of reach. These problems were solved for modern humans, Mithen argues, by a breakdown of barriers between the various cognitive spheres in the brain.

General intelligence, or "G," as scientists call it, is one way to explain this phenomenon: a command module wiring together the cognitive faculties—one ring to control them all. But early humanity also saw the birth of imagination: *If I were a reindeer, where would I go when autumn was coming?* Think of the forearm-size cave lion with the body of a human, carved from ivory by an Upper Paleolithic genius thirty thousand years ago in what is now the German province of Swabia—a person could be an animal, and an animal could be a person. It was the birth of anthropomorphism and probably the original source of my thinking about Stella, sometimes a delightful humanlike daughter to be cooed over, but in another view not so different from a snarling wolf, a half-wild creature—in my mind, she can inhabit both of these personas.

This ambiguity seems to be built in. Whatever the truth of an animal's intelligence, humans seem to be programmed to think there's an "I" in there, something like ourselves, with thoughts and intentions and desires. Anthropomorphism, however imperfect and fanciful from a scientific perspective, happens to be a predictive tool of uncanny accuracy—the kind of mind reading it enabled underlies early humans' ability to kill on a massive scale. Animals were no longer just moving meat, to be observed and pursued in a more or less instinctive fashion, see-stalk-chase-kill. If you knew what an animal wanted to do, you could figure out what you had to do to kill it.

But of course there was another side to this coin. I came to think of anthropomorphism as a kind of original sin: you will have what you want to eat, you will be master of your world, but sometimes your conscience will trouble you, and you will worry about the spirits of the animals that you kill. When I think of the debate these past decades over the animals in factory farms, and over the treatment of dogs in shelters, I'm reminded that these moral complexities—some would say hypocrisies—are ancient and somehow wired in. At one moment, we can think of a dog, or a pig or a horse, as a fellow creature—and the next moment, we can think of it as meat, something that can be thoughtlessly disposed of.

The emergence of anthropomorphism also created a space in our minds—and hearts—for the dog. The remarkable evidence from the earliest dog remains is that, whenever (and wherever) the dog originated, they entered the archaeological record with people. *With* people, not beside people. Some of these early dogs must have been pets, or something like it. In a Natufian grave near Ain Mallaha, in northern Israel, archaeologists found an elderly woman's skeleton holding that of a puppy near her forehead—another moving image of dog love, although one wonders how a four- or five-month-old puppy met its end. The remains are dated to about twelve thousand years ago.

No one knows much about the mythologies of the Magdalenians, and we are not likely to find out. But the dog's presence in early graves, like the one at Bonn-Oberkassel, suggests that dogs had a special status. The dog may have begun as a lurking scavenger, but it was swiftly reimagined as an unusual member of the human community. I kept coming back to something the scientist Ray Coppinger told me: *Dogs are leisure goods.* And one thing hunter-gatherers had—perhaps surprisingly, given our stereotype of their harsh lives—is leisure. They got their protein in massive deliveries, then tried to make it last, and probably worked many fewer hours than their farming successors another few thousand years down the road. Their hunting gifts, providing them with sustenance even when animals were elsewhere, gave them time to think. One of the things they thought about was their dogs. The earliest dog niche was almost certainly the refuse left by seminomadic hunter-gatherers like the couple buried in Bonn-Oberkassel. But evidence suggests another niche—one in the human circle, friend, wordless empath, surrogate child. In other words, the one that continues today. The dog could and does survive without deliberate human care, but for most of human history, it has benefited from the care that it inspires.

Burials provide the most convincing evidence for this claim. Dog burial, both with and without humans, was common among many hunter-gatherer cultures besides the Magdalenian. Sometimes, as in the graves of elderly dogs that couldn't have done much useful work, this seems to be a simple ritual of respect owed to a family member. Darcy Morey writes of a seven-thousand-year-old grave in eastern Tennessee that contains the remains of an especially elderly dog, with arthritis and an unhealed infection from broken ribs, among other ailments. Someone must have cared for this dog, or it wouldn't have survived, and its ritual interment suggests its importance in someone's life. (Wolves too were sometimes buried, and later on, horses.) Many of the dogs buried with humans suggest a spiritual purpose, the dog as a special kind of grave good, to help guide the passage to the next world.

Marion Schwartz, in her excellent *History of Dogs in the Early Americas,* collected many American Indian stories involving dogs. The dog often appears as an intermediary between the world of nature and human communities—a kind of half breed, at home in both. The Cree of northern Canada believed that the dog and the wolf had a contest to decide which would get to live with humans. The dog won—and the howling of wolves outside their camps was an expression of the jealousy that dogs had found such an easy life. In a creation myth of the Penobscot Indians of northern Maine, a heroic ancestral figure known as Deceiving Man—also known as "Master of Beasts and Men Who Was Born in the Sunrise Land"—prepared for the arrival of humans by arranging a council with the animals. Deceiving Man asked them how they would treat the new creatures in their midst. He gave them a chance to make common cause with humans, but they all declined, some with hostility—the squirrel claimed he would bite their heads off. The major complaint was that the humans would make weak allies. Only the dog offered to join the human world and share their meager ration.

The other animals were banished, their power of speech removed, and cursed to fear both humans and dogs. In some stories, like the creation myths of the Shawnee, the great tribe of the eastern heartland, and a tribe in northern California, the creator is accompanied by a dog as a kind of counselor and companion. Schwartz also recounts several stories that seem to explain why the dog should be treated with respect. "It is true that whenever anyone loves a dog he derives great power from it," said an Iroquois storyteller. "Dogs know all we say, yet they are not at liberty to speak. If you do not love a dog he has the power to injure you with his magic."

The dog could also be eaten. The oldest dog remains in North America, found in the Southwest and dated at about ten thousand years old, were found in fossilized human excrement—proof that that dog was a meal, as it has been in many cultures. Lewis and Clark subsisted on dogs during their tough winters in the west—though their own excellent Newfoundland, Seaman, was spared. This amazing, confusing versatility—to be a human companion at one moment and meat at another, a thing rather than a creature with a soul—still complicates our relations with animals today.

Stella's prehistoric past isn't really past—it isn't even gone. Sweet, urban creature though she is, she's also an atavism, built more for the Magdalenian world than for the one she lives in. She's undeniably wolflike, which is one of the great satisfactions of our relationship. On a cross-country ski, she bounds ahead. When I catch up, I see that she's following a fox trail in the snow, something I never would have noticed. She pursues it until she gets tired of breaking through the snow's crust, then bounds ahead to take the lead again. Outdoors, she composes the landscape for me, showing me what to look for. Having her with me is like having another faculty—and I imagine that prehistoric people had a similar sense.

But Stella's nature also causes problems for both of us. She enjoys her concrete world of fire hydrants and chicken bones and likes to greet her public with a whole-body wag, as if every passerby were a long-lost relative. But she gets only enough time in the country to want more, and sometimes, despite the walks and runs and trips to the dog run, I feel that she's just passing time till she gets back there. Guilt, along with plastic bags of dog poop, is pretty much a constant in an urban canine-human relationship. Is this any kind of life for a dog? It is a vicarious, low-level existential crisis—*What does she need, what is she?*—that her imploring eyes seem designed to produce.

The forced intimacies of our urban world must have something to do with the dog's burgeoning personhood. When the dog was in the yard, it was easier to give it any old thing, treat the dog any old way. The dog could find a dead animal, or bury a bone, or chase a squirrel, do its dog things. In the apartment, Stella will dig fiercely at the carpet, making no progress, though at some point we will have to get a new carpet.

Outdoors, it is different. Stella is my avatar in the natural world, blasting through the underbrush, going places I wouldn't go. Off the leash, she leaves kitsch in her wake. Begging for treats under the table, she is ridiculous, if sweet. But finding the high ground to survey the landscape, paw cocked, or blasting through deep snow in a way people (or too many dogs, for that matter) can't manage, she is profound. Over time she has learned to come when called, but outdoors our relationship is more a partnership than a dependency. I couldn't patronize her—she'd run circles around me. Off the leash, she is living.

Stella is built for a different world and reminds me that I am too. The impulses one has in the city—*Pizza or Chinese? What does the weather report say? Umbrella?*—are both overpowering and mundane, the din of modern life that drowns everything else out. But other sensations underlie all the chatter. Worlds like food or sex are dwarfed by the sensations beneath them. And then there are the social emotions, fear and anger and attachments of various kinds that one inevitably explores and manages—or fails to, at one's peril—in the urban world. But other inclinations may be subtler, more difficult to apprehend beneath the scrim of language.

People too were built for the Magdalenian world, or worlds like it—that was the era of our last significant evolution, and the birth of our culture, in which wolves and dogs seem to have played a large part. Our ideas about animals are an important legacy of our life in that environment. And it seems at least possible that we have similar prever-bal understandings, a core of animal knowledge. We developed not only our fantastic categorizing and reasoning faculties but a built-in understanding of geography: how to evaluate a landscape, what course feels right. The low-level ecstasy involved in discovering new terrain, or looking at the play of landscape and trees and water, are natural in-toxications, relics of a previous way of life.

There's nothing I want to kill up in the snow, except at times the snowmobilers. But if I were hungry, that might change. Who knows where such thoughts might take me? *Where Stella is going,* is one answer. She's a connection to a past where nature was a much more important part of human life.

*Ten*

# Mixing the Lab

The site of another of Stella's beginnings, only a few centuries back, is a few hundred miles north of New York. On a flight to Europe, on the seat-back screen with the little pictogram of the plane making its way across the Atlantic, the last outpost marked on the North American map is a place called St. John's Harbor, Newfoundland. St. John's is the largest of countless little ports along Newfoundland's rocky, forbidding coast, and it is where all Labrador retrievers are said to have originated—so it's one of Stella's ancestral homelands. She's a mutt, but she's indubitably part Labrador, jet-black—though in some seasons a reddish-brown undercoat peeks out on her ruff and haunches, a glorious, penumbral imperfection. She's sweet-tempered and friendly to the point of obsequiousness, and focused on people, which is another Labrador hallmark.

Stella is fantastic—she's *my* dog, as I tell her with nauseating frequency—but she's also as common as they come. Labradors are the most popular dog—if you go by Kennel Club registrations—in the world. This is curious, considering the Lab's inherent homeliness. As much as I like to praise Stella for her beauty, the Labrador's calling

card has always been, along with a can-do spirit, a certain plainness.
They've never been particularly successful as show dogs—a Lab has
never won best in show at Westminster. For one thing, they have nothing that needs grooming, really—it would be a bit like taking a comb
and blow drier to a seal. But looks aren't everything. The Labrador
temperament and unassuming intelligence have made it the most popular service and working dog, for a wide array of tasks. They're not as
bright as collies, but the border collie can be like the know-it-all kid in
class with his hand up; the Lab, to crudely generalize, can wait till
called upon, which is a useful quality.

The legend of Stella's nautical ancestry, what little I'd heard about
it, appealed to me. Labs were used in the eighteenth-century fishing
trade, when the shoals off Newfoundland were teeming with codfish,
and they adapted to tough lives, their virtue born of hardship. Stella is
a great swimmer, though not as determined as Putzi, her forebear, who
once paddled after our little outboard in the Charles River for a mile
or more. I imagined that her ancestors were plucked from Newfoundland, and their excellence was passed from generation to generation,
more or less unchanged, until Stella arrived in my apartment.

But that's not quite the way it happened. Stella's story is as much
about creation as discovery. Her reality on my rug owes much to the
fantasy of the past. What happened to dogs in the nineteenth century,
in a sense, was a melting pot in reverse: a loosely organized population
was, in a matter of a few decades, thoroughly reimagined to correspond to this fantasy. Stella was, in some sense, created in the self-
image of certain nineteenth-century Englishmen—her virtues reflect
their virtues. Dogs in the Victorian age were not yet honorary humans,
but they were stand-ins for humans, replicating their masters' inner
excellence and class pride and their vision of a well-ordered society.
Stella's ancestors from Newfoundland played a large part in this drama,
and her story reveals the larger story of the development of breeds in
general. Mapping Stella's circuitous course helped me understand

nineteenth-century dog history—and what is happening now to upend the world that had been created.

For at least three centuries, dogs from Newfoundland were the most celebrated in the British Empire. Originally, all those dogs were called Newfoundlands. Nothing like the Newfoundland or the Lab as we now know them existed in any pure form—crisp designations among breeds were still a century away. But by the end of the eighteenth century, Britain was on its way to producing a homegrown kennel of great dogs, genius farm collies, and fierce bulldogs to become a national symbol, and pointers, and setters, as well as mincing little lapdogs bred by kings.

But as bright as collies may have been, they were familiar, and the work of a shepherd was the opposite of glamorous. By contrast, the exploits of dogs on a far, lonely coast—apocryphal or not—were something to brag about. Something in Newfoundland dogs' nautical expertise and tail-wagging good-naturedness in the face of hardship reminded the British of themselves—and still does today. The empire was a civilizing force—it could take a stew of mongrels and turned them into the best dogs in the world.

Its inhabitants sometimes call Newfoundland "The Rock." For most of its history, it had no roads in the interior. But for a few hundred years, when salt cod was a European staple, it was one of the most important ports in the world. Its dogs were a secondary export—which is where another of Stella's mythologies begins. From the mid-sixteenth century, fishermen from Devon, in the south of England, traveled to St. John's Harbor, on a rocky peninsula called Avalon, every summer to camp and fish for cod in small boats. The Europeans tended to fish for larger cod farther out on the Grand Banks and heavily salt their catch aboard ship, but the English preferred smaller cod that could be preserved with less salt by drying them on the rocky shore. "The English are commonly lordes of the harbors in which they fish, and do use all helpe of strangers in fishing as needes require, according to the custom of the country," wrote Anthony Parkhurst, a Bristol captain who arrived on a reconnaissance mission in 1578. Parkhurst brought along a mastiff and claimed that the cod were so plentiful, his dog could catch them from the beach.

By the mid-eighteenth century, the dogs of Newfoundland had become legend, their heroism on the lips of every Londoner. But their mystique in England was at odds with their existence on the island. In 1766 Joseph Banks, one of the great naturalists of his time (a few years later he would be aboard Captain Cook's first voyage to the South Seas) traveled to Newfoundland aboard a frigate patrolling the coast to make sure the French were observing the fishing treaties. He made a careful collection of Newfoundland's flora and fauna and took the time to set down his thoughts about the island's most legendary animal. "Almost Every Body has heard of the Newfondland Dogs I myself was desired to Procure some of them & when I set out for the Countrey firmley beleivd that I should meet a sort of Dogs different from any I had Seen whose Peculiar Excellence was taking the water Freely I was therefore more surprizd when told that there was here no distinct Breed those I met with were mostly Curs with a Cross of the Mastiff in them Some took the water well others not at all." He heard a report, he wrote, of a man in a distant town who had a distinct breed of what he called the original Newfoundland dogs, but Banks never saw them.

After Banks, most Newfoundland observers seemed to see the island's dogs through the lens of the legend. Dogs from Newfoundland were a long-lived fad, a designer label that celebrated a passel of British virtues: hardiness, good nature, unpretentious intelligence. John Mac-Gregor's 1825 book on the maritime provinces of British America describes the Newfoundland countryside as remarkably similar to that of the Western Scottish highlands and includes a love letter to the local dogs. "These dogs are remarkably docile and obedient to their masters," he wrote. "They are very serviceable in all the fishing plantations and are yoked in pairs and used to haul the wood home. They are gentle, faithful, and good natured, and ever a friend of man, at whose command they will leap into the water from the highest precipice and in the coldest weather. They are remarkably voracious, but can endure (like the aborigines of the country) hunger for a great length of time."

But the truth is that the Newfoundland was a name as much as an actual breed. Any large, excellent, athletic dog was liable to be called a Newfoundland—they were the prize mixed breeds of their day. Newfoundlands tended to be wolflike, heavily muscled but still lithe. They were the explorers' dogs of choice. They didn't look like the supersize, lumbering creatures that they've become in recent years. Some of them, at least, if not inveterate child rescuers, must have been superb athletes.

The Newfoundland had been a superstar for a century by the time the Labrador was separated out as a distinct breed. But at first the breed standard was highly unclear. In 1823 Sir Edwin Landseer painted the first Lab described as such, *Cora, a Labrador Bitch,* a dog that looks intermediate between a black and white border collie and a Lab, with floppy ears and a medium-length, slightly curly coat. That image, like many of Landseer's paintings, was reproduced in lithographs and engravings many times over the next fifty years. But it doesn't seem to have influenced the idea of the breed in the way that his images of Newfoundlands did. Around this time, a certain strain of Newfoundland—smallish, black-coated—began to be plucked out and refined, eventually becoming the dog we know as the Labrador today.

The precise source of this strain, with its oily black coat and distinctive tail, is a harder question. Richard Wolters, whose impressive classic history *The Labrador Retriever* is a coffee-table-size labor of unchecked dog admiration, suggests that the key source was the St. Hubert's dog. A black, pointerlike creature, originally French, the St. Hubert's had crossed the English Channel and was used as a hunting dog in the fields near Devon for enough centuries to breed any

French airs out of it. But Scottie Westfall, whose blog *Retrieverman* is the most authoritative current source concerning dog origins, including the Labrador's, dismisses the St. Hubert's dog as not a real retriever (more like a bloodhound) and not a water dog, either.

The most intriguing theories of the Lab's origins involve dogs from Portugal. Functionally and temperamentally, the Portuguese water dog is an excellent candidate as a Lab ancestor (now with a presidential imprimatur), and they actually did useful work in the fisheries of that country. The sixteenth-century Portuguese were as nautically inclined as the British and maintained a constant presence on the cod banks off Newfoundland—but they tended to stay on their ships. Based on visual evidence and their Portuguese name, the foundation dog may actually be the Cão de Castro Laboreiro—this is Retrieverman's preferred theory. The Cão de Castro Laboreiro is a tough, independent livestock-guarding dog from the north of Portugal. Its dark, often subtly brindled coat of stiff fur and its head shape make it the spitting image of the Labrador today, although its temperament is nothing like a Lab's. Robert Hutchinson, a scholar at the American Museum of Natural History, speculates on the Lab's origins in his book *For the Love of Labrador Retrievers* in a way that makes sense of some unusual details. Just as English sailors brought their mastiffs along on sea voyages as fearsome guard dogs, Portuguese sailors on the fishing fleet may have brought the Cão. Sailors who deserted ship could have taken up residence in the little villages that dot Newfoundland's coast, where they gradually transformed the Cão from a standoffish highland dog into a friendly water dog. That the villages were inaccessible except by boat might have kept the breed reasonably pure. The story explains the name (Labradors never had anything to do with the province of Labrador, and *laboreiro*—"worker," in Portuguese—makes perfect sense, though it seems to derive from the name of a Portuguese town), the appearance, and the fact that, in all the stories, the true dogs seemed to be lurking a couple of villages over, just out of reach.

In 1807 a brig loaded with cod foundered in a gale off Maryland.

A man named George Law helped rescue the crew, who were "in a state of intoxication," he wrote in a later account, as well as a pair of Newfoundland dogs that the brig's owner had requested the captain bring back. "The dog was of a dingy red color," Law wrote. "The slut was black." Their coats were short and thick, like those of the Labs we know today. Law purchased the dogs for a guinea apiece, and they became the foundation of the Chesapeake Bay retriever, the premier American duck dog until the Labrador was reimported from England in the early twentieth century. Law's account is the clearest, most believable description of the kind of dogs that were being exported out of St. John's for the use of sportsmen. Along with other accounts, it suggests that blackness was an occasional quality of just some of the island's dogs. Other descriptions mention black, often with white markings, but also brown and even brindle, and several different sorts of coats.

The most influential account of the dog was in Peter Hawker's *Instructions to Young Sportsmen,* first published in 1814, an early milestone in the development of the British obsession with field sports. Hawker, a well-born army officer, pursued waterfowl on his furloughs with a single-minded passion that verged on madness. His diary is an amazing document of avian carnage, detailing just about every bird he shot or missed. Wounded with a musket ball in the Duke of Wellington's campaign in Spain in 1809—the ball went clean through his thigh, shattering the bone—Hawker was in intermittent pain throughout the rest of his life, but he seldom passed up an opportunity to blast birds when his army duties were finished for the day—a shining exemplar of British pluck. "Breakfasted by candlelight," he wrote in a typical entry. "Walked hard all day in a deluge of rain. Bagged three cock-pheasants; gloriously outmaneuvered all the shooters, came home very satisfied and dined off one of the birds." Firing with a flintlock, he was uncannily accurate, the greatest shot of his generation and apparently one of the greatest in history.

A crucial fact in the creation of the Labrador as a separate breed is that, by Hawker's time, the Newfoundland had drifted. Everyone wanted a dog as furry and lovable as the ones Landseer painted, with the result that somehow their heroic athleticism got left out of the equation. Hawker described the Newfoundland dog of his era with contempt: "Every canine brute that is nearly as big as a jackass and as hairy as a bear is denominated a fine Newfoundland dog," he wrote. The solution was to go back to the original source, and to a particular strain of Newfoundland dogs. "By far the best for every kind of shooting, is more often black than any other color, and scarcely bigger than a pointer," he wrote. "He is made rather long in the head and nose, fairly deep in the chest, very fine in the legs, has short or smooth hair; does not carry his tail so curled as much as the other; and is extremely quick and active in running, swimming and fighting."

The Labs we know today diverge from Hawker's description in that they are shorter in head and nose, and are deep in chest, and belly too. But except for the uncurled tail, Hawker's would be a fine description of Stella, who's chestier than most Labs. In his diary, Hawker wrote with sadness of a favorite three-year-old dog he had to shoot for distemper. "The dog was of the real St. John's breed, with a long head, very fine action, and something of the otter skin, and not the curly haired, heavy brute that so often and so commonly disgraces the name of the Newfoundland dog." After praising the dog's sagacity, attachment, courage, and excellence in the field, he invoked Shakespeare for an epitaph: "Take him for all in all; we shall not see his like again."

Thanks to Hawker, we do see his like today—on the end of every third leash in Manhattan. Hawker may have been Stella's most important inventor. He did not invent the breed (and in modern Labs, the heads have been tending to get shorter), but his description was a template that other sportsmen could follow and follow they did.

In the first half of the nineteenth century, the notion of breed purity had not yet taken hold. Cross-breeding to develop the best possible dog—keeping breeding lines separate and refining them over generations—was a gentleman's art, the province of aristocrats. The era's most popular gundog was the flat-coated retriever, also based on dogs from Newfoundland and crossed with setters that looked a lot like Landseer's Cora. John Henry Walsh (pseudonym: Stonehenge), the editor of *The Field* in the mid-nineteenth century, and with Landseer, the most important inventor of the English dog, was of the opinion that the calm at the crucial moment required by setters and pointers was disrupted by retriever training. "My own experience is that, with a setter or pointer of high courage, it is almost impossible to keep him steady at 'down charge' if he is allowed to retrieve." Contradicting Hawker, Stonehenge maintained that the setter's nose was superior to that of the St. John's dog, so a cross was mandated. The only clear excellence of the pure St. John's dog, whether curly-haired or short-haired, was in its gifts as a water dog—the webbed feet, and coat that sheds water like oil.

Stonehenge's *Dogs of the British Islands* is a tablet on which are inscribed the breed commandments that are still largely followed in the dog world today. Like Darwin, Walsh was a gentleman scientist: trained as a surgeon, he was captured by his sporting passions and brought his scientific bent along with him. Unlike Hawker, who wrote for gentlemen, Walsh was a popularizer, bringing upper-class passions to the aspirational middle. A protoyuppie and avatar of the gear-obsessed warriors of leisure that characterize the sporting world today, he introduced the idea of field-testing guns for his magazine, a practice that brought important technical refinements; he also brewed beer, wrote books about archery and "manly exercise," helped popularize croquet, was an expert horseman, and founded the All England Lawn Tennis Club. But it was with dogs that his influence has been most lasting.

Like many a Victorian, Walsh had the highest order of intentions. He aimed to civilize, to bring order to the profusion of dog varieties that were then in the process of being invented, and to provide standards for the increasingly fashionable dog shows. Informal dog competitions had long been held in pubs and other low-class venues, but the criteria for judging were based more on attractiveness or owner pedigree rather than on any platonic dog ideal. Walsh intended to make sure that the shows produced winners based on standards other than pure whim.

The first recorded dog show was organized by a gun manufacturer and held in Newcastle in 1859, the same year *On the Origin of Species* was published, which isn't exactly a coincidence. It featured only two breeds of dogs, pointers and setters. By the time *Dogs of the British Islands* was published in 1867, dog shows were a national craze. Walsh's standards were far from the rigid and arbitrary decrees of an autocrat—a great deal of observation, discussion, and deep connoisseurship went into their promulgation. "The neck should be long and clean," he wrote of the foxhound. "The least looseness or approach to dewlap or cravat is fatal to appearance." Because order requires numbers, Stonehenge inaugurated a point system for judging the breeds: head 5, neck 5, ears and eyes 5, legs and feet 10, and so forth, adding up to a grand total of 100. Walsh's system was used at the first Westminster dog show, and it's still operant in the dog shows of today.

In his magazine *The Field*, Stonehenge hosted a long-running debate over the dog show dictates as they evolved. One correspondent wrote that a spaniel had won a prize even though it held its "stern up" in an unspaniel-like manner; when the correspondent objected, the dog's owner told him that this was a good point: when hunting in "high turnips, if you could not see the dog, you could see its tail." Everywhere was the Victorian spirit of improvement, of confidence in one's technical prowess. After scrutinizing old portraits of the English setter, Walsh insisted that "we possess dogs far superior to the dogs of our forefathers," though he allowed that this perception was likely due to the failings of the artists rather than the dogs. And often the dog breeders of the era were pursuing dogs of the imagination. "The perfect Setter," wrote one correspondent, "I am sorry to say I have never yet seen."

Stonehenge does not seem to have entertained the notion that the art of breed crossing would ever disappear. It was a tool for improvement and an essential weapon in the sportsman's arsenal. The point was to breed great dogs by any means necessary. "In-and-in breeding"—breeding between close family members—had well-known dangers, and correspondents in *The Field* acknowledged them.

They also actively debated the importance of pedigree. A lively dispute erupted in 1865 over a celebrated Gordon setter named Kent, fine of nose, courageous of spirit, and attractive too, one of the great sporting dogs of his age. But he lacked a pedigree. A writer using the name Experientia thought that this should disqualify Kent for use at stud. "Pedigree is everything," Experientia wrote, noting that, while Kent had bred with some sixty bitches, his offspring had only one second-place ribbon to show for it. Unless a dog had a long, well-known history of excellence—the same kind that aristocrats possessed—who knew what mongrel might emerge? Kent's defenders rushed to defend Kent with glowing encomiums to the dog's prowess and suggested that Experientia was probably a "disappointed exhibitor" whose own pug-nosed setters had failed to please the judges. But the truth was that—in what was no longer a gentleman's hobby but a growing industry—everyone wanted consistency. Dogs that could reliably produce excellent progeny quickly became spectacularly expensive. And one way of ensuring consistency was to make dog breeding a science.

In the eighteenth century, livestock breeding had become a kind of science, largely because of the efforts of a farmer named Robert Bakewell. His farm, a hundred miles north of London, supplied meat to the city, and Bakewell aimed to perfect his Leicester sheep, which he supposedly called "machines for turning herbage . . . into money." He had no interest in the wool, which confounded his fellow farmers, whose business model was to sell both the wool and the meat. He did controlled experiments to produce meatier sheep, measuring the growth of a number of rams given the same amount of feed, then bred from the best ones. His house was full of sheep skeletons and limbs pickled in brine. Some of his animals were said to be as wide as they were long. At one point, he bred sheep with legs so short they couldn't nurse, and he had to reverse course. Bakewell maintained parallel lines of animals and outcrossed for various purposes, but inbreeding was an important tool—a way of fixing an animal's characteristics, of ensuring the consistency he was looking for.

In building better sheep, Bakewell upended the pastoral tradition, and in many ways it never recovered. His work in selective breeding revolutionized the livestock industry and also became an important intellectual touchstone for Darwin, showing how quickly individual variations could be magnified into large differences. His freakishly meaty sheep inspired even more unusual animals, those tractor-trailer-size cows and hogs painted by George Stubb in the early nineteenth century. These were not aesthetics that anyone thought should apply to the dog. But the desire for consistency led to use of the same techniques.

When the ancient upper-class notion of pedigree melded with the selective breeding of animals, the idea of the purebred was born. The dog world, slowly but surely, created an imitation aristocracy. Dogs with a pedigree, wrote one critic of the new system, "are valued more highly than another without any pedigree at all, although the latter might be in superior shape, and might perform equally well in the field. The importance of pedigree is becoming more mournfully recognized every year."

Purebred dogs were not quite honorary humans, but they were getting close. Dog refinement was a scale model of a good society, a utopian experiment. Anxieties about class, race, and social mobility were intensifying with the acceleration of empire, bringing the English into contact with people they would rather not believe they were related to. The dog world reflected the growing prejudices. Mongrels were the uncivilized, the great unwashed, the accidents that should be stamped out. A gentleman wanted a dog that had been civilized, that reflected his station. The "dog fancy," as the dog-loving world had come to call itself, systematized the dog world, creating a rigid caste system.

The kennel registry was intended to protect the purchaser against "the danger of buying mongrels." Thus it removed outcrossing, the traditional livestock breeder's method of ensuring animals' health, in favor of inbreeding, with eventually disastrous results.

The Kennel Club's first show was held at the Crystal Palace in Sydenham in 1873, under the close consultation of Stonehenge. Frank C. S. Pearce, one of Stonehenge's colleagues at *The Field*, was enlisted to prepare its first studbook. It was a massive production, running to more than six hundred pages, and its ambition matched its heft. The book "is intended," wrote Pearce, "to fill up a blank in the history of the canine world."

Pearce asked thirty-five hundred people for pedigrees and ultimately registered four thousand dogs. The champion dogs were allowed to pass on their genes, narrowing the gene pool still further. Though the effect took a few decades, the dogs that Pearce allowed into the registry ultimately had a much better chance of reproducing than those that didn't; they undoubtedly compose a huge percentage of the ancestry of the dogs of today in the United States and Britain. Before Pearce, pedigree wasn't everything; at least it was a matter of debate. But after the Kennel Club's registry was established, pedigree became the central fact of a dog's life, a seal of approval. The old art of breeding—a little of this, a little of that, refinements that were more art than science—was now socially unacceptable.

In the United States, the first Westminster Kennel Club Dog Show was held at Madison Square Garden in 1877, four years after the British show; it borrowed Stonehenge's judging principles. Twelve hundred dogs were entered. Owners were encouraged to supply pedigrees but weren't yet required to do so. A few celebrity dogs were on hand: a pair of General Custer's staghounds, orphaned after his death at Little Big Horn the previous June, and a two-legged dog, "a veritable biped," wrote one contemporary observer, "and withal possessing almost human intelligence." It was an aspirational festival. Madison Avenue was choked with liveried carriages: "Everybody was fashionably dressed and wore an air of good breeding." Dogs that had produced champions were given stunning valuations, the beginnings of the superstar system that would do so much genetic harm. Newspapermen caricatured the dog fancy—already many observers regarded it, with its addiction to new and unusual canine forms, as a kind of madness.

A debate raged in *The Field*, Stonehenge's magazine, over the dangers of dog shows and their distorting emphasis on form over function. "Dog shows are the greatest humbug in the world and are ruining our breeds of dogs," wrote a hunter and dog breeder who went by the initials W.C., bemoaning the emphasis on looks over function. W.C. went on to provide a great retriever: cross a great foxhound with a docile temperament with a setter, then cross their progeny with a really good St. John's dog. W.C. didn't specify what such a dog would look like; to a sportsman, looks were a secondary consideration.

The invention of the modern dog was over with stunning swiftness. Questions remained to be ironed out, but Stonehenge and others wrote the constitution, and after the 1870s, increasingly powerful institutions controlled the definition of the dog. While just a couple of decades before, the spirit had been to breed ever better dogs, the dog world now became one obsessed with the preservation of old forms, with keeping old traditions alive, however fabricated those traditions might have been.

Amazingly, given its celebrity, the dog show world left the Labrador retriever alone for a few decades. One factor in saving the Labrador from this fate (sorry, Stella) might have been its homeliness. The Lab didn't have the flowing coat and elegant gait of some of its cousins. No one thought to show it—it was a utilitarian creature, a tool for hunters. "As his use in this country is almost entirely confined to retrieving game," Stonehenge wrote, "he cannot be included among the nonsporting dogs." But the other crucial factor was that the Lab was an emblem of the aristocracy: plain as it was, the most passionate

Lab lovers wouldn't have considered bringing it to something so common as a dog show. This fact gave the Lab a subtly different status from other dogs that were invented and refined in the nineteenth century— and exempted it from some of the pressures that would so damage other breeds.

S tella's aristocratic lineage was the unlikeliest thing I discovered in my exploration—it just didn't fit with her Tennessee background, the ubiquity of her breed, or her plainness. But in many ways she is an upper-class product. It turns out that the Labrador retriever was the passion of a few upper-class families—which happened to be among the wealthiest in Britain.

Late in June, in a week as beautiful as it is possible to have in Scotland, I visited the grandest of Stella's ancestral homes, a place where the main line of her relatives—the ones who've inherited everything—still reside. Though I had read extensively about it, I was unprepared for the reality of what I found there. The Queensberry Estate—in the Scottish borderlands near Dumfries—is, at some ninety thousand acres, the largest privately owned piece of land in Great Britain and one of four estates owned by the tenth Duke of Buccleuch. The centerpiece is Drumlanrig Castle, a wedding cake of seventeenth-century pink limestone, framed by elaborate formal gardens and a collection of trees from around the world. The castle is a junk-shop jumble of priceless artifacts—there is always something to look at, or play with, or admire, all executed with the highest possible production values. There's a Rembrandt and a Holbein, a superb series of oils of the household staff in the eighteenth century, plus artifacts from Napoleon, Louis XIV, and the heroic, incompetent Bonnie Prince Charlie, who spent a night here on his famous flight. By the time the Labrador arrived here, the party had been going on for quite a while, and dogs had long played a role in it.

It's preposterous to think that a member of my own household could be descended from such splendor, but it's true. All the Labs in the world are descended from a small group of dogs owned by a few families at the very highest levels of the British aristocracy.

Until the dog fancy became an obsession of Britain's rising class, aristocrats and monks were the only people with the wherewithal to maintain distinct breeds. During the eighteenth century, the Duke of Buccleuch played a substantial role in the creation of the Dandie Dinmont terrier—based partly on a gypsy's dog that got caught in a snare at the duke's borderlands estate at Bowhill. Gainsborough painted the third duke, his hands clasped around one of these terriers in 1770. The duke no doubt cared deeply for these dogs—he has an unmistakable look of love on his face—but the actual creator was the gamekeeper at Bowhill, who apparently refined the dogs by crossing otterhounds with the local Scottish terriers.

The Lab entered the lives of the Dukes of the Buccleuch more or less at the same time that it did Colonel Hawker's, and for the same purpose: the Dukes of Buccleuch were obsessive hunters. The fifth duke, at his estates in Dumfrieshire, at Langholm, and at Bowhill, was a mainstay of the northern set of the British hunting aristocracy. His good friend the Earl of Malmesbury was likewise a mainstay of the southern set, and his ancestral home—Heron Court—happened to be five miles or so from Poole Harbor. The Earl of Malmesbury seems to be the original source of the Buccleuch dogs, although records from this period don't exist. The fifth Duke of Buccleuch began his own kennel of Labs in 1835. In 1839 the duke took his Lab Moss to Naples on his schooner. Also on board was Lord Home, accompanied by his dog, Drake. Other dogs imported by the duke in those early days included Jock and Brandy, the latter named because on his voyage across the Atlantic he had been sent overboard to retrieve a sailor's hat and, after two hours in the cold water, had to be revived with brandy—no doubt an amusing story to be told after dinner.

Nell, one of the duke's dogs photographed in 1866 at what seems a ripe old age, is the subject of the oldest photograph of a Labrador retriever or, as Scottie Westfall of *Retrieverman* points out, possibly the oldest one of a St. John's dog. Nell looks a bit like Stella, who has another breed or two in her genome. Other dogs of the era, with their barrel torsos and white muzzles and wise expressions, look similar. They're homely, not showy, and no one would think to show them for another few decades.

The fact that Labs weren't common—everyone from Hawker on had said that the true dogs were rare in Newfoundland—was undoubtedly part of their appeal. The Newfoundland had been ruined by its popularity. But Labs were seen as authentic colonial artifacts, gilded by a couple of centuries of legend, the excellence of which could not have been appreciated by ordinary dog owners. They were good-natured and obedient. Mostly, with proper training, they knew their place.

Shooting was the great passion of the upper classes of the time, a kind of sacrament, giving meaning to otherwise idle lives; it made sense of their land and gave owning it a purpose. The dog was important to this equation, a necessary adjunct. Scotland had produced numerous excellent breeds of dogs, many of which continue to dominate the dog world today. But the Labrador was special, in that it was— even for a few decades afterward—the exclusive passion of the duke and a few of his friends. They seem to have felt an impulse for preservation, for the careful husbanding of an heirloom, something the aristocracy excelled at.

The original studbook, kept in a safe at the Buccleuch estate offices half a mile down from the castle, is a handsome black volume bound in subtly textured leather, about four inches thick. A woman who worked in the estate office brought it out for me, and I sat in a quiet conference room and traced with a finger the story of Stella's ancestors. It was a biblical thing. There, written in black fountain pen, in a firm, elegant, masculine hand, were the true beginnings of the Labrador. At the top of the pyramid were the legendary progenitors, Ned and Avon. Along with their half-sister Nell, these dogs were gifts from the Earl of Malmesbury. "We always call mine Labrador dogs," wrote the third Earl of Malmesbury to the fifth Duke of Buccleuch in an 1887 letter, "and I've kept the breed as pure as I could from the first I had from Poole, at that time carrying on a brisk trade with Newfoundland. The real breed may be known for having a close coat which turns away water like oil and, above all, a tail like an otter."

The earl's dogs became the stars of the duke's kennels. "When Ned arrived at Langholm Lodge, he proved himself a better category than any of the other dogs there," according to a history of the Buccleuch Labradors commissioned by a later duke in 1931, "and Avon was even better than Ned." Both of them were bred to Nell. Pups were never sold but were given to other nobles, expanding the network. I sat at the table in the quiet room and traced the names and bloodlines. Avon and Trick begat Ned, Nep, and Nero. Ned and Dinah begat Bob, Hector, and Nero. Baron and Bess II begat Captain, Carick, Cora, and Cupid. A little later, at the beginning of the twentieth century, there was a dog named Stella. Poor thing, she lived only a couple of years.

The British aristocracy flirted with the dog fancy, arriving in a bustle of excitement at the shows and blessing the proceedings. But Labs themselves didn't enter them in any numbers for a while. The Buccleuch history of the Lab averrs that they were "never shown," with an almost audible sniff. Aristocrats wouldn't participate in such a spectacle was the implication. Labradors were adjuncts to the ducal lifestyle; that was enough distinction.

The Duke of Buccleuch's dogs were distributed to a network of Labrador fanciers that seems to have been growing quickly—new names appeared, along with the Earl of Home and Lord Wimborne, not all of them noble. The dogs were finally registered by the Kennel Club and first shown in 1903—but they were still rare enough that one breeder, seeing a Lab-like dog with a thick rough coat on a quay in Norway in 1908, acquired it on the spot to add new blood to the kennel.

When Lord Wimborne's Duchess was mated with Major C. J. Radyclyffe's Neptune, a pair of yellow puppies resulted, and a new substrain, the yellow Lab, was born. Some of the Buccleuch dogs occasionally had chocolate pups. These dogs, accidental breeds—the result of variations in just a couple of genes—were duly enshrined in the dog pantheon and given full breed privileges.

The minuscule community of Labradors in the early twentieth century would suggest that it might end up as one of the most inbred and damaged breeds. And certainly there was inbreeding. But the Lab didn't win dog shows, so the desire to refine and perfect the breed wasn't as much of an issue. Rather, the Lab was bred for excellence in the field, for hunting and retrieving. There wasn't much pressure, say, to change the shape of its head, as happened with the King Charles spaniel and the English bulldog. Labrador conservators like Lorna Countess Howe, who was instrumental in forming Britain's Labrador Club in 1916, argued against dividing the breed into show dogs and field dogs, an effort that was partly successful. The Lab's identity was always that of a hunting dog—and Lab owners still complain that the dog is given short shrift at AKC shows (failing to realize that this is probably for the best).

I n the decades since Labs were developed, the ducal lifestyle has undergone some changes. Estate life is expensive, and the Dukedom of Buccleuch is essentially a corporation, with farming and sporting and real estate interests. Shooting is not only a pastime—it's a business. "The big estates are managed by the accountants," said a man I met in Thornhill, the little village that grew up to service the castle.

The estate kennel, in continuous operation since the 1890s, has become the kind of luxury that even a duke can't afford. In 2002, when the previous duke died, only one breeding female remained: Millie, "the Duke's bitch," says Roy Green, the sporting manager at the duke's estates. Green came up with a business plan to rebuild the kennel. He brought in David Lisett, one of the best dog trainers in Great Britain, who'd won field trial championships with spaniels in England and Ireland, selected a Lab to mate with Millie, and set about repopulating the estate with dogs.

On a beautiful July afternoon, I drove out on the old Roman road to visit Lisett and his dogs. Like most of the castle's outbuildings, Lisett's house is built of the local stone. The view out his kitchen window extends twenty miles down a valley, the hills mostly treeless, speckled with sheep. He took off his Wellingtons and led me into the living room, telling me about his dogs, Stella's long-lost relatives. Like many canine empaths, Lisett seems happier with dogs than with people. Millie was the last and now the first, a favorite of the family. "Millie would stay in the kennel," he said in his gorgeous sea-lion bark of Scottish accent, "but when the duke and his family were on the Queensberry estate, she'd stay in the house."

Millie was seven when Lisett arrived. (Lisett had been a hunter, which is how he got interested in training Labradors.) The estate hadn't employed a trainer since the 1970s. "It gave me great heart," he said, "because, good or bad, she was the only one that we had." They mated her with a dog Green found, and she managed to have three puppies. One of them, the first Buccleuch dog ever to compete in a field trial, has won four British championships. Now there was a new litter of puppies outside, the fourth generation. "I'll get around to naming them when I get a free minute," Lisett said. A young kennel attendant was watching the puppies play in a pen in a sunny courtyard. Lisett took me through the kennels, past rows of stalls with heated floors, the nursery equipped with cameras so the duke could look at his new puppies on his laptop.

Moss, one of the Buccleuch champion Labs, was out past the kennels, in a fenced-in area with a dozen or so other dogs, including spaniels and Labradors. The younger dogs had their paws up on the fence, looking for a hand to lick. They were used to being doted on, because they were in the midst of their training. Moss hung back but bounded forward when Lisett called her. Now past her prime as a field dog, she was a cheerful, unassuming creature. An alley of 150 yards or so had been mowed in the tall grass on the hillside, next to a fenced area that held rabbits. The dogs had to be taught not to chase them.

Lisett stood in his tweeds and Wellingtons, seeming vaguely military. "Mark," he said, and Moss looked up, ears squared. "She thinks something is about to happen," he said. Then he yelled: "Oooot! Ooot, ooot!" and Moss was down the hill. He brought his whistle to his lips, and Moss, far away, stopped to look back. Lisett pointed left, and Moss, as if by radio control, went into a little copse, nose working in search of nonexistent birds.

After a while she looked back at Lisett, who called her back and then—"Ooot, ooot, oooot"—sent her another hundred yards up above us, over a good-size stone wall, and then back. Her prize was a scratch behind the ears, which she accepted on hind legs, wagging furiously. I felt, watching this remarkable display, some shame about Stella's ineptitude at such activities. But I thought—hoped—that some of the excellence that people like Lisett had bred into prior dogs still had some purchase in Stella's genes, if only someone had the wit to bring it out.

Later I walked past the castle, down some steps next to an elaborate garden, and into the woods. Under a towering willow off the garden was a little graveyard for the dogs of Buccleuch. The willow, like much else on this estate, was impossibly grand, a cathedral in light green and earth tones, the sun filtering through its papery leaves. A dozen or so handsome gray stones poked out of a tangle of dead leaves and branches. Some of the stones were partially encased with moss, making it hard to read the names engraved there. I thought of the small explosions of sadness that their long-ago deaths must have brought. These dogs were loved—by dukes and their servants—and died, and someone cared enough to make these stones for them, not as grand as the marbles in the chapel down the road, but significant nonetheless.

. . .

As the dogs of England flowered, the old Newfoundland way of life changed. At the end of the nineteenth century, with the cod industry in decline, the British government tried to turn Newfoundland into a paradise for sheep. No one talked about the dogs' excellence anymore. In a book of Newfoundland history and description published in 1883, the great dogs of the past had apparently disappeared—although it was probably not the dogs that had changed. "The common dogs are a wretched mongrel race, cowardly, thievish, and addicted to sheep killing," the authors maintained. In 1885 Newfoundland passed a heavy tax on dogs—heavier on the females than on the males, so the bitches were usually destroyed. And in 1895 Parliament passed a law that required any imported dogs—even dogs from Canada—to spend six months in quarantine. The gangplank had been drawn up.

But the pursuit of the true dogs didn't come to an end for another few decades. In the 1970s, Farley Mowat, author of *Never Cry Wolf* and *People of the Deer*, among numerous other Canadian chronicles, attempted to locate the true St. John's dogs. He managed to acquire a magnificent white-chested black dog from Newfoundland, the spitting image of Nell, named Albert. Unfortunately, he couldn't find a female, so he bred him to a female Labrador, producing four puppies. The two females died. One of the males was given to Pierre Trudeau, and one to Soviet premier Alexei Kosygin.

Around the same time, Richard Wolters made a voyage to Grand Bruit, a tiny village on Newfoundland's south coast accessible only by boat, where he'd heard there were a pair of St. John's dogs. And indeed he found two aged males, one thirteen, one fifteen, white-muzzled and wise-looking, belonging to an eighty-five-year-old man whose father and grandfather had both kept water dogs. The dogs liked to sleep, as old dogs do, but they'd still chase a stick. The St. John's dogs of the past were gone from this earth—and yet they weren't gone at all.

. . .

It took a few decades for the Labrador to return to this side of the Atlantic. But in the first half of the twentieth century, as the American wealthy explored their lifestyle options, one of the obvious places to look was to the grand old piles of the British countryside. In the late 1920s the Lab was the most popular shooting dog in Britain. But according to Wolters, at that point only twenty-three Labradors were registered in the United States. In the Jazz Age, Anglophilia was a hallmark of the superrich. The Labrador was a status symbol, the favorite of British kings, and the era's Gatsby mansions, some thought, weren't complete without a kennel of dogs and a Scottish gamekeeper to handle them. Averell Harriman, the son of a railroad tycoon and one of the richest men in America—the closest thing in this country to a duke—imported a Scottish gamekeeper for his upstate New York estate in 1913. His first Lab came in the early 1920s, and he started a full-fledged kennel a few years later. Along with running a Wall Street business and conducting a remarkable career in public service, Harriman was the most influential sportsman of his day. He played a major role in popularizing Thoroughbred horse racing and also conceived and developed Sun Valley in Ketchum, Idaho, the first major ski resort in the American West. While Harriman was away in Washington working for Franklin Roosevelt, his dogs, handled by his Scottish trainer Thomas Briggs, were excelling in the new pastime of field trialing.

The first shoots organized around the Labrador were even grander than those in old England, with huge numbers of driven game. But America had no archipelago of country houses and shooting lodges of the kind that underpinned the culture of British Labs. American Labs were judged against the field talents of American dogs like the Chesapeake Bay retriever, in pursuits such as duck hunting, and in fairly short order they evolved away from the British model. American dogs tended to be bigger, faster, and more athletic, in keeping with the rougher conditions of American hunting. These traits seem to have carried through to today: while Stella is smallish, she's muscled in a way that British dogs, like the ones I saw in Scotland, are not.

*Life* magazine put one of Harriman's field-trial champion Labs on the cover of its December 12, 1938, issue. It was big American-style success, a mass-market coup. But only after World War II did the Labrador—and other dogs—really start to boom. The suburban ideal, with its two cars and two children, required a dog, and the Labrador, with its cheerful, child-friendly temperament, and its echoes of both a working background and the aristocratic life, was the animal in the back of the station wagon. It was the dog in the back of *our* station wagon. My parents got their Lab in 1959 from a small-scale breeder, the same year that a Labrador named King Buck was put on a U.S. stamp. My older brother named her Putzi—he was three at the time. She was a great swimmer, mother of many puppies, white-whiskered, and, truthfully, somewhat plump in her old age. This was where the Lab entered my story, and where Stella picks up the thread.

## Eleven

# Beyond Breeds

The Victorian invention of the dog as we know it was, at least in part, a consumer revolution. It was all about the brand. When you bought a Lab or a dachshund or a West Highland terrier, you knew what you were getting. Moreover, assisted by the marketing apparatus of the American Kennel Club and its associated breeders, you could believe that you were getting a creature blessed by history, one that had stood the test of time.

But the reality of breed refinement today is quite different. One October weekend I attended the American Kennel Club's Meet the Breeds event at New York's Javits Convention Center. Some 160 breeds were represented, amid booths for every conceivable dog accessory and dietary regimen: organic behavior aids, chewable dog toothpaste. The focus of the event was on connecting breeds with their ancestral homelands. Behind the Cavalier King Charles spaniels was an oversize photograph of a castle surrounded by woods—actually, quite like those on the Buccleuch estate. The Borzois lounging on pillows in a tented area, long and elegant but probably not the brightest bulbs, like the czars who had bred them. A man in a tartan kilt and holding a shepherd's crook stood with a small pack of Shetland sheepdogs, alert, confident creatures, like little collies. The dogs don't herd sheep so much anymore, the man told me, though sometimes they're used to herd geese on golf courses.

The antic shapes of many of these dogs correspond to a specific Victorian-era task: ratters, herders, wolfhounds, guard dogs—a Swiss Army knife of countryside work. But virtually none of these dogs still perform the work they supposedly once did. They've drifted, following the vagaries of fashion rather than usefulness. Successive generations of breeders have tweaked and refined them, all with their own taste. But in the last couple of decades, the AKC, the arbiter of these refinements and unshakable emperor of the dog world, has been shrinking—partly because of competing registrations, but also partly because the Victorian fantasy of designated roles seems increasingly remote from the modern world.

Most dog breeds embalm a specific moment in history, a kind of hinge moment, when a pastoral era transformed into an industrial one. The fantastic visual variety of dogs seems more and more like an end in itself—dogs for dogs' sake—rather than some important vestige of the past, a crucial inheritance. The fantasy of country life, which the kennel clubs have assiduously promoted for 130 years, seems stale: what, exactly, is being preserved? The dog fancy was a story that the rising class told about itself, about its own civilizing power and its distinctions from the common run of city dwellers. But now we know pretty much how that story ends. The dogs aren't useful; they're a hobby, like any other.

Worse, the idea that pedigree is a guarantor of excellence is in many instances empty and false—a problem, as any marketer will tell you, for any brand. By now it's a truism, in a way that it wasn't two decades ago, that the closing and regulation of breeds came at an enormous cost to the health of dogs. The Victorians accepted inbreeding—of a kind that would have appalled an eighteenth-century livestock man, or Darwin, for that matter—as a necessary price for ensuring a consistent animal. The population bottlenecks that accompanied both world wars—large dogs were not mouths anyone wanted to feed when they had to feed their own families—amplified these effects, reducing the populations of breeding dogs.

Nowadays people talk about breed extinction, as if dog breeds were species in themselves, refined over ages. In a very few special cases, that may be true. But in many others, the story is more complicated, involving imagination as much as some authentic form that needs to be preserved. Dogs can be fairly easily re-created. What seems like an immutable dog creation is actually the result of continuous human intervention. Beginning in the 1930s, the Portuguese water dog was rebuilt from just a few individual dogs and, many have alleged, judicious outcrossing. The invention of the dog has never really ended.

When I was in England, I went to see Jemima Harrison, whose 2008 documentary, *Pedigree Dogs Exposed,* was the biggest bombshell the dog world had ever seen. With its vivid scenes of canine suffering and graphic footage of canine operations, the film is a powerful piece of work. But interestingly, many of the ideas it presents are not particularly new. There has been intermittent concern about inbreeding since Stonehenge's time. And in the modern era, the drumbeat began with a widely read 1990 piece in *The Atlantic Monthly* by Mark Derr, now a preeminent American authority on dogs, who pointed out many of the genetic problems with purebreds. At that point, the purebred dog world absorbed the criticism and moved on. But Harrison's film had a different effect.

Harrison, a vivacious woman with a big mane of dark hair and a resonant tenor made for broadcasting, was a horsewoman in her youth. She hunted foxes. But when the master of the hunt smeared the traditional fox blood on her cheek, she was disgusted and gave up the sport, though she's far from a vegetarian. Her battle with the Kennel Club is itself a blood sport. She's thrilled by the conflict. We had coffee in the kitchen of her eighteenth-century cottage. While we talked about dogs, we were surrounded by them, seven in all, most the result of her association with a dog shelter in Ireland. Jake was the king—a big, lanky shepherd-setter mix, like a cartoon wolf.

Harrison is far from a doctrinal animal rights activist. She looks the other way when Jake chases down a rabbit in the farm fields that gird the village. The innovation of *Pedigree Dogs Exposed* was that it framed the question of breeding in terms of animal welfare. In Britain, animal welfare is a mainstream issue, hardly the province of academics and extremists, as it can seem in America. The day I visited Harrison, a plan to put an industrial pig farm in a nearby town had brought protests and shouting national headlines: AMERICAN STYLE FACTORY FARMING.

Harrison's film is not subtle. The star, or perhaps the antihero, is a cavalier King Charles spaniel named Sylvie, a sweet little creature with a terrible condition known as syringomelia. Her skull isn't big enough for her brain: "a size-ten brain in a size-six shoc." The condition is horribly painful—in humans, it is among the most excruciating of diseases. Over a moody soundtrack, Sylvie limps along, head askew, tongue lolling out, a profoundly damaged creature. Other spaniels whine in pain, soon to be put out of their misery.

The severity of this condition in the breed is in dispute. Even the Kennel Club admits that as many as 50 percent of King Charles spaniels have the underlying condition, though the club maintains that just 5 percent show clinical symptoms. Some veterinarians believe that a substantial portion of the dogs that appear to be asymptomatic are nevertheless in chronic pain—pain that, being dogs, they can't make known. When they are given painkillers, some spaniels change their facial expressions and personalities in ways that suggest they are experiencing relief. Ironically, the Cavalier King Charles was reengineered beginning in the 1950s to resemble the dogs in the sixteenth-century royal portraits. The goal of changing the skull shape was achieved so fast that the brain didn't have a chance to catch up.

At the 2010 Canine Science Forum in Vienna, Paul McGreevey showed a series of slides demonstrating the pushing and pulling that various areas of dogs' brains have undergone in the interest of breed standards, with uncertain effects on brain function and behavior. Harrison resorted to laymen's language when talking about the King Charles. "It's the cerebellum that's squashed," she told me, "so it squidges out." Sadder, in a way, are the German shepherds, their low-riding sterns an aesthetic refinement developed in the last fifty years. If you look at photographs of the German shepherd taken over the last few decades, you can see its back gradually being ratcheted down to its current rakish angle. Sometimes I see these dogs in the dog run, their splayed hocks unable to generate much power; they struggle to climb stairs. Amazingly, a Kennel Club judge in Harrison's film insists that these slope-backed dogs are superior to working German shepherds, because they more closely conform to the "breed standard."

Dachshunds and basset hounds have gotten shorter and lower, so that if they gain too much weight, they bottom out—an uncomfortable and undignified fate. Then there are the brachycephalic breeds, bull-dogs and pugs—both of which have chronic breathing issues because of their compressed snouts. (Bulldogs' heads are so disproportionately large that 86 percent of them have to be born by Cesarean section.) An overexcited pug will sometimes choke itself when its windpipe gets clogged with its soft palate. It will pass out from lack of oxygen, then wake up when it relaxes. And with their snouts pressed into their faces, pugs have been known to damage their eyes by running into things.

The scale of these genetic problems is debatable, as well as the degree of suffering they inflict on dogs. But even before Harrison's documentary, the Kennel Club acknowledged that inbreeding had caused serious genetic issues. Genetic diversity has been reduced by 90 percent in the last half century. Harrison points to the pug. Although there are some ten thousand pugs in Britain, the effective population is fifty individuals—which makes it, on a genetic level, more endan-gered than the giant panda. In the world of dog fancy, many Genghis Khans have left their genetic imprint on huge swaths of descendants, passing on their faults as well as their excellences. (Labradors didn't suffer the worst of these consequences, as we have seen, because for most of their history, they didn't have to be show champions to be considered excellent.) Certain aesthetic refinements can even be traced back to a single dog. But these practices—breeding best to best, champions that leave many offspring—are the core of the Kennel Club and the AKC. Harrison's point is that they've botched their stewardship, and looking at the evidence, it's hard to argue. Harrison's documentary even makes a controversial connection between the origins of the Kennel Club and eugenics. In truth, the judges and breeders she interviewed seem fairly benign, white-haired drinkers of tea and collectors of china, hobbyists who are shocked to find the world's attention suddenly focused on their little province.

It's difficult to overstate the degree to which Harrison's documentary upended Britain's dog world. An aggressive producer managed to get the program on the BBC's main channel, but the network, having backed it, couldn't get around the hypocrisy of also broadcasting Crufts. Crufts is the equivalent of the Westminster show in the United States, but it is far more culturally central—one of Britain's favorite national sporting festivals, along with Wimbledon and Ascot. So in 2009 the BBC pulled Crufts—which had a slightly bigger audience than the documentary—from its lineup. Crufts had been sponsored by the RSPCA and other humane organizations, as well as dog food manufacturers, but most of its sponsors dropped out as well.

The Kennel Club's leadership made their contempt for Harrison palpable in her documentary, but they quickly realized that mere wagon circling and resistance weren't going to solve the problem. In fact, for both the Kennel Club and its American counterpart, the public crisis had been going on for quite some time. AKC registrations peaked in 1992, but in the two decades since, they have been cut in half. Their once all-powerful system has eroded, at first imperceptibly, then in a rush. In my suburban youth, the word *purebred* still had power, something kids bragged about, like having a Cadillac in the garage; mutts were a rung below. But the distinction has lost a lot of its force.

After *Pedigree Dogs Exposed* was broadcast, the Kennel Club joined forces with Dogs Trust (one of the charities that had withdrawn its support) to commission a report by eminent ethologist Patrick Bateson, president of the London Zoological Society, on issues involving pedigree dogs. I had lunch with Bateson at a bustling Italian restaurant near Piccadilly Circus. Bateson has presided over animal issues since the 1970s, when he chaired a panel that developed standards for animals used in research. (He once dated Jane Goodall—he told me he found her obsession with chimps hard to get past.) Then in the 1990s, he produced a report that led to the banning of coursing red deer with hounds, finding that the chase to exhaustion was cruelty. In Great Britain, the strong associations between class and hunting makes them tabloid fodder in ways that they aren't in the United States.

"Jemima's film changed everything," he told me. His 2010 report, based on extensive interviews with breeders and scientists, supported almost all of Harrison's charges. But it is not a general indictment of breeding practices like *Pedigree Dogs Exposed*. Instead it contains a nuanced discussion of inbreeding, explaining the apparent contradiction that populations can become healthier (as in humans, whose numbers, at some point in our passage from Africa, were reduced to perhaps ten thousand individuals) by purging unhealthy mutations and reinforcing strong ones. The report also pointed out the problems with unlimited outcrossings. And it pointed to the Kennel Club's tacit approval of puppy mills (because it registers those puppies).

The Kennel Club said it welcomed the report. It maintained that its efforts to address these problems had been under way for years, long before Harrison's meddlesome documentary. Amazingly, in some areas, it said the report hadn't gone far enough. It seemed to imply that the Kennel Club was not the problem, but the solution. It had banned the most problematic matings, between siblings and between parents

and children. But it rejected Bateson's recommendation to ban matings between grandparents and grandchildren (which are twice as
close as between cousins), a common practice in the dog world. They
changed breed standards in favor of health for several breeds, including the bulldog and the German shepherd. But whether these efforts
were mere gestures or significant reforms is in the eye of the beholder.

Another of the documentary's antiheros, a defender of the old
order, is Jeff Sampson, the Kennel Club's senior canine geneticist.
I had some sympathy for him. He couldn't be in a more difficult
position, between a revolutionary like Harrison and an entrenched,
conservative leadership that only wants to keep things the same. To
complicate the picture, his scientific expertise, at least in some cases,
must have told him things that he couldn't or wouldn't act upon on
behalf of the Kennel Club.

I went to see Sampson in the Kennel Club's London headquarters.
He is a geneticist by training and became interested in dogs partly because their inbreeding offered a window onto the effects of particular
genetic mutations on disease. He began working with the Kennel Club
because his wife was a dog breeder. We sat in a room decorated with
some of the club's enormous collection of dog art, and he said many of
the right things, if not all of them. He'd worked on a 2003 report (published by Imperial College) that pointed to problems among Kennel
Club dogs. He used the report as evidence of the Kennel's hypocrisy.
"Jeff Sampson has known about the problem for years—he's not stupid," he said. "But acknowledging it is not enough."

Sampson told me that the Imperial College report was a significant event in the history of the Kennel Club, opening a lot of eyes
there. "We were marching toward Armageddon." *Pedigree Dogs Exposed*
merely accelerated what the club had already known, he said, and was
working to reverse. "It probably did some good" in that regard, though
in other ways it did a lot of damage. "We were stunned and weakened
as an organization. It set back a lot of programs."

Where the club is marching now, and how quickly, is another question. Some breeds are beyond help. Others, like the Cavalier King Charles, possibly could be saved with the right kind of intervention—but Sampson seemed unconvinced. Sampson is unambiguous in his statements that the dog creation has gone too far. "My opinion is that there are too many dog breeds," he told me. The less like a wolf a dog looked, the less sense it might make as a dog. On these questions, Sampson, Harrison, and Bateson are in near-perfect agreement. But they disagree over what should be done to implement the changes and who should be in charge.

Bateson's report proposed the formation of an independent regulatory body that could ban breeds whose breeders used harmful practices. But Sampson and the Kennel Club disagreed. "Our view was, and is," Sampson said, ". . . that if we start imposing too many requirements, people will stop registering, but keep breeding them." Moreover, "the obvious solution in the outside world is not necessarily the solution that works best in our little world here." Sampson argues with some passion that the Kennel Club is essential to bringing hidebound breeders into the modern world. It is the only possible agent of effective reform—if breeders went unsupervised, who knew what they might do?

In response, Harrison points out that Sampson's argument is partly a financial one. "It's a conflict of interest," she told me, "because they need the money that comes from registrations." The Kennel Club, she said, has a financial incentive to register as many dogs as it can. This makes it a highly questionable steward for dogs. She believes that the club is playing a political game, saying the right things in public while moving as slowly as possible toward actual measures for change. "There's some nodding in the right direction," she said, "but at the end of the day, they haven't really changed." And Bateson, though diplomatic, is frustrated too. "Frankly," he said of Sampson, "he's a bit two-faced." The club's attitude, he said, is: "If there's a problem, we'll take care of it." He'd been wrestling with the club over how to constitute the advisory panel. "You can't be judge and jury," he told its representatives. Their response, he said, was, "We like to be judge and jury."

But Harrison is clear about her goal. "They're unincorporated and enormously rich, and a very small number of people who are controlling things," she said. "You will not see real change at the Kennel Club until there's regime change." In fact, the dog nation that the Kennel Club pretends to command has changed beneath it. It's undergoing a legitimacy crisis. In the nineteenth century, breeding was a mark of excellence. But now it's a mark of . . . what, exactly?

In the United States, a similar struggle is unfolding, even without a single defining event like Harrison's film. Here animal welfare issues are more vast and varied than in Britain, and the AKC, as large as it is, does not have the same kind of national identity that makes the battle against Britain's Kennel Club so dramatic. American cows and pigs—not to mention the still-vast number of shelter dogs—are raised in such dire conditions that inbreeding issues don't have the same priority as other animal welfare issues. So the dog fancy is not liable to come crashing down—rather, it may very well become a sect with fewer and fewer adherents. AKC membership is declining not only because of breed health problems but because what they're selling—the dog, and the idea of it—has become more complicated. People try to keep old ways close, but the semirural cultures in which these dogs were originally bred will be hard to re-create.

The AKC is desperately trying to reclaim its relevance. Its communications are inflected with humane concerns. In 2009 it allowed mixed-breed dogs to participate in its new agility programs, the first time in 125 years that it had compromised on its pure-breeding ideology. But the mixed breeds were allowed only on a separate-but-equal basis—and one stated reason for opening the door to mutts and their owners was to persuade the owners to make their next dog a purebred. The AKC's policies may look like glasnost, but underneath, the goal seems to be to preserve the ancien régime.

The kennel clubs are still the largest powers in the dog world, and their regulatory power could be a force for good. The AKC sometimes sells itself as a bulwark against PETA and other animal rights groups. But Patrick Burns of the popular blog *Terrierman,* who is one of the AKC's fiercest critics, points out that PETA is nothing more than a press release machine, searching for relevance with ever more outlandish stunts. (A couple of years ago, PETA members showed up in KKK robes at the Westminster dog show, highlighting both the AKC's emphasis on purity of blood and PETA's own confusion about appropriate rhetoric.)

One may dream of peace in the dog world, but it doesn't seem likely anytime soon. Later in my visit, Harrison and I sat at a picnic table in her garden, ate dinner, and talked about the future of dogs. "My fantasy," she said, "is that the Kennel Club or some other organization really takes the opportunity to do something incredibly special for all dogs by recognizing that we have made such a mess of it, and realizing that with reform we can undo that mess. I believe it's possible."

When we walked away for a minute, Jake got up on the table and ate a piece of my steak.

## Twelve

# Future Canines

Even as the Victorian dog creation is losing steam, it has left an amazing legacy. A group of scientists, the two most prominent of whom are Elaine Ostrander at the National Human Genome Research Institute and Robert Wayne at UCLA, is mapping the deep genetic structure of the dog population. The dog genome project is closely tied to the Human Genome Project, but where the results of the Human Genome Project have often been murky (marvelous, but nowhere near as clear in terms of identifying single genes that control for diseases as had been hoped when Craig Venter first began putting his genes through a sequencing machine), the dog genome has provided marvelous insight to the species' genetic structure—and by analogy, to the human genome. Inbreeding is an important component of this genetic clarity. As wrongheaded as it was in other ways, inbreeding helped to organize and simplify the dog genome; it made it easier to compare and contrast components, to find the genes or the areas on the genome that account for differences among dogs.

Canine variety, the greatest among any species, used to be one of the great scientific mysteries. Dog diversity persuaded Darwin and many later scientists up to Konrad Lorenz that dogs must have descended from several different kinds of canids, rather than just the wolf. But dog genetics has turned out to be surprisingly simple. The dog is a basic template, a wolf template, pretty similar across breeds—a good deal more similar than are humans—but infinitely customizable with the variation of a fairly small number of genes. For instance, all small breeds share a single, very early gene mutation. The short legs of dachshunds, bassets, corgis, and twelve other breeds are also traceable to a single genetic mutation, a growth factor gene that's been duplicated and reinserted in another place. Three genes control 95 percent of different types of fur. Floppy ears are the work of a single mutation. Genes that control facial development are another important factor, determining whether a dog has a long, wolfish snout or a plump, abbreviated face made to be babied.

"The process that led to dog diversification is very different from, say, what led to variability in humans," Wayne told me. "And that process really focused on the last few hundred years of history. Beginning in the Victorian era there was intense selection for novelty, for cuteness in dogs, essentially, started by the nobility, who wanted symbols of their wealth and status and who would choose dogs that are literally freaks. And then pathological kinds of mutations began to be fixed in dogs."

Darwin had pointed to this phenomenon, noting that breeders put a high value on "sports," or very unusual puppies in litters. Often, these characteristics were produced by what Wayne calls "single mutations of large effect." Some 70 percent of dog breeds are based on those types of mutations. It's very different from what happened with humans, or indeed, with any other species. "If you look at the top forty genes that influence body size in humans—the top forty—they count for only about five to ten percent of the variation in body size. If you look at the top gene in dogs, it counts for more than fifty percent of the variation in body weight." Dog breeders, he says, didn't gradually select for small variations, building qualities up gradually—for one thing, dogs don't live long enough for such a protracted process. Rather, breeders selected freaks—Darwin's "sports," or what Wayne calls "pathological mutations."

Scientists and breeders have a deep, though far from perfect, understanding of the genes that produce the black of the black Labrador. With a couple of variations, the same basic template produces chocolate and yellow Labs—the equation for Stella. They even understand the variations that produce the white blazes and white paws that disqualify dogs from the Lab ideal.

It's not as simple as flipping switches and creating the dog of your choice, but the clarity of Wayne and Ostrander's work so far suggests a bright future. Morphology is only a small part of their revelations. Using their dog DNA study, Wayne and his colleagues recently produced a detailed canine family tree, mapping underlying relationships. Sight hounds, scent hounds, and herding and guarding dogs, among others, are all related—a finding that may seem obvious to the layperson but surprised the scientists, who assumed that breeders began with a wide variety of canine raw material and created these different qualities through many routes. In a way, their finding aligns with the pre-Victorian species with a few big, simple groupings.

But as fascinating as the new science is about dogs, it tells us even more about humans—particularly when it comes to disease. The dog's pathological mutations offer a kind of clarity that the human genome does not. Dog diseases are not always precise analogs of human diseases, but many are: the dog has 450 hereditary diseases, about half of which are related to similar conditions in people. A fairly rare narcolepsy in greyhounds has shed light on human sleep disorders. A mutation leading to heavily muscled "bully" whippets may correlate to genes producing the impressive physiques of some professional athletes. Some golden retrievers have muscular dystrophy, which has led to promising new treatments for the disease in humans. Some dog genes are even behavioral indicators, like those for OCD, and Williams Syndrome, which tantalizes with a vision of a human analogue to canine tameness (see chapter 4). The fact that the dog shares our environment makes it more interesting to scientists in some ways than the mouse, the traditional animal for studying inherited diseases. Perhaps most important, people want to cure dogs; the emerging science benefits both species.

Again, inadvertently, the dog has been pulled into the human story. The dog fancy's obsession with purity didn't produce what it thought it would—the best possible dogs. In fact, its breeding practices damaged the dogs. But the damage turned out to be highly revealing. From a human creation, hopelessly polluted by human interference, dogs have once again become a model species. Recently, a study on shelter dogs with respiratory ailments found that some of them have a close analog to the hepatitis C virus, whose origins have long eluded scientists. Some researchers now believe that hepatitis may have originated in dogs within the last thousand years.

There's something a bit unsettling in reducing the dog to a disease vector, a pile of inherited conditions to be studied. But these studies don't murder to dissect, as Wordsworth had it—no one gets murdered. And scientific usefulness has beauty, especially to a scientist. Ostrander has spoken of her awe at the pets that showed her these deep patterns. But again, the modern dog's inadvertent usefulness isn't the whole picture of the animal—it's another artifact, a partial view to add to the collage. And it certainly isn't a reason to refrain from reforming the kennel clubs or even overthrowing them. Disease shouldn't be the raison d'être for a culture, as if purebred dogs were so many colonies of lab rats.

What future generations of dogs should be, and who should breed them, are complicated issues containing a hint of futuristic vertigo. Now that the kennel clubs' hold over the public imagination is relaxing, with the general recognition that their breeding regimes created terrible problems, the door is open to new creative impulses, something like the ones that transformed dogs in the Victorian era, but to different ends. The current situation, however, is much more chaotic, with little agreement as to what a dog should be, or what kind of world it should be made for. A dog like Stella, who can run for hours, doesn't make much sense in my concrete stomping grounds, for instance. Should dogs be created for our apartments, and to alleviate our allergy problems? It's already happening.

The first dog to make a break for it was the Labradoodle, or Lab-poodle cross, now a common sight in my Manhattan neighborhood. The Labradoodle was the brainchild of Wally Conran, who in the 1980s formed the guide dog program at Australia's Royal Institute of the Blind. Conran had a request for a guide dog that was hypoaller-genic and had the bright idea of crossing a Labrador, a preferred guide dog due to its calm, affable nature, with a standard poodle, whose ringlet coat tends to be much less bothersome to people with allergies. In the resulting litter of three dogs, one had the desired quality. Dog training involves extensive socialization, and Conran needed homes to foster the dogs, so he advertised them on TV as a new form of guide dog. The Labradoodle's recombinant sweet goofiness and hypoallergenic nature were instantly appealing. Conran then experimented with the dog, creating bi-doodles (second-generation doodles) and tri-doodles, fixing its characteristics much the way Victorian breeders had. He retired from dog breeding a short time later, but he'd lit a spark. A nonsense poem's worth of new breeds have been produced: beagos and bichomos and bodacians, cavapoos, frengles, mastadors, and pug-gles. The clan of those supposedly hypoallergenic poos and oodles is large: airedoodles, basetoodles, cairnoodles, all the way to the Yorki-poo. If nothing else, this new flowering is an exuberant statement of freedom from the old laws of dog.

The problem is that breeding a great dog is only the first step. The world demands popular dogs in industrial numbers—they don't live very long, after all—and the easiest way to produce industrial numbers is with industrial methods. A small operator like Conran can keep control of his creations, but in the wrong hands, breeding regimes could get out of control.

The second most famous designer dog is the puggle (or pug-beagle cross), created by Wallace Havens, a Wisconsin cattle farmer and entrepreneur who ran Puppy Haven Kennel. Havens began his career as a breeding technician. He built a nest egg by inventing a cattle-breeding lubricant, after which he bought his own spread and began experimenting in earnest. Havens's breeding experiments bring to mind those of Robert Bakewell, if not those of Dr. Moreau. He tried, unsuccessfully, to breed an Asian leopard with a Bengal tiger. He bred hedgehogs and miniature donkeys. And he created several new breeds of dogs, some simply the result of breed-to-breed crossing, others whole cocktails of different combinations. Havens used his cattle-breeding skills, which usually don't value a breed's purity. A cattle breeder selects for traits rather than bloodlines. Havens's first dog was the cockapoo, which mixed the cocker spaniel's easygoing temperament with the poodle's hypoallergenic coat. Havens maintained that his dogs were healthier than purebreds, even offering a five-year warranty on his puppies. But marketing was only one part of his enterprise.

He was making something to sell to a huge market, just as in his cattle farm days. He built his business on the dog's twin roles as livestock and as family member—that ancient duality. He treated them as things and sold them as honorary humans. His kennel became essentially a factory farm to produce new breeds. Conditions were fairly gruesome: toothless dogs in cages gave birth to litter after litter, never having a toy or going outside. It was a puppy mill—one of the largest in the country—censured by the AKC and under continual attack by humane organizations.

Havens's kennel was partly staffed by Amish, who've established a beachhead in that part of Wisconsin partly to escape encroaching modernity in their former stronghold in Pennsylvania. Amish country there had been a center of puppy mill activity, because puppies are a cash crop and Amish animal ethics permit the kind of intensive husbandry that maximizes profits. But Pennsylvania's legal environment for commercial breeders had been eroding; Wisconsin offered more forgiving laws.

Humane organizations regularly rescued dogs from Havens's operation—most often, he sold them. Finally in 2008, the Humane Society of the United States bought his breeding operation and closed it down—a good deal for everyone (though some rescue organizations saw it as akin to paying a hostage taker). At seventy-two, Havens was planning to retire anyway. Meanwhile Conran, now in his eighties, has come to regret inventing the Labradoodle, given all the problems that accompany its mass production. "Now when people ask me, 'Did you breed the first one?' I have to say, 'Yes, I did, but it's not something I'm proud of,'" he told *The Australian*. "I wish I could turn the clock back."

Turning the clock back is something many people in the dog world want to do, in some portion of their brains. The Labradoodle can be an excellent dog, but it doesn't answer the question of what sort of dogs should be bred today. If you wanted to build a dog for this moment and not some imagined, rural Victorian moment, what would you build, and what kinds of institutions should control their breeding? Should it be a dog that fits into the lives of urban dwellers—able to tolerate confinement to apartments, and spend long hours on the rug, content to take the occasional excursion to the dog run? Alexandra Horowitz suggested to me that you might want a dog that sleeps all day—she was joking, but there's truth in it. For someone who lives in a Manhattan elevator building and works nine to five, a seminarcoleptic corgi might be the perfect dog. The owner wouldn't feel guilty that, by going to work, he was depriving the dog of companionship. And the corgi wouldn't have a problem, either, being mostly asleep. But that would mean a new stage in domestication—for dumber, more tolerant animals. And who would choose such a dog?

Poor Stella is a magnificent athlete. She can run for a day—which doesn't do her much good in our apartment. I think a lot about the world she deserves versus the one she has—and if I don't, she reminds me to, fixing me with a hard stare when I'm putting on my sneakers. She often gets what she wants, which is a run, or a bike ride, but it's an imperfect substitute for the kind of life she was designed for.

Others in the dog world are focused on rebuilding dogs' prior excellences. Pat Burns, of *Terrierman,* wants to tear down the Potemkin village of the AKC and repopulate the world with real working dogs, dogs that can dig up farm varmints, like his own terriers that he sets after woodchucks on the farm fields around his Virginia home. His deep, scoffing contempt for his adversaries makes him a great blogger. He's forged a cross-Atlantic alliance with Jemima Harrison, creating a two-front war. In some ways, he's also an ideological ally of journalist Michael Pollan, author of *The Omnivore's Dilemma,* as well as all the sheep farmers and heirloom vegetable growers and locavores who are trying to imagine a new relation with the natural world. But he's far from sentimental about the past—he knows what the modern world is, knows that the Wendell Berrys are not about to feed Chicago anytime soon.

And he knows that in some ways the natural world is in better shape than it was, say, thirty years ago: there are more eagles, more deer, and more varmints, which is where his terriers come in. Terrierman uses them for the purpose they were originally bred for: digging for varmints. Their chests have to be narrow enough to squeeze down fox and groundhog burrows, and part of his issue with the AKC is that the dogs it certifies don't have these dimensions.

Burns's cosmology is idiosyncratic, a world entire, woven from skeins of history and philosophy and science. He writes about what your life might be like and what equipment you'd need if the electricity were turned off; why the AKC won't listen to Charles Darwin; why the golden bear hasn't returned to California. His hunting is a practice that leads to all sorts of corollaries. He's a truth seeker and a truth teller. His dogs anchor his thinking to what's happening to nature in the modern world.

Burns's passion reminds us that to have a relationship to the natural world, we must imagine it, then believe in it, and then live it. One of the main intellectual threads of the last decade has been our need to take ethical responsibility for our food choices and for our carnivorousness. Despite their element of moral playacting, these ethics raise an important truth, which is that we're not on the farm anymore. And getting back there involves, as much as anything else, imagination.

Dogs, as always, are players in this drama—side players, a parallel story. The Victorian era's field-and-farmyard uses for dogs—"hunting in a field of high turnips"—no longer exist in our world. But then what uses are appropriate for dogs today? The dog world is alive with such anxieties, hand-wringing about the future of the dog. Which can seem a little silly, as dogs are patently not going anywhere.

Developing a serious fixation on dogs in all their capacities often demands a move to the countryside. But the countryside is also, in many ways, an artificial environment. It's a nostalgic invention. And it's not a place where I could make a living—it's a vacation, not an answer to this conundrum. Dogs are caught up in human thinking. Stella's incongruous urban lifestyle is a hypocrisy I'm ready to live with—a minor suffering I inflict with open eyes and mitigate as best I can.

Stella is only a dog. I often think that she wants to take me back to a world where we're walking in the path in the forest, where her eyes— and nose—are more important than mine. But getting back there is far from easy.

# Thirteen

# The Great Migration

Stella is what's known as a rescue dog. As such, she's a product of the sprawling, conflict-riven, highly ad hoc system that supplies most of our dogs. Many owners deservedly take pride in having adopted a dog from a kill shelter or an otherwise troubled situation, telling horror stories about its former confinement and abuse, followed by their blessed intercession, after which all live happily ever after. It's one of the good feelings about owning a dog in the modern world. And for many urban dog owners, the knowledge that they have saved the dog from life in a cage or worse helps justify keeping it cooped up in an apartment for most of the day. But in truth, our moral heroism is not of the highest order. Stella wasn't a middle-aged pit bull with a mean streak, say, or a toothless retiree from a puppy mill—she was a beautiful, glossy-coated, twelve-week-old puppy, a rescue dog that anyone would have rescued.

Dog shelters existed in my imagination from earliest childhood, serious and confusing. We didn't want our puppies to end up at the local shelter, and, to my knowledge, they never did. It was a place where you could go to adopt a dog, but it was also death row—the clock was ticking on its dogs, and no sentiment could save them. You could go and pick one for yourself, but the rest would die. What a horrible choice to have to make—when you walked in, they were all prospective family members. As my childhood mind understood it, if unwanted dogs weren't euthanized, then the world would be overrun with dogs. But that was too much death for a young mind to deal with.

And that's more or less where my understanding of these matters remained until Stella arrived in our lives, and in fact for some time thereafter. The notion that she'd been plucked out of some fetid kill shelter and somehow miraculously been delivered to us was a wonderful myth, but one I only partly bought. I knew that getting Stella was to some extent an act of shopping. But it gradually dawned on me that our shelter experience, as much as it was about saving dogs, was also about great marketing. We'd driven all the way out to Long Island to get a dog, when, in fact, there were plenty of needier dogs right in Manhattan— dogs that might actually be in danger of being euthanized.

As always, the killing went on in the distant exurbs of my mental frame, something I could have told you was happening if you asked but that I otherwise almost never thought about. But dogs are euthanized every day in New York City—more than two hundred dogs a week in 2010. And a small army of people are trying to save them. Each weekday afternoon between five and six P.M., New York's Animal Care and Control (ACC) facility on 110th Street—the semipublic agency responsible for handling the city's strays and unwanted or problem animals—e-mails a list of dogs at risk for euthanasia to a group of rescue organizations, which then tries to take as many dogs as they can off death row, placing them in other shelters or in foster homes.

Eleven thousand dogs a year is a big number, but it's probably less by a factor of ten than the statistic in 1970. But if you think that a dog has the same moral status as a person, as many of the ACC's angriest critics do, then this statistical decline is small consolation. A dog is a life, and a lesser genocide is still genocide, not something to celebrate.

On the Internet, skeins of vitriol are directed at Mayor Michael Bloomberg; at Jane Hoffman, head of the Mayor's Alliance for Animals; and especially at the ACC's director, Julie Bank. Capital letters are used liberally. "Ms. Julie Bank = DISGRACE," wrote one commenter beneath a post titled "Bloomberg and Julie Bank, How Do You Sleep At Night?" Several sites feature pictures of the condemned animals, which are mostly alert, young, healthy-looking pit bulls (at least they look healthy in the pictures), either strays or dogs surrendered by their owners. Most of them peer at the camera with the pit's distinctive look of confident inquisitiveness—adorable. These pictures were, of course, hard to look at, one reason I didn't look at them, and possibly one reason the people fighting the ACC become so overwrought.

I couldn't imagine who would want such a job—to have killing these animals be part of your job description, and then to be reviled for it. In fact, no one seemed fully committed to taking on the management of New York's dogs as a public responsibility. There was something furtive about it—which makes dealing with the problem even more difficult. The ACC has limited public funds and its fund-raising is anemic, augmented by a block grant from Maddie's Fund, a no-kill charity founded by the entrepreneur who started PeopleSoft, a large software company, in the 1980s. Maddie's Fund insists, as a condition of its grant, that dogs not be euthanized due to lack of space. According to the ACC's critics, the organization was getting around this stipulation by euthanizing dogs that had minor illnesses like kennel cough—in order to receive the money to care for, and sometimes kill, more dogs. It's a classic vicious circle: the ACC has the word *care* in its name, but its Web site makes only a half-hearted attempt to portray itself as a true humane organization.

The rescue community refers to this dilemma as the care-kill paradox. In the last two decades, heroic efforts have been made to solve it, but it still torments those who are in charge of the nation's stray dogs. It was clear to me that the ACC's function would have to be provided

by *someone*. But the loudest voices (if not the most numerous) argue
that dogs' honorary personhood means they must be saved, and if they
are not, it's because of sloth, incompetence, and lack of imagination.
To these critics, the animal control complex is a malign bureaucracy.

The extreme politics and raw emotions surrounding the treatment of dogs on 110th Street belies a surprising fact: by many measures, the treatment of dogs in New York is a success story. In the
Bloomberg administration, under the leadership of Jane Hoffman—a
white-haired, cheerfully efficient former corporate lawyer who founded
and now heads the Mayor's Alliance for Animals—the number of
dogs euthanized in New York has steadily declined: from a whopping
74 percent of the more than forty thousand dogs taken in 2002, when
the mayor's alliance was founded, to 33 percent today. Given that the
euthanasia rate in some urban shelters a couple of decades ago could
be well over 90 percent, those would be numbers to brag about (if they
didn't still look like genocide to some).

The credit for this accomplishment certainly belongs to some
degree to Hoffman and her colleagues. But euthanasia rates have been
dropping in other large metropolitan areas too. It's part of a larger
cultural transformation. The system is far from perfect, but dog overpopulation, where it exists, is a different kind of problem from what it
was three decades ago.

Dog overpopulation began in the suburbs. In a survey in the late
1950s, residents of Levittown, America's ur-suburb, identified stray
dogs as their number-two problem—just behind the danger of nuclear
annihilation. Those were the days of Lassie, with her commitment to
the family and her empathic understanding of her master's wishes.
Lassie's dual citizenship in the human world and the natural one was a
big part of her appeal. A dog on a leash or behind a fence—even in
Levittown—couldn't do what Lassie did. Unleashed dogs were part of
the suburban fantasy.

In our household, Putzi wandered wherever she wanted to go—

she sometimes trotted a mile or so for an assignation with the king dog of the neighborhood, an enormous, splendid, toffee-colored Rhodesian ridgeback owned by a local doctor. Our method of birth control was, essentially, to keep the dog in the house when she went into heat, which was an imperfect solution—my mother still holds me responsible for one of her escapes, when I'd been specifically ordered not to let her out, which led to a litter of puppies. But that wasn't the worst thing in the world. Besides, dogs taught kids about the cycles of life, from the humping stage (occasions for great mirth) to the wet little lumps, eyes shut, crawling to nurse at their mother's teats. Spaying and neutering, while not exactly cruel, seemed selfish—why alter something so basic for the convenience of not having to deal with puppies?

Not a bad life for a dog. But it was producing a truly enormous number of excess dogs, and something had to be done with them. So they were euthanized. Big shelters produced big trash barrels of dead dogs, which were then sent to a rendering plant. In some ways, those dogs were the lucky ones. Others could end up as laboratory subjects.

It was pure numbers, the language of industry, that first began to speak of the horrors of the animal shelter world. In the 1960s, automobile traffic may have killed 10 percent of American dogs, due to their leashless, fenceless existence. By 1973, 13.5 million cats and dogs—more than 20 percent of all cats and dogs in the United States—were killed in animal shelters. This number, so large it looks like a misprint, spoke to something broken or misaligned in American life; our good society was malfunctioning.

The staggering number of dogs dying in shelters reflected the staggering number of dogs being born. Between 1963 and 1974, sales of dog food tripled, the result not only of superior Mad Men–style marketing but also of the substantial growth in the pet population. In 1974, according to a National League of Cities report, when mayors were asked what citizens most frequently complained about, 60 percent said dogs and other animal control issues. In the early 1970s, it was acknowledged that dogs provided solace for the depredations of a complex, depersonalized, and alienating society.

Having conquered the suburbs, dogs moved into the cities in huge numbers, bringing unconditional love to the lonely and dog poop to everyone. "New Yorkers are partial to dogs," wrote a *New York Times* columnist in 1974, "which they harbor in all sizes and shapes, keeping them imprisoned most of the day in tiny apartments and bringing them out morning and evening to evacuate on sidewalks." Dog poop became one of the scourges of the ungovernable city and a major issue for Mayor Ed Koch. As Michael Brandow notes in his entertaining *New York's Poop Scoop Law,* the debate over the measure amounted to a civil war over dogs. The seminal animal rights activist Cleveland Amory called the 1978 poop scoop law "a carefully planned first step toward banning dogs from New York City altogether." And the city's befouled streets did indeed lead to a more general questioning of the dog's place in the urban world, asking whether apartment life was any kind of existence for a dog and whether the billions of dollars devoted to caring for pets could be better spent on human problems. As always when dogs are concerned, the rhetoric became remarkably heated. "Like the Jews of Nazi Germany, we citizens, including the old and infirm, are being humiliated by being forced to pick up excrement in the gutter," wrote the head of the New York Dog Owners Guild. But Ed Koch finally engineered a grand bargain that, by making the sidewalks safe for pedestrians, made the city safe for dogs—at least ones that didn't end up in the shelter.

What went on in shelters was unthinkable—industrialized killing of perfectly healthy animals on a massive scale, a precise analogue to the depredations of the factory farm. And as with factory farming, the core of the system was institutional secrecy—the barrels of dead dogs were an abomination, but as long as they were hidden, the system could function. That was the way it worked for decades. In truth, no one wanted to think about it—just as no one wants to think about where bacon comes from. And it was one of the dubious achievements of America's industrial society that the vast majority of people didn't have to think about it. The killing went on out of sight.

Changing the system involved getting people to think about the unthinkable, which wasn't easy. It was Phyllis Wright, a vice president of the Humane Society, who most effectively called attention to the problem, while devising a solution that many now revile. During the Korean War, Wright had been the U.S. Army's head dog trainer; she then played a Cesar Millan–like role on local television. She was a dynamo, with no squeamishness and an ability to look head-on at the problem. She was concerned with mitigating suffering, not necessarily with saving dogs—she tested various methods of euthanasia to see which was most painless. Mother Wright, as she was known, could be a stern moralist, and she took aim at people like my family, with our FREE PUPPIES signs, which conceded a world of suffering and death. "People who let their dogs and cats have litters in order to show their children the 'miracle of birth' should come witness the 'miracle of death' performed in the back rooms of animal shelters all over the country."

Wright and the Humane Society did more than anyone else to popularize the notion that spaying and neutering should be nearly universal, and that measure, more than any other, began to solve the problem of too many dogs. In 1968 the ASPCA adopted a policy of spaying and neutering the animals that passed through its shelter. In 1970 some 10 percent of dogs were sterilized; by 1990, the number was 90 percent. But that wasn't the only tool in Wright's arsenal. She personally took part in more than seventy thousand euthanasias, a questionable legacy—no-kill advocates now accuse her of being the architect of the "catch-and-kill" animal control strategy.

The disappearance of the free-ranging American dog is part of a more generalized taming and ordering of the suburban world. No one thinks of letting their dogs run free outside (even if it weren't against the law in most places) any more than they would tell their kids to go play in traffic. Kids have playdates and soccer leagues and tutors; dogs go to the dog run or get walked. People have to plan for them, think about them—just like our children.

The disappearance of unleashed dogs from the suburbs has given rise to a new ecosystem. In my neighborhood in the 1960s, deer and even raccoons were comparatively rare. Now they're as common as pigeons. As for wild turkeys, as mean as they can be, a flock wouldn't last long in a standoff with a couple of determined dogs. And the dog's close cousin the coyote has arrived in large numbers, dominating eastern areas where it never set foot before. A young coyote even appeared at the entrance to the Holland Tunnel, below the windows of my office, and proceeded to lead police on a three-day chase around the West Side.

It's a conundrum: rescue dogs are more popular than ever, but on the East Coast there are far fewer dogs, and especially puppies, that aren't pit bulls, to rescue. So where do shelter dogs come from? The people at North Shore told us that Stella came from Tennessee, which at the time seemed exotic—a long way for a puppy to travel. But I hadn't been paying attention. Dogs in New York, just like people, tend to be from somewhere else. Purebreds can come from anywhere—a breeder upstate, or New Jersey, or Pennsylvania, and often even farther afield. And so can mixed breeds.

After we brought Stella home and began to meet the other participants in the dog parade, we discovered that Stella's exotic background was anything but unusual. Almost as a rule, mutts that aren't part pit bull are from red states: Virginia, North and South Carolina, Kentucky, and Tennessee. Some dogs come from as far away as Puerto Rico. North Shore is the largest shelter around, and plenty of dogs are in evidence there, some looking quite a bit like Stella, and many from Tennessee—another set of cousins, along with the ones at Buccleuch.

The archetypal story of a modern dog is an odyssey. Liberated from a high-kill shelter in some rural backwater, or rescued in a raid on a puppy mill, it then makes a trip on a semiunderground railroad of trains, planes, and automobiles, shelters and halfway stations. The huge, teeming, mostly not-for-profit marketplace is operated by cadres of truly passionate animal lovers for little or no recompense; collectively, this network is the most important institution in dogdom. Shelters like North Shore are crucial nodes in that network. The rise of the Internet has made it ever more granular and individualized. Sites like Petfinder.com and Petsmart.com now place more dogs than do shelters, and they help shelters find homes for their dogs far from their brick-and-mortar locations. Breed-specific rescue groups can scoop up breeder and puppy mill discards—dogs that used to end up in shelters—and allow people to choose the characteristics they want while also having the satisfactions of rescue. And the AKC, of course, has been eager to get involved with this business, maintaining its brands while trying to stay relevant in a changing world.

Most fundamentally, the dog market is an ongoing transaction between the red states and the blue states, and it's based on the same basic differences in core values that make our presidential elections so dramatic. The flow of dogs, in general, is from south to north, and from flyover country to the coasts. In many places in the south and west, a dog's life just isn't worth as much as it is on the coasts. In the language of Wall Street, this situation presents opportunities for arbitrage, except that the arbitrage is moral. The transaction is especially beautiful morally because the adopter is not only saving the dog from some callous shelter but also denying the transaction to a puppy mill—an industry built to fill the demand for dogs in the blue metropolises. These are the tidal forces that picked Stella up and deposited her on our rug.

In the mid-1980s Mike Arms, director of operations at North Shore, pioneered populating New York with out-of-town dogs. Arms had started his animal career at the ASPCA, after a stint in the military. It wasn't a calling—he went through an employment agency. But his military background might have been an asset. A lot of the staff had similar résumés: his boss was still called colonel. The ASPCA's bureaucratic coldness at that point—its central job was to euthanize New York's unwanted dogs, and it was killing about 140,000 per year in decompression chambers—made him want to seek another line of work. But then one day he saw a dog struck by a car in the Bronx, and the callousness of the bystanders—who were taking bets on when the animal would expire and tried to prevent Arm from taking the dog for treatment—gave him a mission. He knew which side he was on. When North Shore, which had been a no-kill shelter since its inception just after World War II (it was limited-access; it didn't take just any home-less dog that anyone wanted to surrender), offered him a job in adop-tions, he took it. North Shore was a dog marketplace for the central Long Island suburbs, but it also rescued dogs from death row in the ASPCA's facilities in New York City. To start, they were adopting out about eight hundred animals a year. In a decade or so, it was forty thousand.

The secret, says Arms, was that they "started to run it as a busi-ness." North Shore was the first shelter to market and advertise exten-sively. It would do promotions and give away Timex watches or pumpkin pies at Thanksgiving—anything to get people in the door, to overcome the stigma of the shelter and compete with puppy mills and pet shops. In the animal welfare community, marketing was considered sacrilege: it compromised an animal's dignity to be hawked with a cheap watch. But to Arms, the problem was not to care for the animals or to make a case for their personhood; it was to get them out the door. "Animals need your intelligence," he said, "not your heart."

But then the dogs began to dry up. "Between the leash laws and spay/neuter," Arms said, "the young animal count was diminishing. They couldn't meet our demands. They couldn't meet the public's demands."

So Arms got in touch with a humane society director he knew in Greenville, South Carolina. The organization was killing, on average, two hundred puppies a week, Arms told me. "And so we made an agreement with them. We would take their surplus puppies, provided they let us help them build a spay/neuter clinic. And everybody who brought in a litter of puppies, the clinic would spay the mother for free." Arms's trip to Greenville was the beginning of a dog migration that has since grown to a flood. Shortly afterward Arms met a woman in Knoxville named Linda Hutchison who worked in a vet's office. After seeing what happened to unwanted dogs, she developed a passion for saving them. Arms brought her to Long Island and taught her about North Shore's work, and in 1992 she started a shelter called Precious Friends—the place where Stella started her journey.

Precious Friends is in a warehouse in a little industrial park in downtown Clarksville, Tennessee, just up the hill from the floodwaters' crest a couple of springs ago. Clarksville is at the junction of the Cumberland and the Red rivers, an hour north of Nashville. It started its life as a river town, but now its sleepy downtown is something of an afterthought. It is part of an army base, a support facility for Fort Campbell, home of the 101st Airborne Division, which sprawls on 102,000 acres just north of the city into Kentucky. Thirty thousand military people are stationed at the base, along with 63,000 family members, though at any given time more than half the troops might be overseas. Most people in Clarksville are connected to the base in one way or another.

The base makes for a lot of drama at the local shelters, because an army is the classic transient population: soldiers get shipped out or go back to civilian life, and the puppy that anchored the family in the little ranch house on the base is not permitted in the condo in Nashville. "The problem is that the South has a whole different opinion of dogs," Hutchison told me, shaking her head. "Down here they're property."

Linda Hutchison is semiretired now, but she still oversees Precious Friends' operations. She's an indomitable person with a blond bob and a perma-smile, a useful quality when dealing with unwanted animals. Like many people in the rescue movement, her humane

concerns are anchored in a personal understanding of suffering. Decades ago, as a newlywed, she was riding a horse in a parade when
she was hit by a truck and knocked against a phone pole. Her injuries
were horrible—her back was broken in several places.

The pain never completely disappeared—but she eventually got
well enough to crawl under an abandoned house looking for a litter of
puppies or hoist a bag of dog food. Saving dogs became the mission
that drove her. When she forged her connection to North Shore, some
people thought the dogs she collected were going east to laboratories.
That was one of the horror stories of the age—the dog jobber with his
van, carting the dogs off to be cruelly vivisected—more horrible because it sometimes happened to be true. Hutchison actually got a letter
from a New York Chinese restaurant that was interested in puppy meat.

Precious Friends eventually became a clearinghouse for dogs in
kill shelters all over the South. "We get 'em from Alabama, Georgia,
Louisiana, Mississippi, Missouri," Hutchison said. They'd hear about
a shelter and find out what they could take. Sometimes they'd send a
truck out to meet them halfway. Hutchison, a crusader for spay/neuter,
is committed to her cause, but if an epidemic of canine parvovirus ar-
rives, as happened a couple of times in the past, every dog might have
to be euthanized—it's simply too expensive and time-consuming to
treat them. Hutchison is soft-hearted, to a point—she brings her work
home in the form of dogs, five currently—but she also has a professional's distance. "The save-them-all attitude leads to an impossible
situation," she said. "You've got to look at the big picture."

Now, in Kristen Brooks, a golden-haired, thoughtful woman of
twenty-seven, she's found someone who can deal with these pressures.
Brooks's husband is an artillery officer at an FOB in Afghanistan—"he
can't even tell me where," she told me. She stays focused amid the controlled chaos of the shelter, the din of the puppies in the next room,
though sometimes she has a faraway look in her eyes. "The first time he
went away, I had so much anxiety," she said. "I had to learn how to

focus on my job." Now she's learned to compartmentalize, something that helps in dealing with the dogs. She's hyperefficient without being overbearing, an island of sanity, controlling what she can.

In a corner of the warehouse, in free-standing pens, Brooks pointed out a pair of low-riding, shaggy Lab mixes, adults. Their names are Oscar and Sophie. They belonged to a soldier who was killed in Afghanistan the previous month. For reasons that are hard to account for, the soldier's wife gave them away before she told her two young children their father was dead. That must have been a hard day. Brooks couldn't turn the dogs away. And now they're bound for Long Island—their involvement in a tragedy with national resonance makes them adoptable. Their comical shapes give an odd edge to their sad circumstances.

A little while later a shopping cart arrived carrying a load of Stella's relatives: four Lab puppies, eight weeks old or so, pushed by a rough-and-ready-looking woman in a red shirt with long gray hair. From the next county over, she's a regular visitor to Precious Friends. Dog rescuers like her are freelance operators, providing a community service by word of mouth. This is how Stella arrived here, where she was inspected for rashes, vaccinated, and shipped off to the next stage.

Everyone in the shelter world talks about the moral obtuseness of some of their clients: *Come over and get this dog, or I'm going to leave it by the side of the road.* It's a game of chicken, taking advantage of the rescuers' tender feelings. One way people deal with the guilt of giving up a dog is to lash out at those who are taking it. Others with unwanted puppies dispose of them more cruelly. Once, Hutchison said, some kids saw a moving, squirming bag hanging from a tree near the Red River. They managed to get it down and found a litter of week-old puppies, which they delivered to Precious Friends. Lucky little dogs. The standard euthanasia down here is an old pillowcase, some rocks, and a river bridge at night. Or they get thrown in a Dumpster, or buried alive. "We're not living back in that time when you shoot your dog or drown your puppies," said Hutchison, shaking her head, because the problem is that she *is*. It's a basic values conflict. Civilizing people about animals can be a big and frustrating job.

In the afternoon, Brooks took me over to see David Selby, a dark-haired Andy of Mayberry character in a neat uniform who at the time was the city's animal control officer. Selby's job is exasperating and entertaining in equal measure. People release snakes and gators into the wild, which then arrive in surprising places. Last year a man facing foreclosure released his pet wolves into the woods—and they promptly started terrorizing livestock. Wrestling with the human creatures is even tougher. Selby tried to pass a law prohibiting dogs from riding in the backs of pickups, an eminently sensible idea that is barely think-able out here. Selby is amazed at the thoughtlessness of his neighbors. "Most southerners," he said with a shrug, "treat animals like property. If you don't want 'em anymore, take 'em out and shoot 'em, or dump 'em in the woods." That sweltering summer people were leaving their dogs staked out without water or in the car, where the temperature can quickly get to sauna levels and beyond. "You try to educate 'em, make people understand," he said. He told me about a woman who'd been breeding golden retrievers in her basement. Withered creatures at age three, already with cataracts, they'd never seen the light of day.

Most aggravating, Selby told me, are "the ten people a week who come in and say, 'I'm moving. I want you to find a home for my dog.'" What he wants to say is, *Let me look up the definition of companion animal.* Instead, he tells it to them straight: the dogs will likely have three days, if that, and that's it. They get ticked off, he told me. *You ain't gonna give my dog a chance?* "Well, what kind of chance did they give it?"

The dogs have three days here, though the ones Selby deems adoptable may stay indefinitely. He took Brooks and me into his ken-nels to look at ones that might fit Precious Friends' qualifications. A couple of fierce-looking brown, brindled pits had been confiscated for terrorizing their neighbors. Fearsome creatures, they were doing what they'd been taught, the only thing they knew, but they probably couldn't be saved. A couple of cages down were a pair of winning, personable, floppy-eared hounds. A boy on a bike selling cookies had passed their house, and they'd chased him for two miles, knocked him down, and left him in the hospital with multiple stitches. The owner was arrested and was now out on bond. Those dogs too had lost their chance. In another cage was a blue-eyed white shepherd that could have been a twin of one that Brooks just sent to North Shore. She had a shot, but it wasn't a sure thing.

Selby is a compassionate man, a dog lover and concerned for his neighbors, despite their conflicting ideas. But the dog population around here is too large. Last year they took in eight thousand dogs. "Forty-two percent were euthanized," he told me, fixing me with his eyes, as if to make sure I understood that he was ready to be judged for this number. I'd heard much worse, but that's still a lot of dogs to kill. "You keep knocking your head against the problem," he said. Now he's hooked in with a North Shore–like organization called Rescue Waggin', which will take some of his dogs to the West Coast. "We'll see if that works," he says.


*What's this country coming to when a man can't shoot his own dog?* I thought often of Ray Coppinger's bumper sticker, so jarring to eastern ears, when I was in Clarksville, because that northern Tennessee country hadn't come to any such thing. In some places in the South, shooting dogs that have somehow transgressed, as well as those that are old and sick, is practically an institution. It can be a matter of necessity—many places have no public animal control facilities, so for nuisance dogs, there is no other option. But it's also a deeply held cultural attitude. To many a southerner, the kind that David Selby deals with every day, the notion that a dog is entitled to humanlike treatment is simply loopy. The dog belongs on the farmyard, and the farm belongs to the farmer, and that's the way it's always been.

Everyone out here still talks about places back in the woods where nothing much has changed except the models of the cars. It's something to be proud of and afraid of simultaneously, a wellspring of the culture—and no doubt partly mythological. And yet for all the cruelty, the backwoods must be a paradise for dogs. What would a coonhound rather do than tree a coon? I imagine rural dogs lying in the dirt, waiting for the next thing to chase.

Freedom means something different in a place like this, even for a dog. You might end up in the woods, on the trail of a coon, happy as a dog can be; or you might end up at the end of a chain in the hot sun and the cold rain, barking at any human who comes near. The notion of controlling these outcomes can seem crazy. If a dog ends up suffering, that's just what happens. Why get the government involved?

It's the city people who don't understand that softheartedness would get in the way of getting the farmwork done, and then everyone would starve. Seamus Heaney's bitter coming-of-age poem, "The Early Purges," gets at this sense, from a different rural culture:

> And now, when shrill pups are prodded to drown
> I just shrug, "Bloody pups." It makes sense:
> "Prevention of cruelty" talk cuts ice in town
> Where they consider death unnatural
> But on well-run farms pests have to be kept down.

Empathy for animals is a luxury that rural folk cannot always afford. It isn't that they don't appreciate their dogs, the ones put in the bucket under the spigot. You have to put those unlucky ones out of your mind.

To many people out here, it seems that the regiments of the nanny state are marching in from the North and East, much as the bluecoats did a century and a half ago, bringing their unwelcome, restrictive laws, telling people how to run farms. Dogs are in a complicated position, as always. Everyone wants at least some baseline regulation of puppy mills. They shouldn't be like chicken farms: chickens are raised to be chopped into pieces, while dogs are going to live in people's homes. The consensus is growing that dogs shouldn't become honorary persons merely at the point of sale—that would be more hypocrisy than the public could bear. In 2009 Tennessee passed commonsense puppy mill legislation by a huge margin. Even in Missouri, a state where puppy sales are a major industry—30 percent of the national business—the Humane Society of the United States managed to pass a referendum limiting puppy mill activities.

But in Texas and North Carolina, puppy mill legislation has been checked by the agricultural lobby, which realizes that once a dog gets its nose under the tent, cows and chickens and pigs may soon follow. Wayne Pacelle, head of the Humane Society of the United States, in his elegant suits, looks perfect on Washington's K Street (he was the Humane Society's chief lobbyist for a decade), but in many states he's an alien, bringing alien ways, sensible though they are for animals. As an undergraduate at Yale in 1985, Pacelle formed an animal rights organization and, with the idealism of youth, said some pretty radical things. In an interview for a book called *Bloodties*, author Ted Kerasote asked him whether, in the future, the practice of pet keeping might be abolished. "If I had my personal view," he said, "that might take hold. In fact, I don't want to see another dog or cat born."

But that was a long time ago. Since then Pacelle's youthful arid animal philosophy, and his dream of a society without human guilt or hypocrisy in relation to other creatures, has been deeply submerged if it still exists at all. Dogs are central to the Humane Society: its puppy mill work is amazing and supplies a steady stream of good public relations. The Humane Society's huge fund-raising effort is based on the perception, only partly accurate, that one of its central activities is caring for homeless dogs and cats.

HumaneWatch, an organization run by Rick Berman, a PR man who works frequently for the farm lobby, is trying to decouple dogs from the Humane Society's broader animal mission. Its newspaper advertisements broadcast the fact that the Humane Society spends less than 1 percent of its budget supporting animal shelters. Berman accurately diagnosed his clients' issue: a humane concern for dogs could be a gateway drug that leads to stronger stuff, like concern for pigs and chickens. He wants people to focus on their pets and not on what's happening in the factory farms. But with its enormous war chest and its shrewdly ecumenical message, the Humane Society may have reached a place that Berman and his allies can't reach even in heartland states, pressing commonsense reforms about animal treatment. Who doesn't believe that animals should be able to turn around in their cages?

Because some of the commonsense regulations that have been proposed are hard to argue against, HumaneWatch's sell against the Humane Society is that these kinds of initiatives are the first step in a wholesale revision of the rural way of life.

Who knows what kind of life Stella might have had in the land of her birth? Maybe no life at all—everyone says black dogs are not the preferred dogs to adopt out here (although one then wonders why so many seem to be produced). Or maybe it would have been some kind of country idyll, chasing rabbits and riding in the back of a pickup truck. But instead, she got on a van going to New York City.

The day after I met with Brooks and Hutchison, the North Shore van was being loaded with dogs for New York. James and Claire, the drivers, are an antic pair—a comedy duo with no straight man. Claire was wearing sunglasses and has a broad Long Island accent. James has a stud in his tongue. I asked them about their driving rituals. "The driver has control of the radio," James said. "She likes country, but it scratches my ears till they bleed." They're hugely entertained by each other, which, on a drive of seventeen hours or so, can come in handy. Out on the road, with all those dogs, they're celebrities—anywhere they stop, everyone wants to see the dogs, a wish they occasionally grant.

It was a happy day, but tense. Every dog had a number and a history, written in the puppy book, a black binder on one of the old school desks. Brooks and a veterinarian were at the table, administering shots and checking for rashes. In a shelter, puppies' health inevitably decays. It was like Noah's Ark, a procession of animals going to populate a new world. The Lab mixes Oscar and Sophie gamboled out the door into the bright sun, with no idea where they might end up. They got bigger cages than the rest, like celebrities with special dressing rooms. Then came a litter of Great Pyrenees mixes, huge already at nine weeks, with paws the size of softballs. Their hocks quivered on the stainless steel table as Hackett and Brooks checked their teeth and administered their vaccinations. Then they were slung over the shoulder of a shelter worker, and out the door they went, looking back at their old world as they moved toward their new one.

Next came the Labs. A lot of them were white-toed, with white blazes on their chests, reverting to their original St. John's form. The truck was filling up. Already it was bedlam, a rolling dog party. This had been Stella's journey. She's never liked to ride in cars, and I often think, with no evidence, that her passage from Tennessee to North Shore had something to do with it—a minor scar. The turbulent formative months of shelter dogs—they're caged and institutionalized, no matter how much loving attention is provided—is a flaw in the system. An animal's early life, as much as its genes, defines who it is, and animals that have been mistreated, or even simply caged, can end up with all sorts of issues. These issues don't necessarily change our love for our pets; if anything, they can augment it. But it's one of the ways in which the rescue system, so admirable in many respects, is imperfect. If you had to design a way to produce the nation's dogs, this wouldn't be it. Lobbyists for commercial breeders argue that these problems, along with dog shortages in many places, suggest that regulations on breeding should be relaxed. But that'd be like letting the fox into the henhouse.

After all the dogs were loaded, we got into Brooks's SUV to drive out into the countryside—Stella's homeland was somewhere out there.

We were going to visit Shelly Greenlee, a frequent source of Precious Friends' dogs, who lives in Houston County, where there is no animal control authority. Hutchison's grandson Cody, a wiry twenty-two-year-old, was driving. He'd been to school for underwater construction, but his plans to work on the Gulf Coast rigs had been thwarted by the BP disaster. The trip was an adventure for Brooks and Cody too, even though it was only thirty miles from Clarksville. As we drove along, Brooks pointed out a convict weeding in black-and-white-striped prison livery. Tobacco was drying on trailered ricks. Outside Lucky's, a gas station and convenience store where we stopped for a drink, a man in a long white beard sat in a lawn chair with a couple of black and white dogs at his feet, watching the world go by. Some teenagers cooled off by jumping off a bridge into Yellow Creek. Just by looking at them with my New York eyes, I was making their life a cartoon, just as they might if they saw me running down for the *Times* in my bathrobe, or saying the word *latte* (even I cringe), or putting on my bicycle helmet for my ride to work.

Greenlee's house is just past the Montgomery County line, a quarter mile into Houston County—one of the most remote outposts of the New York dog republic. A blue plastic tarp covered her roof, and a couch and chairs stood on the front porch, moved there to make room for the forty dogs inside. Greenlee is a wiry woman approaching fifty, with a tanned and weathered face and long, graying blond hair. A couple of horses stood behind the house. One, Greenlee told me, was twenty-eight years old, destined for the knacker until she intervened. The other was totally blind. "This is the misfit house," she said.

A former army brat, Greenlee is queen of this peaceable kingdom, with its fiercely protective ethic, though she still has emissaries in the regular world. She grew up around Clarksville, got married, moved away, drove a truck for years, got divorced, moved back, and was called to this work, which is a mixed blessing. She knows what she does is necessary, but it's a heavy weight she's carrying. "They call me the witch out here, 'cause they'll bring me a half-dead animal, and I'll nurse it

back to health," she said. "Dogs need human nurturing." She serves as
a vet, stitching up animals for free. The physical part is hard enough,
eighteen-hour days. Her dogs, some of which seem bigger than she is,
drag her around on their leashes, dislocating her shoulder. "They're
good people out here, a lot of poor people, good hunters who eat what
they kill," she said, hands on hips. But others, she said with a shake of
her white hair, were just interested in blood, "seeing the coon hit the
ground, and the dogs setting upon it."

Or they take their aging coonhound up for its last hunt and set it
loose. Or they shoot it and maybe fail to kill it. Or they drop off a pregnant dog on Greenlee's lawn. She is a connoisseur of these horrors,
man's inhumanity to dog; she knows her enemy. Coming home from
her missions, she sometimes sees a car stopped on the bridge in the
night. "I know what they're doing," she said, eyes narrowing. "A bag in
their hand, with a few rocks in it, tied shut. I do not like most humans.
I do not."

She sleeps in a Sandpiper trailer, which is also the nursery. She has
a beagle mom, an abandoned hunting dog that she spent weeks trying
to catch, with a few week-old puppies. Squirming little things, their
eyes trying to blink open, they will eventually be New York dogs, when
they're old enough for North Shore to ship them.

Greenlee wouldn't let us see inside the house, but brought out a
procession of dogs, hard-luck cases, each with its own story. They were
well groomed and well fed—a little too well fed, in some cases. A pair
of little Lhasa apsos emerged, puppy mill breeders who'd outlived their
usefulness; their tongues lolled out of their toothless mouths. Next
was a cute and cowering little pit—she was covered with scars, missing
pieces of her ears. Her legs looked like they'd been chewed on. She'd
been used as bait, practice for fighting dogs. Each time Greenlee went
back into the house, a tremendous, house-shaking baying ensued, a
magical sound that I felt in my chest.

Once, Greenlee told me, a neighbor pointed to her horse and
said, "Jeez, he's just an eating machine. Why don't you just have him

put down?" Greenlee said, "Hey Bill! You're limping a lot on that leg—yep, maybe someone should put you down too. At least he keeps my lawn mowed pretty good. You know, we all have something wrong with us, every last one."

Cody was eager to get back to Clarksville because he had a date that night. Driving back through the lush countryside, he pointed out the pond where he caught his first catfish—it almost pulled him in while his father was readying the net. Then: schools, tract houses, traffic signals. "Now I feel like we're back in America," Cody said.

# Fourteen.

# The Birth of Empathy

The kinds of attitudes that drove Stella on her surprising migration from rural Tennessee to the heart of Manhattan are also a product of the Victorian age. The eighteenth and nineteenth centuries saw the rise of a new empathy for animals (reflecting the new science of animal intelligence); it retreated in the early to mid-twentieth century, but it has now returned with greater force. And the dog is again a signal species—its place in our homes is an argument for how other animals should be treated. It's a great awakening that's still a work in progress.

The Old Testament is fairly stern on the subject of dogs. In fact, it seems to single dogs out for particular derision. In no sense is the biblical dog an honorary human (though some particularly problematic people are said to be lower than dogs). Mostly they're associated with filth and carrion, threatening to eat corpses that haven't been properly buried.

Descartes, for all his philosophical radicalism, essentially gave a modern imprimatur to the biblical understanding of our dominion over animals, saying that reason was the essential quality from which all other human rights descended. The Enlightenment arrived at the dog in 1789, when Jeremy Bentham reacted against Descartes, comparing the capacities of animals with those of certain incredibly valuable members of the human group. "A full-grown horse or dog," he wrote, "is beyond comparison a more rational, as well as a more conversable animal, than an infant of a day or a week or even a month, old. But suppose the case were otherwise, what would it avail? The question is not, Can they reason? nor, Can they talk? but, Can they suffer?"

Bentham, who had a "beautiful pig" at his house at Hendon that he liked to scratch with a stick, or chuck under the chin, like a dog (though he was, most passionately, a cat lover), made in passing a powerful argument that reason, by itself, was a very infirm foundation on which to base morality. The crucial quality was an animal's feelings, he maintained—specifically of pain.

Scientists like Romanes and Morgan could debate the degree to which dogs could think. But finally it's laughable—a form of madness, really—to argue that animals can't feel pain. And implicit in the notion of animal suffering is an assumption of animal consciousness. The struggles of a dog that was being vivisected weren't merely reflexes. Bentham opened the door to animal consciousness; feeling implied a feeler. Benthamism also famously reduced life to arithmetic, putting pleasure and pain on a ledger. The balance sheet approach was perfect for the coming industrial age, obviously not by coincidence. Bentham's conception of animal suffering was a useful idea, but it wasn't always a beautiful one. He made compassion scalable.

Until fairly late in the Enlightenment, empathy was confined to the smallest of circles: the family. No one thought to manage the suffering in the whole world—that was God's job. And even to try would have been a fool's errand—suffering could no more be prevented than the tides.

One of the things that flowered in the modern mind was an appreciation of the horror of pain, as James Turner's excellent social history *Reckoning with the Beast* points out. William James wrote in

1901 that a moral transformation had occurred in the century past: "We no longer think that we are supposed to face physical pain with equanimity."

Expanding the circle of human concern to animals was certainly altruistic, based on the realization that they too could suffer. But the impetus for the humane revolution was only partly concern for the suffering of animals. The other crucial factor was that newly civilized people didn't want to witness these things—the kinds of things that the lower classes, the unenlightened, seemed to take particular pleasure in, according to the classist conventional wisdom of the time. Civilized people certainly felt sympathy for the feelings of the animals, but also horror for those who weren't enlightened, for people who wanted to see bulls torn apart by dogs, a brutal and appalling practice in which some of the dogs died too, a primal, bloody conflict.

This atavism was something the self-consciously civilized class saw as their mission to stamp out wherever they found it. Concern for animals was a badge of refinement, a commitment to the progress of civilization—a luxury, and often a kind of snobbery. And it was an urban concern. In nineteenth-century London, as in any city, no matter how starched your collar might have been, you couldn't get away from seeing a drover beat his horse. Everything was visible. The early empathy movement was partly a way to make the city safe for the civilized.

In America, the unlikely focus of this nineteenth-century obsession was a wealthy, drifting middle-aged heir named Henry Bergh. Born in 1813 to a Manhattan shipbuilder, Bergh attended Columbia College but didn't graduate; he worked perfunctorily at the family business, while maintaining an active presence on the elite social circuit of New York, Saratoga Springs, and Washington D.C., with his wife, Matilda. Bergh was a stiff man with an elongated face and an extravagant mustache, but his fierce dignity and self-possession prevented him from seeming ridiculous. He had exquisite manners and a gift for language. In 1847 he ended his career pretenses and embarked on a three-year tour of Europe, where his eyes began to open.

In Spain, Bergh and Matilda attended several bullfights and were appalled by the brutality. At one of them, twenty horses were gored to death, and eight bulls were killed, to the delight of the crowd, but not to the two Americans. "Never before has a similar degree of disgust been experienced by us," he confided to his diary, "or such a hearty degree of contempt for people calling themselves civilized and at the same time Christian." A trip to Russia awakened his interest in a career in diplomacy, whereupon he managed to get Lincoln's secretary of state, William Seward, also a New Yorker, to appoint him head of the American legation in Moscow. Bergh's refinements served him well in the position—he was a favorite of the tsar, who even once lent him his yacht.

One day on a grand avenue in St. Petersburg, Bergh's carriage, with its liveried coachmen, turned a corner, and angry shouting caught his attention. A cart horse had come up lame in its right foreleg, and the droshky driver was shouting and beating it on the neck with a stick. Bergh ordered his coachman—in French, the St. Petersburg lingua franca—to stop and tell the droshky driver to cease beating his horse. "Can't he see the poor brute is injured?" Bergh said, as recounted in *Heritage of Care*, Marion Lane and Stephen Zawistowski's 2007 history of the ASPCA. The droshky driver at first was incredulous, but then, apparently dazzled by Bergh's elegant coach and liveried coachman, put away his stick. The effectiveness of this tactic delighted Bergh, who used it many times afterward. In this one area, he could bend the world to his will—which turned out to be what he was searching for. "Encouraged by my success," he later wrote, "I made up my mind that when I returned home I would prosecute those who persecuted poor dumb brutes and would try to compel justice to the lower animals from whom man derives two-thirds of the benefits he enjoys."

Early humanitarians were kooks and eccentrics, like Humanity Martin, who lived up to his name. But the tender sensitivities of the rising class, and the unruliness of the growing cities, were powerful drivers of the new sensibility. Bull baiting was the first target of organized humanitarians. Animal cruelty of this kind was seen as leading to all manner of other vices. The British SPCA, formed in 1824, became mainstream within three decades, attracting a steady procession of royals, including in 1837 the Duchess of Kent and her daughter, Princess Victoria. This was trickle-down humanity, the civilizing mercies flowing downward from the upper classes in the form of educational tracts and lectures and revised schoolbooks.

It was into this glamorous world that Bergh arrived in 1865, and he liked all of it. He liked royalty and their evening-dress universe, and he liked the SPCA's "glittering roster of luminaries," he wrote. He admired Humanity Martin's willingness to bear ridicule in pursuit of his chosen end, seeing it as evidence of his strength of character and nobility. When he returned to New York, Bergh leveraged his social connections, pounding the cobblestones to enlist a quorum of New York's aristocracy to sign a kind of petition, self-consciously modeled on the Declaration of Independence, if not exactly with Jefferson's prosody. "The undersigned," he wrote, "sensible of the cruelties inflicted upon Dumb Animals by thoughtless and inhuman persons; and desirous of suppressing the same—alike from considerations affecting the moral well being of society, as well as mercy to the brute creation: consent to become patrons of a Society having in view the realization of these objects."

Bergh's new organization, the ASPCA, was given statutory power to enforce new animal welfare laws. Humane agents—"Bergh's men," as they were known—spread across New York City, the scourge of dog catchers and horse beaters—but most visible was Bergh, his sad-eyed visage and impeccable dress the symbol of his new enterprise.

For all its universalist ideals, the new animal welfare movement was a distinctly upper-class passion—it was good and merciful, but it was also "smart," a fact that pleased Bergh. "Already it is fashionable to defend the friendless dumb brute," he later wrote. However much his heart bled for the mistreated brutes, early animal welfare was also about who would rule the city, whose codes would be in the ascendant.

As much as making the city safe for animals, Bergh made the city safer for refined, aristocratic sensibilities. He was a class warrior.

Dogs, at first, were not at the center of Bergh's concern. New York was overrun with them. While rag merchants and others who couldn't afford horses used dogs to pull carts, and some were used to power rotisseries, mostly they were just there, in swarms. Periodically, the dog catcher would come in his wagon and take them to the pound. The majority were put in iron cages and swung out on a crane, to be drowned in the East River, a hundred at a time. It was an image of bedlam, the seething heedlessness of the modern city, not far from brownstones where lapdogs lounged. But unlike horses and livestock, dogs and cats were seen as a threat, because of rabies. Bergh (accurately) insisted that the fear of rabies was highly overstated and irrational; he called for an end to the indiscriminate slaughter of "these harmless and confiding friends of mankind."

At that time, the dog was being reinvented as an accessory of aspirational life, an impulse in harmony with Bergh's project—the new fascinations with dog breeding and humane treatment came together. He spoke at the first meeting of the Westminster Kennel Club in 1877, stressing in the cacophony of Madison Square Garden that such wonderful creatures could have been bred only by people who truly cared for their welfare. A portion of the proceeds of the event, $1297.25, went to the ASPCA in order to found a home for dogs. The next year Bergh skipped the speech and wrote a letter. "The purpose of all cultivated thought is to seek for the highest development," he said. "To this end institutions of learning are established, and mankind are ennobled thereby. There seems to be no just reason why this spirit of intellectual progress should not apply to all the sentient beings that come under the dominion of man." Bergh went on to enumerate dog excellences: fidelity, courage, vigilance, gratitude, generosity. "Go on, gentlemen, in your noble undertaking, for it means progress, beauty, refinement."

Across town at the city pound, conditions were anything but noble. Dog catchers, notoriously brutal and conniving, even kidnapped family pets for ransom. The city, under constant fire from Bergh for the pound's appalling conditions, asked him several times to take over its animal control responsibilities, but he resisted. Bergh wasn't necessarily against euthanasia. But he saw, presciently, that caring for stray dogs was work that the public should pay for itself; taking the job would dilute his own organization's advocacy mission.

When Bergh died in 1888, the Victorian world was almost at twilight. Cities were being wired with trolleys and elevated trains, and the animals that once filled the streets had been moved to the outskirts. The public drama over enforcement of animal cruelty laws was nearing its end. And the urban chaos of the early nineteenth century, when streets had been shared by livestock and drovers and gentlemen alike, had become rationalized. The brutal work of providing meat for the ever-growing population was now performed out of sight, where a public man like Bergh wouldn't encounter it. Cruelty took place in locales where it didn't compromise the city's civility. Sometimes it burst forth, as in Upton Sinclair's famous exposé, but most people were happy to avert their eyes and not contemplate where their meat really came from. After Bergh's death, dogs and cats moved to the center of the ASPCA's mission. In 1894 the ASPCA contracted with the city to take over its animal control responsibilities.

After Bergh, the animal welfare movement lost much of its energy, as well as its central place in the nineteenth-century mind. It had managed to change the treatment of animals, partly by pushing them out of public view. Its last important battle was over vivisection, a Continental specialty, regarded with horror and alarm, but not all that common in Britain or the United States. Around 1870, the war against it began in earnest. Scientists—with their burgeoning cultural confidence—asserted that it was necessary for their work. But the humane community and much of the public howled in outrage over the apparent hypocrisy: men of science, in their white coats, with their gleaming instruments, were the supposed flower of civilization, and yet they were the most brutal. The racks used to restrain the dogs are chilling to look at, torture machines bringing to mind some of the contraptions used in Henry VIII's time. It was an Orwellian contradiction—injuring is helping. But at first the scientists weren't helping much of anything—their research was too basic.

By the 1880s, nineteenth-century research using vivisection had produced very little in the way of actual cures. Even the progress of bacteriologists like Louis Pasteur failed to impress the antivivisectionists, who questioned the science. Pasteur's 1885 discovery of the cause of rabies was a worldwide sensation. But the humane community reviled his work in particular. Bergh had argued that rabies was caused by animal cruelty. When four Newark boys who'd been bitten by a rabid dog were taken to Pasteur in Paris for a cure, humane advocates denied that the animal was rabid. In place of bacteriology, the humane forces stressed sanitation, which had, in fact, greatly improved public health over the past half century.

The schism between the humane and the scientific worlds was widening. To doctors, the suffering of some animals was simply the cost of doing business. How were you supposed to make progress if you didn't make sacrifices? But the humane forces saw that choice as a perversion of morality: choosing to cause animal suffering meant losing morality. Since the mid-nineteenth century, the technical complexity of science had been expanding at warp speed—and it was an alienating development. What had once been done by gentlemen in their libraries was now done by men in special coats in the bowels of impressive new university buildings. Scientists were a new kind of priesthood, an elect, who insisted on the primacy of their own values against the soft morality of ordinary people. They were suspiciously remote from the cozy home-and-hearth notions so comforting to the Victorians. And they thought nothing of carving up a dog or a horse to find out—what?

Then in the 1880s, using techniques that they'd honed while practicing on animals, doctors in England saved a series of patients by removing brain tumors, which had previously been uniformly fatal. The rabies vaccine came in 1885. Along with rabies, diphtheria was one of the terrors of the Victorian world, a terrible strangling disease that killed four in ten of the infants who contracted it. But an international group that had isolated a germ that caused the disease discovered that it was soluble in liquid, then used Pasteur's attenuation technique to create a vaccine. The vaccine, first tested on a human in Paris in 1891, worked. Ultimately, animal lovers were forced to choose between their civilized and civilizing concern for dumb animals, and their tender feelings for their own children. In the debate over the diphtheria vaccine, scientists could appeal to the most sacred and inviolable human feeling: love for children. "Determine, if you can, how many dogs lives and how much dogs suffering it would take to equal the lives saved and sufferings prevented in our children by this mode of treatment," wrote Dr. John Madden, a Milwaukee physiology professor, in arguing against antivivisectionists. "A hundred weeping mothers," wrote Charles Richet, a physiologist and serotherapy pioneer, in a provivisection tract, showing a keen rhetorical gift, "a hundred unfortunate children with gaping throats, suffocating, gasping, the death rattle at hand—that is what these sensitive souls declare is nothing beside one rabbit which has had to receive a little blood of a dog into its abdomen."

After the diphtheria vaccine, the door to the laboratory—and to the animal shelter's euthanasia room—was closed, and no one looked inside for a few decades. The vivisection debate never completely disappeared, but the arguments against it lost most of their force. And more generally, the humane movement reached a kind of steady state of concern for dogs and cats. It was part of the web of American institutions, not leading or following but doing its part.

For now, the ASPCA provided a pretty good solution to the cruelty problem, at least compared with what came before. The cage, that image of nineteenth-century bedlam, of the pain and fear and loneliness that accompany a city being born, passed into history. Strays and unwanted pets were killed—sad but necessary work. A painless death for these poor creatures was the best that could be hoped. For the next fifty years, the lives of animals in shelters became a secret guilt of the modern world, a dark place in the many-roomed mansion of the industrial economy. Few imagined that unwanted dogs shouldn't be euthanized; the world was just arranged so that ordinary people wouldn't have to think about it.

# Fifteen

# The Rights of Dog

The 1970s were the decade when all manner of cultural consensuses broke apart, and liberation movements blossomed in the wreckage. People suddenly wanted to know what kinds of horrors were perpetrated in their name. Dogs too (and animals in general) had their day. Phyllis Wright of the Humane Society and others had prepared the ground by calling attention to the gargantuan size of the unwanted-dog problem. But the real sea change in the status of dogs, the one that would give birth to the no-kill movement, began in 1979 with one dog. She was Sido, an eleven-year-old, fox-faced tan and white sheltie mix whose mistress, Mary Murphy, was found dead in her apartment, having committed suicide. Sido was taken to the San Francisco SPCA, which at that time provided the city's animal control functions. Murphy intended her death to be a suicide pact; she stipulated in her will that Sido should be euthanized. The provision was humanitarian, by her standards and those of the day: Sido was her dog; who could love her as she did? She worried that the dog would end up in an animal experimentation lab—a reasonable concern.

For decades dogs had been killed in huge numbers in American shelters, but people were only just beginning to take notice. The San Francisco SPCA's new director, Richard Avanzino, saw dogs not as possessions but as beings, something like people, with their own inherent rights. "We didn't think the dead hand from the grave should be able to determine the life of this precious being," he told me recently. "I hadn't bought into the litany that death is a humane exit for our companion animals, that we are doing them a kindness by taking their lives."

Avanzino, who is now president of Maddie's Fund, refused to surrender Sido to the estate's executrix, Rebecca Wells Smith, who promptly sued to gain possession of the dog. So Avanzino set about making Sido into a celebrity, which wasn't difficult, as she was a vivacious, confident, winning creature who bonded with reporters. Sido and Avanzino were photographed frolicking, riding in his car, and touring the Marin headlands near the Golden Gate. Sido slept in Avanzino's bed. Smith rounded up significant forces, including the Humane Society, which maintained that euthanasia was a perfectly acceptable outcome for a dog. But Smith's team was no match for Avanzino's sunny relentlessness, masterful public advocacy, and use of a technique borrowed from civil rights activists—he said he'd go to jail rather than surrender her.

The publicity made Smith seem like the Wicked Witch. And Sido's charm—"it was as if she'd been ordered from central casting," Avanzino told me—made killing her seem monstrous. Who would want to hurt that little dog? In a stampede of sentiment, the state legislature passed a bill, specifically designed to save Sido's life, banning almost all will-stipulated euthanasia.

The campaign to save Sido prefigured many of the themes of the dog rescue movement that subsequently emerged. The dog was presumed to have rights independent of the wishes of its owner. It called into question the shelter's view that euthanasia was a humane and unobjectionable way to manage society's homeless dog population. And it showed how the use of publicity—especially showing dogs' eyes to elicit human concern—could be the most powerful weapon in the humane movement. Three thousand people wanted to take little Sido home, but Avanzino took her himself—she lived for another five years. The case changed public attitudes.

Meanwhile animal shelters had an endemic institutional neurosis. Shelter workers didn't want to think of themselves as killers—quite the opposite—but nonetheless they killed. That paradox has been at the core of the shelter system ever since 1894, when the ASPCA first contracted with New York City to perform its animal control duties. Public ignorance about what went on in the shelter was beneficial. Workers had the sense of being an elect, of doing something that the public wouldn't do for itself. Their "defense mechanism," said Avanzino, was to tell themselves, "'It's not our fault, we really care, but we're the instruments, a solution for an irresponsible public.'" And they took pride in being able not only to manage the grim job of killing but to grasp the moral complexity that it required. Tufts sociologist Arnold Arluke calls it the caring-killing paradox.

Sido's case changed this situation by shining a light on the shelter world. "What I realized," Avanzino told me, "was that if you tell people of the animal's distress, the emergency rescue instinct of the American people rallies, and they step forward, and they're very generous and kind and supportive." But simply shining that light turned out to be complicated. Shelter workers tended to think that the public could not bear that much reality.

Sometimes when a person handed an animal over to a shelter, they would bluster a simple "now it's your problem" and be done with it. But in far more cases the transaction was a kabuki of blame displacement: a family member was said to have an allergy, or a neighbor complained about barking, or a landlord didn't allow dogs. Often the dog itself got blamed—it had failed at being a pet. Those who would give up their animals always had someone to pass the responsibility along to, where the buck would stop.

The secrecy of the shelter was like the secrecy of the laboratory, or the factory farm, or the military industrial complex—rooms in the mansion that were necessary but best kept hidden. In the 1950s and 1960s, we were supposed to believe in the system. You could choose how much blood you wanted on your hands—choice being one of the benefits of our industrialized economy.

But Avanzino's radical idea was that the public, rather than being cordoned off from in this work, could be part of the solution. An avuncular man, a peacemaker, he began to involve the public in the work of saving dogs. By reconceiving the role of the public, he changed the practice of the SPCA.

The old order was finally broken apart by Ed Duvin, who worked for Avanzino at the San Francisco SPCA. In a 1989 manifesto called "In the Name of Mercy," he condemned the shelter system as "a vast killing machine," and, in what must have been a conscious echo of the factory farm, he called the shelter system "an assembly line of slaughter." He used the language of business, or organizational goals, and put numbers on the hypocrisies that Avanzino had pointed out. "How can they have the audacity to primarily blame the public for the killing," wrote Duvin, "when some four percent of the total shelter budget is spent on education."

Duvin didn't spare the public. He suggested that the killing be brought out into the open so that the public could know the consequences of its irresponsibility. "The breeding of companion animals, including pure breeds," must become stigmatized, "as those who breed for any reason are complicit in perpetuating the confinement and killing of precious beings."

"In the Name of Mercy" is an amazing manifesto, spraying fire in all directions. The truth it held self-evident, a leap at the time, was that every animal deserved consideration—that these weren't statistics, but individual lives. It was especially scathing to shelter workers, but that was only half of its brilliance. The other half was to provide a plan to rebuild what it had just torn down. The SPCAs would have to give up their animal control contracts. Duvin proposed that their role be replaced by volunteer programs, and he urged community outreach,

communication in industry at a national level, more professional management, and better statistics so that progress could be measured.

The next year, 1990, Avanzino began to put Duvin's ideas into practice. He gave up the SPCA's animal control contract with the city, which
was the crucial step. No longer would it be responsible for euthanizing
animals or dealing with every hard case that came in. Instead, its mission would be purely to save animals and to convince the public of the
importance of this mission. That is, Duvin and Avanzino set the city and
the nation on the road to no-kill. They aggressively pushed spay/neuter
programs, at reduced or, in some cases, no cost. They began programs
for off-site adoptions, both to adopt animals and to advertise their
wares—these precious dogs. They fostered out some animal inmates to
make room for others and to stretch their budget. With socialization
and training, they taught people how to live with their animals, and
they trained animals to live with their people. Volunteers were key: not
only did they help with the workload, but they tended to adopt more
than their share of animals, and they brought in their friends to do the
same. Rather than a grim place on the outskirts of town, the shelter
became a part of the community. Soon the number of healthy animals
that were euthanized in San Francisco dropped to zero.

San Francisco, as is so often the case, was the paragon, with a hint
of utopia that was exceedingly difficult to capture elsewhere. Consider
nearby San Mateo, which had an impressive record of progress in its
care of dogs and cats. In 1970, it had opened a low-cost spay/neuter
clinic, at a time when most people were only just beginning to see its
value. Despite the town's long-standing commitment to reducing the
number of euthanasias, however, its Peninsula Humane Society was
killing some ten thousand pets a year in secret—their bodies were held
in a refrigerated room, to be picked up by a rendering company and
turned into fertilizer. "There's not a day goes by that you don't think of
walking away from this misery," Chris Powell, the shelter's executive director, told the *New York Times*. But it was difficult to get people to care.

"I'm sick of it," animal lover Kim Sturla, who worked at the shelter, told one paper. "We want to get out of the business of killing animals and back to protecting them." In 1990, she and her colleagues proposed a moratorium on breeding dogs and cats, for consideration by the town board; if passed, it would be the first such statute in the nation. She bought two-page ads in three local papers, exposing the secret of the shelters: the ads showed barrels of dead animals, paws hanging over the sides. The headline read, "We Couldn't Do It Without You." She invited TV cameras and newspaper reporters to the shelter to see what daily life there was like. Live on television, she and her staff injected four kittens and three dogs with lethal amounts of sodium pentobarbital. "You have to see it to experience the immorality of it," she said. Some reporters couldn't watch. It was a stunning piece of political theater, and it certainly got people's attention.

Both she and Avanzino were reacting to the horror of having to euthanize animals they loved, animals they'd sworn to care for. Where Avanzino saw the problem as institutional, Sturla, along with many other shelter workers, saw the problem as the moral obtuseness of the American public. The burden of killing those animals in secret had become too great, and she wanted the public to take responsibility for it. "We tried to tell the public with numbers, but it didn't work," she told the *Times*. "It's time to take a two-by-four and hit them over the head."

Today Sturla runs a sanctuary called Animal Place outside Sacramento, where livestock and poultry that have somehow escaped the assembly-line carnage of the industrial meat complex live out their days, along with roosters that have run afoul of their neighbors. In moral terms, it's absolutely pure. Sturla no longer has any blood on her hands, of any species. But in terms of life-saving, it's a drop in the bucket. Places like this are like monasteries, where people devote their lives to the beauty of an idea. Some animals are saved, and Sturla and her colleagues can be certain that they are part of the solution—but as to saving the world, it's magical thinking. It's a beautiful symbol, but it leaves to others the complicated ethics and practical institutions of dealing with the number of animals killed in our industrial society.

As of April 1994, San Francisco was officially no-kill, meaning that no healthy animals were being euthanized for space. Dogs that were once statistics became individuals, then anecdotes, which is the point of dog rescue. At least here, Duvin's vision was fulfilled. The shelter had gone from a place of darkness and fear to a place open for all to see. It had an army of volunteers, a much stronger fund-raising picture, and oceans of favorable publicity. But most important, the image of the shelter as a place of sadness, where an adopter could easily think that as he chose one dog he was consigning others to death, was over.

The movement didn't solve the whole problem—which created a new kind of problem. In the aftermath of Avanzino's success, many SPCAs and private shelters had a eureka moment. They clarified their mission, canceled their city contracts, and slept a lot better. They would no longer be the dumping ground for unwanted animals. But they also took in many fewer animals. They shifted the responsibility back to the public, by forcing the government to take the responsibilities. Meanwhile pet overpopulation continued to be a problem. The result could be an epidemic of strays with nowhere to go—the precise problem that the SPCAs had been created to deal with in the first place.

Often the killing continued at city-funded shelters. No-kill ignited a war of words: conventional shelter workers added back in what they felt the term elided. "They're not saying the animal's not going to die," said Roger Caras, then head of the ASPCA. "They're just saying, we're not going to kill it."

This schism within the rescue world has made its politics more fraught than ever, a struggle between those inside the rescue institutions and those outside. The angriest outsider is San Francisco attorney Nathan Winograd, who joined the San Francisco SPCA in the late 1990s, then ran the SPCA in Tompkins County, New York. He transformed it from a chronically underperforming shelter to the best one in the country, achieving remarkable numbers, saving 100 percent of the healthy, friendly animals it took in.

Then Winograd moved into advocacy, holding up his Tompkins

County success against the middling numbers produced by most other SPCAs. But whereas Duvin and Avanzino wanted to reform the shelters, educating the bureaucrats who run them, Winograd often seemed to want to blow them up. "Animal sheltering," he wrote in *Redemption,* his 2007 book that's become the manifesto of the no-kill movement, "is an industry whose leadership mostly fails." *Redemption,* a work of stunning passion, supercharges Duvin's rhetoric. Where Duvin banked his rage, Winograd's broadside is contemptuous, scoffing, and righteous. At its core is the idea that pet overpopulation is a myth, half-consciously propagated to justify shelters' euthanasia of large numbers of healthy pets. Winograd chronicles the bad consciences of shelter workers, the rationalizations and defense mechanisms that allow them to paper over the horrible truth and that prevent them from instituting programs that might help. Where Avanzino is a man of bluff, sunny optimism, Winograd seethes. Ed Duvin had partly forgiven the shelter system because its denizens were naïve—they simply didn't know any better. But ever since San Francisco led the way in 1994, killing animals had become a choice—and what did this make the shelter workers now?

The power of no-kill shows no signs of ebbing. But it is possible to look at the dog carnage of the 1970s and come to a completely different conclusion about what kind of relationship should exist between dogs and people.

Ingrid Newkirk already had a lot going on in her life when her eyes were opened to the suffering of animals. Born in Surrey, England, she'd married race car driver Steve Newkirk and moved to suburban Maryland, where, in 1972, she was working toward becoming a stockbroker. A neighbor had moved away and left several cats to fend for themselves, and before long Newkirk found herself with a load of kittens in her backyard. She took them to the local shelter—and was shocked, upon returning later, to find that they had all been euthanized. She had had no idea that such a thing was going on. "I decided

I needed to do something about it," she told Michael Specter in a 2003 *New Yorker* article. She took a job in the shelter, and what she found there was worse than euthanasia—it was an environment of shocking callousness, an animal hell on earth, with dogs and cats being kicked or stepped on or locked in freezers.

Newkirk's time in the shelter transformed her view of euthanasia. Rather than the ending of a life, it was a blessed release from pain. She would come in early to perform extra euthanasias rather than leave the work to less-skilled colleagues, who would miss veins and prolong those poor animals' sufferings. Some days she'd kill dozens of animals. She didn't believe dogs or other animals had rights—cruelty and neglect were simply an offense to human values. But then she met Cleveland Amory, the most visible animal activist of the 1960s and 1970s, who had funded Paul Watson's Sea Shepherd Conservation Society, and gradually became radicalized. In the late 1970s, working at the Humane Society in Washington, D.C., Newkirk met activist Alex Pacheco, who introduced her to Peter Singer's 1975 book *Animal Liberation*.

Singer's work provided an intellectual underpinning for instincts she already had, positing a moral equality between humans and other creatures. The book's provocative title suggests a peaceable kingdom in which animals will somehow be free. But for animals, suffering was the issue. In a 2009 blog post titled "Why We Euthanize," illustrated with gruesome photographs of abused dogs and cats, Newkirk wrote of "holding them in my arms and gently helping them escape an uncaring world without trauma or pain." To Newkirk, our modern industrial society is the problem, and euthanasia is a necessary kindness. "As long as animals are still purposely bred and people aren't spaying and neutering their companions, open-admission animal shelters and organizations like PETA must do society's dirty work." Later she would call shelter workers "dark angels."

Newkirk's clarity about her ideals, and her ability to act on them, can seem a little inhuman. Her certainty is breathtaking; she had herself sterilized at age twenty-two because she saw having a baby as selfish. "Having a purebred human baby is like having a purebred dog," she told Specter. "It's nothing but vanity. Pure, human vanity." In her angry early rhetoric, animals often seemed to be machines for suffering, and ending the suffering was always an option. Her thinking was Bentham for the late industrial age—the more suffering widgets you turned off, the less suffering there would be.

In many ways, Newkirk has been more radical than Winograd. (Though more recently, Newkirk has cuddled up to dogs and their people as in her 2007 book, *Let's Have a Dog Party;* an organization like PETA can't survive without the goodwill of pet owners.) But where Winograd blames the bureaucracy and its operators, Newkirk's anger is at the inhumanities of the public and the entire culture. She feels we've botched the dominion thing and should retreat from it—we aren't equipped for such responsibility. Out at the edges of her philosophy is an animal politics that puts up an unbridgeable wall between animals and people. "The bottom line is that people don't have the right to manipulate or to breed dogs and cats," she wrote in the magazine *Animals* in 1984. "If people want toys they should buy inanimate objects. If they want companionship they should seek it with their own kind." Her vision is far from utopian, for either animals or humans. How animals should live after they've disengaged is not her concern. And indeed, when animals are liberated, the strongest possibility seems to be that they'll go to the country . . . to that same happy farm where parents have always told children unwanted animals go. PETA has reportedly killed a shocking number of the animals it's taken in, upward of 90 percent—an unusual view of animal liberation.

Everyone I spoke to who is involved in dog rescue and animal sheltering acknowledged the usefulness of Winograd and the no-kill forces' angry, shaming rhetoric: they exert a pressure, which is necessary, even if his ideas about how to reform the country's animal bureaucracies leave something to be desired. But the traditional sheltering institutions have found that the rhetoric creates an environment of political conflict in which the needs of the animals—which is, after all, the point—can easily be forgotten; it impedes fund-raising and gets in the way of the very community-building activities that Winograd is advocating. At bottom, the old question persists: Did shelter workers help animals by euthanizing them? For their part, even after all the progress that has been made, Winograd and his allies see the humane establishment as morally callous incompetents—or worse.

Ed Sayres, current head of the ASPCA, is by his own admission a man of numbers. He's also, according to Nathan Winograd, an animal killer who should be fired. "Nathan always wants regime change," Sayres said with a slight smile when I went to see him in his quiet office, a surprising oasis in a grimy garmento neighborhood on Eighth Avenue in the West Thirties. "You can't always have regime change." In many ways, Sayres and Winograd, both alumni of the San Francisco SPCA, represent two sides of the modern animal rescue movement. Sayres has devoted his career to reforming the shelter system from the inside. The ASPCA relinquished its animal control responsibilities in 1995, but the new agency that was formed to care for homeless animals, Animal Care and Control, was massively underfunded—its budget was less than a dollar per capita, as opposed to three dollars in San Francisco. Using his San Francisco experience, Sayres worked to deepen the partnership between the ASPCA, along with other humane organizations, and Animal Care and Control, with impressive results.

We sat at a conference table, in a hush befitting the CEO of a $100 million operation, as Sayres laid out his animal philosophy to me. Dogs are dogs to him—he has a few himself—but they're also numbers. He talks in terms of threat matrixes, triaging the dogs in the shelter system by length of stay and cost of care: first kennel cough, then ringworm, then more complicated conditions. These dogs are savable, but they are difficult and expensive to save, and the clock is ticking. Then different seasons produce different conditions. In the summertime, puppy season, shelters are full, and adoptions slow down. Events like

Hurricane Katrina make a difference. "These are nuances that advocacy rhetoric doesn't capture," he said. "Nathan has taken a very hard line, not a very informed line" about such issues.

He walked me through the numbers. "From day one," he told me, "no-kill doesn't mean no euthanasia." He came up with a number on the meaning of no-kill—to some, his original sin. "I said okay, how are we going to do this? I tried to analyze it, give it a statistic so people could follow it." At that point, no-kill meant 68 percent saved, a huge improvement on what had been done before and possibly the best that could have been done. But looked at another way, the definition made no-kill into another euphemism, like "putting to sleep." The 68 percent solution. "We didn't end the euthanasia of complex treatable conditions," Sayres told me. "We have basically insulated all healthy, adoptable animals, guaranteeing them a loving home."

But the no-kill people want to talk in terms of beings rather than numbers. And when someone like Sayres talks in terms of practicalities—saying, *There is nothing more we can do*—they tend to hear rationalizations and think, *This is worse than pulling the plug on Grandma*. The no-kill forces see it as a system too. But from the beginning, they were convinced that the people within the system weren't as committed as the people outside.

New York City is now "just touching" the statistic that San Francisco achieved in 1994, Sayres told me in 2010. But that success, while satisfying, is also complicated. Sixty-eight percent no longer looks like success to anybody in the shelter community—that number is closer to 80 percent. San Francisco's current number is 86 percent—and even that is too low by some lights on the movement's left edge. When the city and the alliance made their agreement, they'd set a goal to achieve no-kill by 2008. Now that deadline has been moved to 2015.

The slow, steady progress that Sayres speaks of is cold comfort to the no-kill forces. The rescuers question authority and resist participating in the system, believing it makes bad decisions for individual animals. They want in, want a full say in the decision making, want to keep

shining a light into the shelter system. One of the dogs they hoped
would lead them in was a dog named Oreo.

The proliferation of pit bulls is the most complicated problem facing the shelter system. Everywhere in America they're overrun-
ning the shelters. They're David Selby's biggest problem in Clarksville,
Tennessee, and they're the biggest problem at the ACC on 110th Street
in Manhattan. As statistics for other dogs have steadily improved, those
for pits have held steady or gotten worse. Seventy-five percent of pit
bulls or pit mixes that arrive at American shelters are killed; close to a
million pit bulls were killed in American shelters in 2010. The shelter
community has made heroic efforts to find families for these dogs.
Avanzino, ever the brilliant marketer, tried to solve the problem by re-
christening the dogs St. Francis Terriers, but the new name didn't solve
anything. And the ASPCA tried for a time to market the dogs as New
Yorkies, an effort that lasted all of three days.

Pit bulls are wonderful dogs, I hasten to add, and in my experience much more loyal than Stella, who's off, as a friend says, with the
nearest truck driver she can find. But if they are mistreated, pits can
have a relentlessness and dog-on-dog aggressiveness that is alarming. Their powerful jaws are a physical fact. As an adolescent dog, Stella
was chased down by three pits in the dog run—the kind of scrum that
she normally loves, but with her it usually doesn't escalate to such an
intense level. After that incident, Stella seemed to develop a breed-
specific aversion—she gave almost all pit bulls a wide berth. This kind
of impression drives pit bull owners nuts. To them, it's a form of stereotyping, akin to racial profiling.

A heavy tangle of myth has grown up around the pit bull—that
they have locking jaws that can hold on and chew at the same time,
that they can suddenly "snap" and become violent. But those abilities
are entirely imaginary, as the fierce legions of pit bull defenders will
tell you. Pits are more recently purpose-bred than other American

dogs—they began to appear in large numbers in American shelters in the mid-1980s, accompanied by a renewed interest in dog fighting—for fearlessness, and for grabbing and holding on. Vicki Hearne, the late animal trainer and writer whose books are crucial for anyone who thinks about animals, praised their gameness—they're ready for anything.

These are the pit's strengths, just as retrieving is the strength for a Lab (though not, alas, for Stella, dogs, she constantly reminds us, are individuals). And nature and nurture—or abuse—can combine to produce dangerous dogs. Almost half of American and Canadian fatalities involving dogs in the last three decades were caused by pit bulls, as were half of the attacks involving child facial disfigurements and two-thirds involving adults. Such accidents have more to do with how the dogs' owners raised them than with anything intrinsic to the dogs—but it's sometimes hard to separate the breed from the story. According to *Animal People*, Denver, one of the few big cities that hasn't had a dog fatality in the last couple of decades, has had a ban on pit bulls in effect—with a brief break—since 1989.

Given the pits' prominence in the mythology of the black and Hispanic inner city, their canine nature-nurture issues quickly become debates about people. In an inner-city context, pit bulls can be used to protect and intimidate. So pits, among other things, are a race-class battleground. In Tennessee, they're often a dog of the poor, both black and white, in the backwoods and in cities. In huge swaths of the East and West coasts, they tend to be the only dogs left unfixed, because their owners don't get around to it, and because they choose, especially with male dogs, to leave them that way. Pits also have a place in the inner city's underground economy. A litter of pit puppies, if all goes well, might bring in a thousand dollars or more. Spaying or neutering reduces this potential windfall. But if the offspring can't be unloaded, they end up in the shelter.

Pit bulls no doubt get a very bad rap—raised properly, they are as sweet as any other dog. (The most fearsome dogs of my childhood were

German shepherds, whose bite is, if anything, more powerful than that of the pit.) But in many areas a good percentage of pits are not raised properly—and a powerful dog that was bred for fighting, with an uncertain upbringing, as is the case with so many shelter dogs, is an occasion for worry, no matter what your position on the nature-nurture question. The same would be true if our shelters were filled with unwanted German shepherds or Rottweilers. But today pits are the most numerous dogs in shelters—each year, according to *Animal People*, 33 to 45 percent of pit bulls in America will enter a shelter. Pits are being adopted at a surprisingly high rate: 16 percent of the dogs adopted from shelters in the last five years have been pit bulls, according to *Animal People*. Yet that's still only denting the shelter population. So changing the pit's image, removing its fearsome and largely false mythology, is unfortunately not an adequate solution to the problem as it currently stands. Out in Clarksville, David Selby doesn't even try to find homes for pit bulls. He's worried about their strong jaws, and how they might have been treated as puppies, and what the liability might be for adopting out a dog that goes on to do harm. It's a painful choice to euthanize them, but it makes his life easier.

When it comes to pit bulls, the save-every-dog rhetoric of the no-kill movement sounds like dreaming. The population of New York's Animal Care and Control Center on 110th Street, said the ASPCA's Gail Buchwald, can be close to 100 percent pits. These are the dogs that are still in grave danger of getting euthanized. You could, if you had the resources, cage them for the rest of their lives, or—what? The question, even in the voluminous discussion of the no-kill world, has no clear answer. In the no-kill world, it's a matter of faith that there's a family for every dog, and that somehow they'll find each other. The idea is to hold on to the dog until the right family comes along.

But faith doesn't empty the cages—people do. At the ASPCA on East Ninety-second Street, says Buchwald, the struggle is to keep the number of pits below 50 percent. The staff is trying everything. Recently, they've run a campaign to persuade pit owners to have their male dogs sterilized without castration—some owners consider testosterone an important feature and see a dog without its testicles as imperfect. Most of the shelter's long-term residents, in immaculate glass-windowed cages with little blowholes big enough for a dog's nose to sniff a hand, are pits. If they're here, they're nice-tempered enough to potentially get adopted. The workers barely conceal their anxiety about the dogs that no one has picked, like parents of a child who has a hard time making friends. There's nothing they can do but watch. "I want you to meet Pearl," says Buchwald, then orders the pit bull mix to sit, which she does happily. "She came here with a litter of puppies. The puppies got adopted, but we still have our Pearl. She's been with us for quite a while, so it's time to get her adopted." Pearl is a victim of canine stereotyping—she's a dog anyone would be lucky to have. But she's also a victim of the fact that there are too many pit bulls, more than can possibly be adopted, no matter how much marketing genius is applied to their case.

Buchwald, a slim, attractive woman, has been at the ASPCA for ten years. She'd been to business school at Wharton, worked in marketing at Unilever and then Pfizer, marketing Viagra, and then began to think of changing her life. She'd been volunteering and wanted to do something mission-based. The ASPCA is a big business, with a $100 million budget, more challenging in many ways than selling Viagra. The ASPCA brand was "a double-edged sword," she says. The shelter is still, to many minds, the place where they kill dogs.

"We're in retail," says Buchwald. "We compete with every other agency or channel or outlet for animals." The drawback of her facility is that, at East Ninety-second Street, it's located across from public housing and draws little foot traffic. So it sends out adoption wagons and buys advertisements, anything to get people to visit. Buchwald takes me upstairs into the area where animals are prepared for adoption. In one of the cages are six puppies that look, but for slightly larger ears, exactly like Stella. In fact, they're her cousins. "Tennessee dogs," says Buchwald. To all appearances—every week, it seems, I meet a new Tennessee Lab mix in the dog run—Lab mixes are as numerous and vigorous as the dogs that Peter Hawker imported from Newfoundland. But as all of them are spayed or neutered as a condition of their adoption, they won't be making a mark on future generations.

The Lab mixes have been brought here specifically to help rescue the pit bulls: they attract potential adopters, who might end up falling in love with a pit. This is the way retail works. "If we don't create a diverse inventory for our consumers," says Buchwald, "we will be driving them to other outlets. The Internet is full of puppy mills masquerading as family breeders, backyard breeders. If the public thinks we're only in the pit bull business, they won't come in."

Pit bulls are the hard cases of the dog rescue world, and Oreo was one of the hardest. Black and white, as her name implies, she had been thrown off a sixth-floor rooftop in Red Hook, Brooklyn. The perpetrator, a twenty-two-year-old named Fabian Henderson, was eventually convicted of animal cruelty and sentenced to only six months' probation, which infuriated the animal rescue community. Maybe his aim was to perform do-it-yourself euthanasia—most dogs wouldn't survive such a fall. But Oreo did survive. She was brought, with two broken legs and internal injuries, to the crowded ward at the ASPCA's Ninety-second Street shelter where, slowly, she got better.

Oreo, in a sense, was a direct descendant of Sido, but she evolved in a different environment. Like Sido, Oreo was what shelter marketers call a "perfect case," tailor-made to raise public awareness. She'd been the victim of spectacular cruelty—enough to attract the attention of the newspapers—and she was photogenic, and a happy ending for such a creature would be edifying and educational and valuable publicity for the ASPCA. But whereas Sido was charming with everyone, having been raised in comfort, Oreo was an inner-city pit, and her hard life had produced in her a deep anger. She could be sweet, but she was unpredictable.

The ASPCA nursed her back to health and tried hard to save her and rehabilitate her, but her inner scarring seemed to make it impossible. She'd lunge unpredictably at her handlers—people who knew her well. No one thought Oreo could be adopted out—the risks and potential liabilities were simply too high. So the decision was made to euthanize her.

To Winograd and his allies, Oreo's case activated the old caring-killing paradox. There are far from enough refuges in the United States to accommodate every problem dog. Several of Michael Vick's dogs were taken to such places, symbols of what the system *could* do, rather than what it did in most cases.

To Winograd and his allies, every being is precious, not only the cute and cuddly. Didn't Oreo, who had never hurt anyone as far as anyone knew, have as much right to life as any other dog?

Thirty different people and organizations had offered to adopt Oreo, yet the ASPCA had refused to give her up. Why? "Nathan [Winograd] and people who adhere to that philosophy have very little experience in animal handling," Ed Sayres told me. The ASPCA's belief is that, for a dog like Oreo, euthanasia is the best option. Sequestered from people and dogs, what kind of quality of life could such a dog have? In Italy, which is now completely no-kill, difficult dogs, and others too, spend their whole lives in cages—which seems crueler than the alternative.

Winograd's forces have argued that the behavior tests that the ASPCA conducted on Oreo were invalid, that the dog hadn't been given enough time, that the shelter was a flawed environment in which to administer them. Any decision made by a shelter, he believes, is a rationalization based on institutional calculations of convenience. The preciousness of these beings' lives should mean that there are always other choices. But someone has to make the choices, not only for Oreo but for all the difficult dogs that end up in shelters. Despite all the passionate concern of the no-kill forces, the numbers don't yet add up. Saving Oreo might have made headlines, but it wouldn't have solved the problem of where all such dogs should go.

Oreo was euthanized on November 13, 2009—a year in which New York's City's euthanasia numbers dropped to historic lows. Oreo achieved fame, sympathy, and something like love in her less than two years, not that she knew what it all was. More than an anecdote, she had become a story, a tragic one, rife with villains and ambiguities. She could have never lived safely and comfortably with people and died a difficult dog, a complicated symbol in a conflict of ideas. As many as one hundred other dogs were euthanized that week in New York City, mostly unmourned.

Does every dog, even the most ornery, deserve its day? That's the question that Oreo's death sentence raises. Stella ends up with table scraps and belly rubs and five walks a day, while Oreo got a needle in his shoulder. Some dogs get $10,000 cancer treatments, and other dogs don't even get names. These differences in outcome, and the continuing euthanasia of healthy dogs, appear to many people as a vast, systemic injustice, one that has as much claim on our consideration as any in the human world. But the movement to put an end to these hypocrisies doesn't seem likely to end anytime soon. This isn't simply a matter of institutional resistance, or the numerous people who think that dogs and other animals should stay on their side of the fence and we on ours. It's also because it's not at all clear what a world where dogs and other animals are given such consideration might look like. The worlds that some animal liberationists wish for can seem like fairy tales, pigs and cows and chickens wandering the streets. Some even think that pet keeping itself is a sort of slavery. If we ever get to these animal utopias, the dog—the honorary human—will have played a crucial role in leading the way. But those places seem a good ways off.

## Sixteen

# Dog Years

While we were away in Britain, Stella stayed with a friend in the country. The day we got back she seemed fine, though possibly a little subdued—her greeting was less frenetic than usual, which would have been a blessing except for the anxiety it produced. *What's wrong with her?* Projecting, as always, I wondered whether she might be angry at us for leaving her or, worse, for taking her away from her green utopia and back to the concrete city and her customary spot on the rug. That was our life and therefore hers now: tough luck, Stella.

But the next morning she was weak and listless, and her nose was dry. She could barely get to her feet. I had to force her to go for her morning walk. Then it got worse. She seemed to age a decade or more in the space of a day, with no appetite. She was an immovable black lump, heaving slowly. The next morning I managed to get her to the vet—she resisted going in the door with the last bit of her strength. I lifted her onto the stainless-steel examination table—just like the one at Precious Friends, where her voyage had begun—and her legs quivered unsteadily, her claws scratching at the metal.

The diagnosis was quick and happy: it was Lyme. What a relief—all of us had had it. The antibiotics made quick work of it, and in a day, she was back to her old powerfully athletic, occasionally unmanageable self. Which wasn't to say that it was over.

Stella wasn't even three then, but I thought of the illness—her first—as a premonition, the beginning of her old age. You could see, in her temporary weakness, how deceptive the life force is, how far things can go. That event reminded me that Stella's vibrant physicality, so much a part of my thoughts about her, couldn't last. One day it would be gone. My eyes were moistening, but for myself as well: how old would I be then?

In a footnote to one of his poems about the deaths of his dogs, John Updike wrote, "Sometimes it seems the whole purpose of pets is to bring death into the house," a sensationally cruel observation in part because there's truth in it. A dog's mortality is never far from its owner's mind—it's the central flaw in this best-friend business, the problem with its honorary personhood. The dog is on a different schedule. Stella will get off the train—that long, lonesome whistle—while our little party, in all likelihood, continues on. Even now, in her youth, her mortality is something to dwell on. No one is ready for their dog to go.

And the dog doesn't know where it's going—the elemental dog joke turned into a tragedy. In "Another Dog's Death," Updike writes about the last days of one of his animals:

> I took a shovel into the woods and dug her grave
> in preparation for the certain. She came along,
> which I had not expected. Still, the children gone,
> such expeditions were rare, and the dog,
> spayed early, knew no nonhuman word for love.
>
> She made her stiff legs trot and let her bent tail wag.
> We found a spot we liked, where the pines met the field.

The sun warmed her fur as she dozed and I dug;

I carved her a safe place while she protected me.

I measured her length with the shovel's long handle;

She perked in amusement, and sniffed the heaped-up earth.

Sad stuff. But for the dog, this excursion to her final resting place was a happy time (though it would have been improved if Updike had brought a picnic of fried chicken); the day of her death was a day like any other. Suddenly the switch is turned off.

This state of being-in-the-moment is what's so compelling about dogs. It's hard for a human to get to it. Even in their most difficult times, dogs are cheerful and ready for experience. A dog can't figure out that it's being measured for its grave. The three-legged chow that walks on my street every day doesn't know the number three or have any sense that anything is wrong with her at all (and as I write, the dog is sixteen and still fit). It's not that a dog accepts the cards it's been dealt; it's not aware that there are cards. James Thurber called the desire for this condition "the Dog Wish," the "strange and involved compulsion to be as happy and carefree as a dog." This is a dog's blessing, a dim-wittedness one can envy.

A dog's death throws into high relief the human complexities of time passing, children growing, the hard facts that adulthood forces upon us, the way all that we love and build finally comes to ruin, and—yadda yadda yadda. It can seem a little overwrought, but that's the territory. It's the third act of an opera, when everything has been played, and all the big emotions come out. So get out the hankies, because you're not going to be able to hold it together. You know it's coming. It's intense and wrenching—and inevitable, and totally ordinary. A dog's death is a stock scene—which explains the plainness of Updike's title. What else is there to say about a dog's death? They're all different and all exactly the same.

These foreshortened dramatic possibilities herd the dog toward one of its favored playgrounds, which is kitsch. Updike's teary poems drive right up to the edge of it. Loving a dog means, among other things, making peace with kitsch, if you haven't already. You don't have to make goo-goo eyes at every puppy picture you see in a magazine or bake your dog birthday cakes. But if you resist too much the power of the big primary-color emotions that surround the dog, you're missing the experience.

I tried to resist. I confess that when I heard that the shelter Stella came from was named Precious Friends, I recoiled. I mean, precious friend, yes, sure. But the name threatened to swallow the rest of my relationship with my dog, predigesting it, reducing it to treacle. It produced a drowning feeling, as if my dog's life—and mine—were passing before my eyes as a series of greeting cards. Dogs are a national religion, with a catechism composed by Hallmark, so heresy is necessary. I suspect some people resist the dog culture with such passion precisely to avoid the kitsch, the appalling melodrama: if you give in to it, you're trapped in a narrative you can't control. You feel like a dope, buying into it. The emotions around the dog can be as neotenized as the animal itself.

Rather than an end, kitsch can be a starting point. Errol Morris's 1978 documentary, *Gates of Heaven*, about two California pet cemeteries, is a staggering movie, one of the great documentaries, though that term is too small to contain it. It's also a freak show, with 1970s period outfits and products and interiors and landscapes so vivid you could watch it, entranced, with the sound off.

There's something patronizing in Morris's depiction of these dog lovers. Your first thought is *Who are these kooks who care about a dog cemetery?* But this freak show is just a frame for a heavy, mysterious picture. What is a dog's body? Why bury anybody—or anything? What does it really matter what happens to a body when life is gone? Where does my relationship with those creatures go when they are only meat and, soon, given the worms and all, not even that? *What was in there?* It's the mystery of the flesh. Much like Darwin's dog and the umbrella, these questions are the beginning of religion—they're still the great mysteries, demanding endless internal debate—even for those who think the notion of a higher power is just a bit fantastical.

The greatness of *Gates of Heaven* is that it moves past kitsch. The fact that Morris's people seem delusional doesn't detract from the power of their speculations—in an odd way, it augments it. You can't dismiss their loopy philosophizing; everyone is concerned with these questions. The dead dogs—they're not even flesh anymore—get the human plot started. They're an emptiness in the center, a black hole around which is arrayed a galaxy of human obsessions.

My first thought, as a dog lover, is: *There but for the Grace of God go I.* Or, being a bit more realistic: *There I go.* My relationship with Stella features plenty of inadvertent comedy, the constant talk, the welter of thoughts, the way that she noses her way into my grandest, most preposterous philosophizing. Those people in Morris's film—their claustrophobic offices and living rooms overflowing with tchotchkes, their cat's-eye glasses and fleshy faces staring earnestly into the camera, talking about the place of dogs in their lives—are my people. Much as I like to think that kitsch has no purchase in my world, it's found its way in—and it's sleeping on my rug.

Just inside the door of Precious Friends in Clarksville is a Rainbow Bridge pet memorial. Such memorials exist wherever pets are found these days. All of them are based on a poem, or a prose poem, of very questionable literary value. No one knows who wrote it, though it has several claimants. It surfaced in the early 1990s, as the current dog regime was gaining force, a homegrown mythology that made sense of many a pet owner's issues, having watched their animals decline and die.

When an animal dies that has been especially close to someone here, that pet goes to Rainbow Bridge.

There are meadows and hills for all of our special friends
so they can run and play . . . All the animals who had been ill
and old are restored to health and vigor; those who were hurt
or maimed are made whole and strong again, just as we remember them in our dreams of days and times gone by.

The animals are happy and content, except for one
small thing; they each miss someone very special to them,
who had to be left behind.


In the denouement, the dogs run to their owners, and then they
cross the rainbow bridge together, to be reunited ever after. It's crudely
moving, though a large part of its power is like that of a finger down
the throat—a mythic reflex, pure wish fulfillment, its consoling purpose unconcealed. It's Kmart heaven, a little flimsy, purpose-built to
fill a mass need, easy to discard after it's done its work. But seen from
another angle, it's a little tuft of grass growing up through an asphalt
parking lot: not so impressive, hardly a plant at all, except when you
consider its arid surroundings.

Since the very beginnings of culture, dogs have always been associated with death. Partly, it must have to do with their carrion-eating
proclivities. Dogs are like circling vultures, supremely knowledgeable
about things that are dead. You don't want to leave a corpse unattended
when dogs are around, is Old Testament wisdom. But there are other
reasons for the connection too.

Dogs are harbingers of the passage into the next world. If you can
hear the hounds of hell barking, that's where you might be going. Or
your dog might be able to hear them, with its preternatural perceptions, its mysterious insights. In England a couple of centuries ago, a
dog barking on a still night was said to portend a major illness in the
family. Britain and the United States have extensive black dog myths—
the black dog is supernatural, huge, with glowing eyes. If you happen
to see it, start to make your arrangements, because you're toast. The

local refinements are endless. The most famous American variation concerns a dog that sometimes appears in the Hanging Hills near Meriden, Connecticut. The dog, small, sleek, black, and cheerful in many accounts, seems an awful lot like Stella, except that it makes no sound and leaves no footprints.

In 1898 New York geologist W. H. C. Pynchon wrote down the black dog story after he'd seen the dog twice. According to the legend, if you see the dog once, you will have a joyful experience. Seeing it a second time means misfortune may soon befall you. A third sighting means you're not long for this world. Pynchon, so the story goes, encountered the dog a third time on a winter hike. Shortly afterward, he slipped on some ice and fell to his death. I drive past the Hanging Hills frequently—they're off Route 91, about halfway from New York to Boston. It's probably not the best place to stop and take Stella for a walk.

Dog burials, and dog burials with humans, are actually remarkably common in the archaeological record, in many different civilizations besides the Magdalenian and the Natufian graves mentioned in chapter 9. The Egyptians occasionally mummified dogs—along with just about everything else. At Ashkelon, in Israel, a cemetery contains hundreds of dogs, to all appearances ordinary village or household dogs that died of natural causes. There are dog burials all over North America. The earliest known is at a site called Kloster, in southern Illinois, dated to about 8500 B.C. The Peabody Museum at Harvard has two well-preserved dog mummies: a white long-haired dog that could pass as a collie, and a black and white terrier-size animal. They were found in White Dog Cave in northern Arizona, buried there by people known as the Basket-Makers in about A.D. 100—they also liked to weave dog hair into burial shrouds. The dogs were interred with a family—a couple and an infant—in a single grave. And in the grave of a couple in Newfoundland is a pair of large Eskimo dogs, like modern-day huskies. In many sites, dogs were buried just like people—early honorary humans even in death. Where dogs are buried with people, archaeologists assume they were killed to accompany their masters to the next world—to show them the way.

Dogs know the way to the next world—and often have some say in who inhabits it. A dog guarding a bridge or a body of water—sometimes composed of tears of the grieving, sometimes of blood—is a common motif in many cultures. (Cerberus, a little ridiculous with his three heads, is the most rococco of these creatures.) Many Old and New World cultures thought the Milky Way was a path that led souls from this world to the next. In some traditions, dogs have their own path in the sky that runs parallel; in others, like that of the Delaware (the tribe that once inhabited Manhattan), they guard a bridge on the Milky Way, deciding who gets to cross. The Cherokee thought it was the route that a little dog traveled after being discovered stealing cornmeal; the smudged white path was said to be the cornmeal falling out of its mouth. It's called, in their language, Where the Dog Ran. Sirius, the dog star, is the most well-known legacy of these mythic traditions. The brightest star in the sky, Sirius is ever searching for his master, Orion.

The consonance among myths from cultures far-flung in time and geography suggest some kind of deep structural connection. Some scholars believe that such mythologies made the trip across the land bridge from Siberia to Alaska along with people and their dogs, then filtered out across the Americas, changing and evolving as they went: an odd echo of the dog's development from a small group of pioneers in Asia to the variety we see today.

I was ready to believe that, but I also wondered whether the success of these myths might be based on what Updike observed: that dogs bring death into the house? Think of all the cogitation in *Gates of Heaven,* and the arguments over euthanasia in the dog shelter world, and the involvement of Stella in my own thinking about mortality, the counting of years and the adding up. Dogs might know the way to the next world because they get there more quickly than we do, and that idea is never far from our minds.

. . .

In the modern world, whatever your belief in the afterlife may be, you try to postpone getting there by any means necessary. This can get rather expensive, even for honorary humans. The Animal Medical Center, on East Sixty-second Street at the river, is a state-of-the-art hospital, one of the seats of this culture's dog rituals. Dogs are people here—called patients.

The Animal Medical Center is a temple of anthropomorphism and of this whole honorary-human business. It's right on hospital row by design. "They wanted it to be on equal footing," said Robert Liberman, the chairman of the board, whom I ran into in the lobby. He told me about the close collaboration between animal and human hospitals, about studies undertaken in collaboration with Sloan-Kettering. A plaque in the lobby memorializes an A-list of donors—Fanjuls, Kissingers—but pride of place goes to the Vincent Astor Foundation. (The neglect of Mrs. Astor's dogs in her senility contributed to the conviction of her son Tony for taking advantage of her condition. I can't help but wonder whether if in her lifetime Mrs. Astor had diverted some of her love from the dogs to Tony, things wouldn't have gotten quite so out of hand.)

Upstairs in the rehabilitation center, a working animal, a yellow Lab, was being treated by two young technicians. The dog, maybe nine years old, had nerve damage from an infection in her back. One of the technicians had a pair of electrodes pressed to the dog's haunch, stimulating the muscles. The other was massaging its chest—Reiki, she said. They were all lying on a heap on a mat, and the dog seemed as happy as a dog can be. Across the room, a black Lab named Radar, with a mysterious muscle condition, had just finished a workout on a treadmill in a water tank. Outside, his owners waited on a bench.

Susan Phillips Cohen, the director of counseling at the center when I visited, helps people make sense of this bad bargain. A small, cheerful, white-haired woman, Cohen went from person to person in the hospital's waiting room, gauging the emotional distress of the pet owners who came in. "We don't consider old age a disease here," she told me. "We want to be the place that doesn't say, 'It's a ten-year-old dog, there's nothing we can do.'"

The dog's honorary humanity is negotiated in the hospital's waiting room. Here a dog "really is family," said Cohen. For the family, "the choices they're going to make, the protection they're going to give, the nurturing they feel they owe, are the same as for a family member."

Cohen tries to clarify the issues in people's minds, which is not easy, given the confused place of the dog in many urban lives. Dog illness brings up all their stuff. "They realize at this moment how many of their eggs they've put in this basket," she said. "'How did I get here? Why didn't I have children? I hate my job.' Because with a dog, you have someone to come home to who appreciates you just the way you are."

Caring for a dog at the end of its life and grieving after it's gone is in some ways more complicated than grieving for a person, because the question of what a dog *is* is far from settled. An honorary human, or just an animal chattel? This is part of what is unsettling about *Gates of Heaven*—can a dead dog just be a thing whose remains should be sent to the rendering plant? How you make these determinations is pretty much up to you—the Milky Way is, after all, just a lot of stars. Some will say *It's only a dog* and explain that real grieving is best left for people. So the grief process may be, to some degree, kept inside.

And if you choose to use the gleaming medical equipment of the Animal Medical Center to keep your dog alive, you face a similar set of questions. How much should you spend? How much is your dog's life worth? Especially if you grew up in a world where visits to the vet were far from annual, the use of a dialysis machine in caring for a dog whose kidneys are failing can seem a little crazy, as if some border has been crossed.

The hospital's position is "to be as accurate and honest as we can be about what we can do," said Cohen. It leaves the impossible calculus of dog years versus human dollars up to the owner—and you could max out your credit cards over a weekend and still walk home with a bag of ashes. Some friends recently took a ten-year-old dog with bleeding intestines to another prominent New York animal hospital. The doctors discovered a tumor and told them that removing it would give the dog a 90 percent chance of survival. So my friends were trapped in a cascade of escalating medical decisions—five days and several procedures later, the dog was euthanized. The bill came to more than $14,000. They're heartsick over the loss of the dog, and the money too—and furious at the hospital. But at what point, once you start, can you turn back? One lesson: a hospital that makes money on procedures may not be the best adviser on when it's time to pull the plug.

On our way downstairs, we passed a room where I'd had our previous dog euthanized. It's actually, if such a thing exists, a fabulous place to have a dog put down, at least for the human—the dog, no doubt, would rather stay home. There's a view out over the dark, swirling waters of the East River—my river of tears—and on the far side, a sward of green, dog paradise.

Scout was a West Highland terrier, Angela's dog when we met, an exuberant, somewhat cantankerous creature, beloved companion of our New York youth, unwitting enabler of our prolonged adolescence. He was fourteen and tired when we had to bring him here, after a tumor and a torn ligament and a winter of rather expensive medical wrestling with a stubborn breathing problem, all this along with taking care of our young son, who'd displaced him in his princely status, poor thing.

Before we brought him in, a vet asked, with wide caring eyes, "Is there anything else you want to do?" There was, of course—the hospital's high-tech armamentarium, its MRIs and minimally invasive techniques, a hospital they'd be happy to have in Darfur—but we didn't.

I put a rubberized smock over my lap—in the city, one is never quite free of a dog's elimination needs—and told Scout about his happy afterlife on that lawn across the water, which I didn't believe a word of and he at any rate couldn't understand—that same human gurgling he'd heard his whole life. The vet gave him one injection to put him to sleep, another to stop his heart. And that was Scout, whoever he was. At some point I would be along to join him—he had crossed the bridge, and eventually he would show me the way.

But not for a while, with any luck.

Right, Stella?

# Acknowledgments

The secret of a dog is that it's ready to be helped—and this is a lesson I've learned well. I had a great deal of help in preparing this book.

First, I'd like to thank Colin Dickerman and Karen Rinaldi, who took a chance on this book, and also to Ann Godoff, who welcomed it to Penguin Press. Colin, my editor, has made this book immeasurably better, from its woolliest concepts to its organization to the smallest details of language. Jared Hohlt, my colleague and editor at *New York* who edited the original article there, gave a close reading to two drafts, truly above and beyond, and contributed a huge amount to this book (and to my work in general) in myriad ways—I can't imagine what it would have been without him. And this book simply could not have happened without David Kuhn, my agent and friend, whose interest in my writing and belief in this project were crucial in getting it off the ground.

An account of my trip to Scotland was originally published in *Condé Nast Traveler* magazine, and for their help I'm very grateful to Klara Glowczewska, the magazine's editor, and my old friend Peter Stevenson, who edited the piece.

I especially want to thank Adam Moss, editor in chief of *New York* magazine and my boss in my day job, who allowed me to write this book, and whose original title ("Your dog is not a human being") gave the article and later the book a clarifying focus, helping make it what it is.

Thanks are also due to the writers I edit, who have taught me (however imperfectly) to write (and who didn't get *too* visibly annoyed when I bent their ears about my own writing struggles), including, but not limited to, Mark Jacobson, Ariel Levy, Vanessa Grigoriadis, Steve Fishman, John Heilemann, Gabriel Sherman, Chris Smith, Joe Hagan, and Jennifer Senior, among many others. Ari and Vanessa read the book in manuscript—a mark of true friendship—and provided highly useful feedback.

A few people went above and beyond the call of duty to facilitate my explorations, and I deeply appreciate it. Among them were Korrina Duffy at Brian Hare's laboratory at Duke; Roy Green, the estate manager at Buccleuch, who gave me and my family a tour we'll always remember; Kristen Brooks at Precious Friends in Clarksville, Tennessee; and Devera Lynn at North Shore Animal League.

Many of those who helped me most are quoted in this book. Three people whose conversations were very valuable are Donald McCaig, the dean of American dog writers, whose perspective on the history of the AKC I found highly useful; Janeen McMurtrie, a Minnesotan dog trainer who writes the *Smartdogs* blog and provided early insight into the conflict between the flyover states and the coasts over dogs; and Dr. Stephen Zawistowski, historian and all-around dog savant at the ASPCA, who walked me through the story of Oreo and much else.

At Kuhn Projects, Billy Kingsland was always a pleasure to deal with. At Penguin, Kaitlyn Flynn made things easy. At *New York,* Kat Ward was always helpful.

Much of the fieldwork for this book was done in the houses and backyards of family and friends. Accordingly, I'd like to thank my brother James and his wife, Laura (and their dogs, Putzi and I suppose Skip too—he's never bitten me, at any rate); my brother Sam and his wife, Mittie (and the fierce, goat-killing, lovable Rusty); as well as my dog-loving nieces and nephews, Michael, Cathy, Camilla, Caroline, Daniel, and Stewart.

I also want to thank the various members of our long-running North Fork summer commune, now on temporary hiatus: Jane Clark, Pete Wilkinson, and their daughter, Alice Wilkinson (and their Labradoodle, Murphy); John Seabrook, Lisa Reed, son Harry (and the aptly named Foxy). John provided highly useful comments on the manuscript. Sheryl Lukomski (and Maurice), Terry Reed, Richard Cleves, Monica Missio and son Nicholas; and Elizabeth Royte, Peter Kreutzer, and their daughter Lucy, a determined dog trainer, as Stella requires. Randy Harris photographed Stella, while his dog, Marshall, entertained her.

My neighbors Bill and Kathy Finneran have made our Manhattan lives much easier and more pleasant than they might otherwise have been. Thanks as well to Fred Childs and Laurie Jones—Fred especially for his knowledge of Labradors and for saving me much embarrassment by teaching me how to say Buccleuch (it's *buk-loo*).

I especially want to thank Teri Hackett and Ray Manikowski, whose genius Australian shepherd, Roxy, was an important inspiration for this book, and whose current dog, Nell, may be even smarter (if a bit crazier).

Saving the best for last, I want to thank my son, Charles, with whom I regularly talked through this book's contents, who was its first reader, and who provided many excellent suggestions. And finally thanks to Angela Britzman, my wife, whose support and forbearance throughout this project have been truly amazing, and who taught me most of what I know about dogs and so much else.

# Note on Sources

## CHAPTER 1: ENTERING THE WORLD OF DOG

This book is, as much as anything, the history of an evolving discipline: canine studies. So
many of the books I cite in this incomplete and selective bibliography are both
sources and subjects. The first book to make the case that something is going on
between dogs and people that is worth paying scientific attention to was Alan Beck
and Aaron Katcher, *Between Pets and People* (G. P. Putnam's Sons, 1983). Simultaneously scientific and proselytizing, in its breadth and approach it was an important
starting place for me.

James Serpell, *In the Company of Animals* (Cambridge University Press, 1996), served a
similar purpose in different fields, posing a series of powerful questions about the
place of animals in our culture. A collection that Serpell edited, *The Domestic Dog*
(Cambridge University Press, 1995), is a soup-to-nuts snapshot of dog evolution,
behavior, and the human-canine relationship; though now a bit out of date, it's still
a useful entry point for several areas of canine study. Arnold Arluke and Clinton
Sanders, *Regarding Animals* (Temple University Press, 1996), grounded in fieldwork
in shelters and laboratories, is an eye-opening introduction to the sociology of animals in the United States. Jon Katz, *The New Work of Dogs* (Random House, 2003),
answers the question in my book's title much more specifically than I do, and provides as well a rich picture of dogs and people in modern America. And Patricia
McConnell, *The Other End of the Leash* (Ballantine, 2002), in addition to her other
books and her blog, is invaluable in understanding the human-dog relationship
and the neurotic interspecies interchange it can entail.

## CHAPTER 2: THE FAMILY DOG

Alan Beck and Aaron Katcher's *Between Pets and People* is still the most important book
about the health effects of dogs, though the scientific literature is abundant.

E. O. Wilson, *Biophilia* (Harvard University Press, 1984), a playful, poetic work by sociobiology's central thinker, helped open the door to the idea that a connection with nature might be important to human well-being. The Freud material is drawn from multiple sources, the most important of which is an essay about Freud and his dogs in Todd Dufresne, ed., *Killing Freud: Twentieth-Century Culture and the Death of Psychoanalysis* (Continuum, 2003). Stephen Budiansky, *The Truth About Dogs* (Penguin, 2001), expands on the notion that the dog is a kind of social parasite; the book is useful to argue with, even if one doesn't agree with it.

## CHAPTER 3: THE SEARCH FOR STELLA'S BRAIN

Ádám Miklósi, *Dog Behaviour, Evolution, and Cognition* (Oxford University Press, 2007), is now the standard reference in canine science (written by its seminal scientist) and covers the field in detail. Alexandra Horowitz, *Inside of a Dog* (Scribner, 2009), covers dog cognition in a way that is useful in understanding a reader's own animal. Most of the studies I've cited are fairly easily found on the Internet using Google Scholar or a database like JSTOR. My discussion of training draws on several books, the most important of which are W. R. Koehler, *The Koehler Method of Dog Training* (Howell Book House, 1969); Karen Pryor, *Don't Shoot the Dog!* (1984; reprint Ringpress Books, 2002); and Cesar Millan with Melissa Jo Peltier, *Cesar's Way* (Three Rivers Press, 2006), all of which, at times, provide valuable advice on dogs.

## CHAPTER 4: HOW THE MATCH WAS MADE

Vilmos Csányi, *If Dogs Could Talk* (North Point Press, 2005), is an engaging account of the beginnings of canine science—one that will please certain dog lovers and exasperate many scientists in its unabashed celebration of the author's own dogs' cognitive excellences. The material on wolves is drawn from multiple sources but especially from L. David Mech, *The Wolf: Ecology and Behavior of an Endangered Species* (Doubleday, 1970). L. David Mech and Luigi Boitani, eds., *Wolves: Behavior, Ecology, and Conservation* (University of Chicago Press, 2003), encompasses many of its most recent findings and directions.

## CHAPTER 5: LEAPING TOWARD HUMANITY

Most of my discussion about dogs' disputed ability to understand human pointing is based on scientific papers and interviews. Daniel Dennett's *The Intentional Stance* (MIT Press, 1987), is a dense but rewarding study of the underlying issues. Michael Tomasello's lucidly iconoclastic *Why We Cooperate* (Boston Review, 2009) and *Origins of Human Communication* (MIT Press, 2008), while they hardly mention dogs, show how the dog's unusual talent for understanding human cues fits into the larger picture of animal and human cognition.

## CHAPTER 6: DUMB ANIMALS

Raymond and Lorna Coppinger, *Dogs* (University of Chicago, 2001), probably the most important book on dogs published in the last couple of decades, permanently altered the paradigm of dog development. Clive Wynne's *Animal Cognition* (Palgrave MacMillan, 2001) and *Do Animals Think?* (Princeton University Press, 2004), are witty dismantlings of the anthropomorphic tendency in animal psychology.

## CHAPTER 7: DARWIN'S MUSE

As well as drawing from his books *On the Origin of Species, The Descent of Man,* and *The Expression of the Emotions in Man and Animals,* the material about Charles Darwin is based on two remarkable online databases, the Darwin Correspondence Project (http://www.darwinproject.ac.uk) and The Complete Work of Charles Darwin Online Darwin Correspondence Project (http://darwin-online.org.uk), which make research in a specific topic, like dogs, much easier than it used to be. Darwin protégé George John Romanes's magnum opus, *Animal Intelligence* (D. Appleton, 1888), wrongheaded though some of it is, is delightful reading for a dog lover. Published two decades later, Edward Lee Thorndike, *Animal Intelligence: Experimental Studies* (Macmillan, 1911), shows how quickly consensus moved away from Romanes's views. The discussion on changing ideas in animal psychology is drawn from many different sources, but my standard reference is Robert Boakes, *From Darwin to Behaviourism* (Cambridge University Press, 1984), which covers most of the field's significant thinkers at length.

## CHAPTER 8: THE MIND RETURNS

For details about B. F. Skinner and his feud with Noam Chomsky, I relied on Daniel W. Bjork, *B. F. Skinner* (American Psychological Association, 1997). Jane Goodall, *In the Shadow of Man* (Houghton Mifflin, 1971), contains little about dogs but is a transcendent work of anthropomorphism, science, and literature in elegant harmony. Her young adult book, *My Life with the Chimpanzees* (Minstrel, 1996), contains much more about her dog Rusty, as does Dale Peterson, *Jane Goodall* (Houghton Mifflin, 2006), a voluminous, satisfying biography.

## CHAPTER 9: THE WOLVES THAT CAME IN FROM THE COLD

The best book I could find on the literally fragmentary field of early humans is Steven Mithen, *After the Ice* (Harvard University Press, 2004), a study of the archaeological record and the cultural developments it might suggest from the height of the last ice age up to about eleven thousand years ago, when village-based cultures began in earnest. Among other works, I drew facts and analysis from Matthew H. Nitecki and Doris V. Nitecki, eds., *The Evolution of Human Hunting* (Plenum Press, 1987). Likewise, Mithen's *The Prehistory of the Mind* (Thames and Hudson, 1996), is a riveting narrative of the development of human intelligence, on which I've based some of my speculations about the role of anthropomorphism in creating the dog. I also found fact and inspiration about our intuitions of nature in Steven Pinker, *How the Mind Works* (W. W. Norton, 1997). Dog archaeology is advancing more swiftly than ever, which means that most of its findings and certainties are in dispute. But the most complete book-length account of the various discoveries, along with a rich reading of the human-canine relationships these findings might suggest, is Darcy F.

Morey, *Dogs: Domestication and the Development of a Social Bond* (Cambridge University Press, 2010).

## CHAPTER 10: MIXING THE LAB

Richard Wolters, *The Labrador Retriever* (Petersen Prints, 1981), is the standard reference on the history of the Lab. Robert Hutchinson, *For the Love of the Labrador Retriever* (BrownTrout, 1998), covers some of the same history with a different emphasis. And *Retrieverman*, a blog by Scottie Westfall, prosecutes many questions concerning the Lab's origins, as well as the origins of quite a few other breeds, in fascinating detail. I used several other sources for the Lab's early history, including A. M. Lysaght, *Joseph Banks in Newfoundland and Labrador, 1766* (Faber and Faber, 1971), an edition of the explorer's diary, but there's no single trove.

Harriet Ritvo, *The Animal Estate* (Harvard University Press, 1987), is an indispensable starting point for anyone thinking about the culture of animals. Diana Donald, *Picturing Animals in Britain* (Yale University Press, 2007), makes visible the psychic changes in the English mind through images by that country's greatest artists, Edwin Landseer especially. Peter Hawker's diary, available online at Google Books, is a journey into a strange lost world. Also available on Google Books is John Henry Walsh, *Dogs of the British Islands* (Horace Cox, 1872). Walsh, also known as Stonehenge, more than anyone else invented modern dogs. *The Dogs of the British Islands* encompasses much of the debate in Walsh's magazine *The Field;* reading his book is almost like watching the invention of the dog in real time. Donald McCaig, *The Dog Wars* (Outrun Press, 2007), an account of the struggle to keep the American Kennel Club from registering border collies and thereby safeguarding their working talents, is indispensable in assessing the institutional power of America's biggest dog organization.

## CHAPTER 11: BEYOND BREEDS

There are several useful books about dog genetics. The one I found most helpful was Elaine A. Ostrander, Urs Giger, and Kerstin Lindblad-Toh, eds., *The Dog and Its Genome* (Cold Spring Harbor Press, 2006). But the research has been moving so fast that parts of it already feel out of date. Patrick Bateson's report is *Independent Inquiry into Dog Breeding* (Halesworth, Suffolk, U.K.: Micropress, 2010).

## CHAPTER 12: FUTURE CANINES

The best resource about the animal rescue world, and just about the only keeper of certain statistics, is *Animal People*, a monthly newspaper edited by Merritt Clifton, which is also available online and as an e-mail newsletter. Arnold Arluke, *Just a Dog* (Temple University Press, 2006), is a richly reported, indispensable inquiry into the moral drama of our relationship with dogs; it informs parts of this and the next two chapters.

## CHAPTER 13: THE GREAT MIGRATION

There is no single comprehensive history of the dog rescue movement, but Nathan Winograd, *Redemption* (Almaden, 2007), is both a passionate polemic and a fairly detailed history of the origins of no-kill. Michael Brandow, *New York's Poop Scoop Law* (Purdue University Press, 2008), is a snapshot of a particular era of dogs that I found really helpful.

## CHAPTER 14: THE BIRTH OF EMPATHY

Marion Lane and Stephen L. Zawistowski, *Heritage of Care* (Praeger, 2008), provides a fairly rich history of ASPCA founder Henry Bergh. William F. Stifel, *The Dog Show: 125 Years of Westminster* (Westminster Kennel Club, 2001), gives a great short portrait of the first Westminster Dog Show and the early days of the American dog fancy, as well as of Henry Bergh. Other details about Bergh's life may be found in James Turner, *Reckoning with the Beast* (Johns Hopkins University, 1980), a fantastic book about animals and pain in the Victorian imagination that I relied on for my discussion of vivisection.

## CHAPTER 15: THE RIGHTS OF DOG

Ed Duvin's essay "In the Name of Mercy," the founding manifesto of the no-kill movement, is available online in many places. (Here's one: http://www.bestfriends.org/nomore homelesspets/pdf/mercy.pdf.) Nathan Winograd's *Redemption: The Myth of Pet Overpopulation and the No Kill Movement in America* (2007) is both a fierce polemic and an indispensable history of the no-kill movement. Peter Singer's *Animal Liberation* (1975) is the link between animal rights and the other liberation movements spawned in the 1960s, and still the movement's most important work. Martha Nussbaum's *Frontiers of Justice* (2006), which I didn't discuss in the text, is the best discussion I found of how animal's interests could be related to those of humans and how those interests might be embodied in law.

## CHAPTER 16: DOG YEARS

Marion Schwartz, *A History of Dogs in the Early Americas* (Yale University Press, 1998), provided the core of the material about dog myths.

# Index